HOLT, RINEHART AND WINSTON

Making Sense of Numbers

A RESOURCE FOR PARENTS AND STUDENTS

HOLT, RINEHART AND WINSTON

A Harcourt Classroom Education Company

Austin • New York • Orlando • Atlanta • San Francisco • Boston • Dallas • Toronto • London

To Parents and Students

Making Sense of Numbers: A Resource for Parents and Students is an easy-to-use workbook that teaches and practices basic pre-algebra skills in fractions, decimals, ratio, proportion, and percent. Each worksheet uses a simple and direct format that includes an objective, step-by-step solved examples, and practice exercises.

Making Sense of Numbers is organized into six units. Teachers may direct students to read and complete selected worksheets in one or more units to remediate weak skills. Students may be directed to complete worksheets outside of class with the guidance of their parents or guardians. In this case, teachers may also provide answer keys for parents or guardians to monitor the child's progress.

Copyright © by Holt, Rinehart and Winston

All rights reserved. No part of this publication may be reproduced or transmitted in any form or by any means, electronic or mechanical, including photocopy, recording, or any information storage and retrieval system, without permission in writing from the publisher.

Teachers may photocopy complete pages in sufficient quantities for classroom use only and not for resale.

Printed in the United States of America

ISBN 0-03-064284-1

4 5 6 7 170 04 03

Table of Contents

Unit 1 — Order of Operations and Number Theory ..... ix–x

Chapter 1 Order of Operations
- **1-1** The Order of the Four Basic Operations 1
- **1-2** Parentheses and the Order of Operations 2
- **1-3** Using Exponents 3
- **1-4** Exponents and Multiplication 4
- **1-5** Exponents and the Order of Operations 5
- **1-6** Using Formulas 6

Chapter 2 Number Theory
- **2-1** Divisibility of Whole Numbers 7
- **2-2** Tests for Divisibility 8
- **2-3** Factors and Prime Numbers 9
- **2-4** Writing a Prime Factorization 10
- **2-5** Common Factors and the GCF 11
- **2-6** Multiples of Whole Numbers 12
- **2-7** Common Multiples and the LCM 13

Unit 2 — Fractions 15–16

Chapter 3 Fraction Fundamentals
- **3-1** Fractions for Numbers Between 0 and 1 17
- **3-2** Fractions for Numbers 1 and Greater 18
- **3-3** Writing a Mixed Number as a Fraction 19
- **3-4** Writing a Fraction as a Mixed Number or as a Whole Number 20
- **3-5** Modeling Equivalent Fractions 21
- **3-6** Equivalent Fractions: Higher Terms 22
- **3-7** Equivalent Fractions: Lower Terms 23
- **3-8** Lowest Terms of a Fraction 24
- **3-9** Fractions on a Number Line 25
- **3-10** Comparing Fractions: Like Denominators 26
- **3-11** Comparing Fractions: Unlike Denominators 27
- **3-12** Ordering Fractions 28
- **3-13** Estimating Fractions 29
- **3-14** Reading a Customary Ruler 30
- **3-15** Negative and Zero Exponents 31

Making Sense of Numbers

Chapter 4 Addition of Fractions and Mixed Numbers

- **4-1** Modeling Addition of Fractions 32
- **4-2** Adding Fractions: Like Denominators 33
- **4-3** Adding Fractions: Unlike Denominators 34
- **4-4** Adding Mixed Numbers: Like Denominators 35
- **4-5** Adding Mixed Numbers: Unlike Denominators 36
- **4-6** Estimating Sums Involving Fractions 37
- **4-7** Problems Involving Fraction Addition 38
- **4-8** Problems Involving Mixed Number Addition 39

Chapter 5 Subtraction of Fractions and Mixed Numbers

- **5-1** Modeling a Subtraction of Fractions 40
- **5-2** Subtracting Fractions: Like Denominators 41
- **5-3** Subtracting Fractions: Unlike Denominators 42
- **5-4** Subtracting Mixed Numbers Without Renaming 43
- **5-5** Subtracting Mixed Numbers With Renaming 44
- **5-6** Estimating Differences Involving Fractions 45
- **5-7** Problems Involving Fraction Subtraction 46
- **5-8** Problems Involving Mixed Number Subtraction 47
- **5-9** Problems Involving Either Addition or Subtraction of Fractions or Mixed Numbers 48
- **5-10** Adding and Subtracting With Fractions 49
- **5-11** Adding and Subtracting With Mixed Numbers 50
- **5-12** Problems Involving Both Addition and Subtraction of Fractions or Mixed Numbers 51

Chapter 6 Multiplication of Fractions and Mixed Numbers

- **6-1** Modeling a Multiplication of Fractions 52
- **6-2** Multiplying Two Fractions 53
- **6-3** Multiplying a Fraction and a Whole Number 54
- **6-4** Multiplying Several Fractions 55
- **6-5** Multiplying With Mixed Numbers 56
- **6-6** Estimating Products Involving Mixed Numbers 57
- **6-7** Problems Involving Fraction Multiplication 58
- **6-8** Problems Involving Mixed Number Multiplication 59
- **6-9** Problems Involving Addition, Subtraction, or Multiplication of Fractions or Mixed Numbers 60
- **6-10** Adding, Subtracting, and Multiplying With Fractions 61
- **6-11** Adding, Subtracting, and Multiplying With Mixed Numbers ... 62
- **6-12** Solving Problems Involving Multiplication of Fractions or Mixed Numbers Together With Addition or Subtraction 63
- **6-13** Renaming a Customary Measure of Length by Multiplying 64

6-14 Renaming a Customary Measure of Weight or Liquid Capacity by Multiplying 65

Chapter 7 Division of Fractions and Mixed Numbers

7-1 Modeling a Division by a Fraction 66
7-2 Reciprocals 67
7-3 Dividing With Fractions 68
7-4 Dividing With Mixed Numbers 69
7-5 Estimating Quotients Involving Fractions and Mixed Numbers 70
7-6 Problems Involving Fraction Division 71
7-7 Problems Involving Mixed Number Division 72
7-8 Problems Involving Addition, Subtraction, Multiplication, or Division of Fractions or Mixed Numbers 73
7-9 Adding, Subtracting, Multiplying, and Dividing With Fractions 74
7-10 Adding, Subtracting, Multiplying, and Dividing With Mixed Numbers 75
7-11 Problems Involving Division of Fractions or Mixed Numbers Together With Addition, Subtraction, or Multiplication 76
7-12 Renaming a Customary Measure by Dividing 77
7-13 Renaming a Customary Measure by Multiplying or Dividing 78
7-14 Exponents and Division 79

Unit 3 Decimals 81–82

Chapter 8 Decimal Fundamentals

8-1 Understanding Decimals and Place Value 83
8-2 Locating Decimals on a Number Line 84
8-3 Rounding Decimals 85
8-4 Comparing and Ordering Decimals 86
8-5 Writing a Terminating Decimal as a Fraction 87
8-6 Writing a Fraction as a Terminating Decimal 88
8-7 Writing a Fraction as a Repeating Decimal 89
8-8 Reading a Metric Ruler 90

Chapter 9 Addition and Subtraction of Decimals

9-1 Adding Decimals 91
9-2 Estimating Decimal Sums 92
9-3 Solving Problems Involving Decimal Addition 93
9-4 Adding Decimals and Fractions 94
9-5 Subtracting Decimals 95
9-6 Estimating Decimal Differences 96
9-7 Solving Problems Involving Decimal Subtraction 97

Making Sense of Numbers

9-8	Subtracting Decimals and Fractions	98
9-9	Adding and Subtracting With Decimals	99
9-10	Solving Profit Problems	100

Chapter 10 Multiplication of Decimals

10-1	Multiplying a Decimal by a Power of 10	101
10-2	Multiplying Decimals	102
10-3	Finding a Power of a Decimal	103
10-4	Estimating Decimal Products	104
10-5	Solving Problems Involving Decimal Multiplication	105
10-6	Multiplying Decimals and Fractions	106
10-7	Adding, Subtracting, and Multiplying With Decimals	107
10-8	Changing to a Smaller Unit of Metric Measure	108
10-9	Writing Numbers in Scientific Notation	109

Chapter 11 Division of Decimals

11-1	Dividing a Decimal by a Power of 10	110
11-2	Dividing Decimals	111
11-3	Decimals, Division, and Zeros	112
11-4	Estimating Decimal Quotients	113
11-5	Solving Problems Involving Decimal Division	114
11-6	Interpreting the Quotient	115
11-7	Dividing Decimals and Fractions	116
11-8	Adding, Subtracting, Multiplying, and Dividing With Decimals	117
11-9	Changing to a Larger Unit of Metric Measure	118
11-10	Writing Numbers Between 0 and 1 in Scientific Notation	119

Unit 4 *Ratio, Proportion, and Percent* 121–122

Chapter 12 Ratio and Proportion

12-1	Writing Ratios	123
12-2	Writing Rates	124
12-3	Solving Problems Involving Ratios and Rates	125
12-4	Solving Problems Involving Distance, Rate, and Time	126
12-5	Determining Whether Two Ratios are Equal	127
12-6	Solving Proportions	128
12-7	Solving Problems Involving Proportions	129
12-8	Solving Problems Involving Similar Geometric Figures	130

Chapter 13 Percent Fundamentals

13-1	Writing Percents Less Than 100%	131

13-2	Writing Percents Greater Than 100%	132
13-3	Writing Percents as Fractions	133
13-4	Writing Fractions as Percents	134
13-5	Writing Percents as Decimals	135
13-6	Writing Decimals as Percents	136
13-7	Recognizing Equivalent Fractions, Decimals, and Percents	137

Chapter 14 Operations Involving Percent

14-1	Finding a Percent of a Number	138
14-2	Estimating a Percentage of a Number	139
14-3	Solving Problems by Finding a Percentage of a Number	140
14-4	Finding the Percent Rate	141
14-5	Using Proportion to Find a Percent Rate	142
14-6	Solving Problems by Finding a Percent Rate	143
14-7	Finding a Base Number When its Percent Rate and Percentage are Known	144
14-8	Using Proportion to Find a Base Number	145
14-9	Solving Problems by Finding a Base Number	146

Chapter 15 Applications of Percent

15-1	Percent of Increase	147
15-2	Percent of Decrease	148
15-3	Calculating Tips and Total Cost	149
15-4	Calculating Sales Tax and Total Cost	150
15-5	Solving Discount Problems	151
15-6	Solving Successive Discount Problems	152
15-7	Solving Markup Problems	153
15-8	Solving Simple Interest Problems	154
15-9	Solving Compound Interest Problems	155
15-10	Solving Commission Problems	156
15-11	Finding Probabilities	157

Unit 5 Integers 159–160

Chapter 16 Integer Fundamentals

16-1	Positive and Negative Numbers	161
16-2	Comparing and Ordering Integers	162
16-3	Finding Opposites and Absolute Values	163

Chapter 17 Addition of Integers

17-1	Adding Two Integers With Like Signs	164
17-2	Adding Two Integers With Unlike Signs	165

17-3 Adding Three or More Integers 166
17-4 Solving Problems Involving Integer Addition 167

Chapter 18 Subtraction of Integers
18-1 Subtracting Integers 168
18-2 Solving Problems Involving Integer Subtraction 169
18-3 Adding and Subtracting With Integers 170

Chapter 19 Multiplication of Integers
19-1 Multiplying Integers 171
19-2 Adding, Subtracting, and Multiplying With Integers 172
19-3 Solving Problems Involving Integer Multiplication 173

Chapter 20 Division of Integers
20-1 Dividing Integers 174
20-2 Solving Problems Involving Integer Division 175
20-3 Adding, Subtracting, Multiplying, and Dividing With Integers 176

Unit 6 Rational and Irrational Numbers 177–178

Chapter 21 Rational Number Fundamentals
21-1 Recognizing and Writing Rational Numbers 179
21-2 Comparing and Ordering Rational Numbers 180
21-3 Finding Opposites and Absolute Values of Rational Numbers 181

Chapter 22 Addition and Subtraction of Rational Numbers
22-1 Adding Rational Numbers 182
22-2 Problems Involving Rational Number Addition 183
22-3 Subtracting Rational Numbers 184
22-4 Problems Involving Rational Number Subtraction 185

Chapter 23 Multiplication and Division of Rational Numbers
23-1 Multiplying Rational Numbers 186
23-2 Problems Involving Rational Number Multiplication 187
23-3 Using Integer Exponents to Multiply Rational Numbers 188
23-4 Dividing Rational Numbers 189
23-5 Problems Involving Rational Number Division 190
23-6 Using Integer Exponents to Divide Rational Numbers 191

Chapter 24 Square Roots
24-1 Finding Squares and Rational Square Roots 192
24-2 Approximating Irrational Square Roots 193

Unit 1 — Order of Operations and Number Theory

Chapter 1 Order of Operations
- **1-1** The Order of the Four Basic Operations. 1
- **1-2** Parentheses and the Order of Operations. 2
- **1-3** Using Exponents 3
- **1-4** Exponents and Multiplication 4
- **1-5** Exponents and the Order of Operations. 5
- **1-6** Using Formulas 6

Chapter 2 Number Theory
- **2-1** Divisibility of Whole Numbers. 7
- **2-2** Tests for Divisibility 8
- **2-3** Factors and Prime Numbers 9
- **2-4** Writing a Prime Factorization 10
- **2-5** Common Factors and the GCF 11
- **2-6** Multiples of Whole Numbers 12
- **2-7** Common Multiples and the LCM. 13

Making Sense of Numbers

Unit One

NAME _____ CLASS _____ DATE _____

1-1 The Order of the Four Basic Operations
UNIT 1

OBJECTIVE: *Finding the value of an expression that involves whole number addition, subtraction, multiplication, or division*

The four basic operations of mathematics are addition, subtraction, multiplication, and division. Finding the value of some expressions involves two or more of these operations. The order in which you perform the operations is very important.

The Order of the Four Basic Operations

First multiply and divide in order from left to right.
Then add and subtract in order from left to right.

EXAMPLE Find the value of each expression. a. $16 + 8 \times 5$ b. $24 - 6 \div 2 + 1$

▶ **Solution**

a. $16 + 8 \times 5$
   $16 + 40$ *First multiply.*
   56 *Then add.*

b. $24 - 6 \div 2 + 1$
   $24 - 3 + 1$ *First divide.*
   $21 + 1$ *Then subtract.*
   22 *Then add.*

Find the value of each expression.

1. $20 - 9 + 7$ _____

2. $16 + 30 - 22$ _____

3. $25 - 6 + 14 - 4$ _____

4. $15 + 5 - 14 + 6$ _____

5. $18 \div 3 \times 2$ _____

6. $15 \times 10 \div 5$ _____

7. $12 \times 6 \div 3 \times 4$ _____

8. $16 \div 8 \times 4 \div 2$ _____

9. $27 - 12 \div 3$ _____

10. $14 + 9 \times 2$ _____

11. $48 \div 6 - 2 \times 2$ _____

12. $9 \times 8 - 6 \div 3$ _____

13. $21 + 12 \div 3 + 1$ _____

14. $32 - 2 \times 4 + 12$ _____

15. $36 - 16 \div 4 \times 4$ _____

16. $40 \div 2 \times 4 - 2$ _____

17. $72 \div 3 + 6 \times 3 - 2$ _____

18. $4 \times 10 \div 5 - 1 + 3$ _____

Making Sense of Numbers   Unit 1   Order of Operations and Number Theory

NAME _____ CLASS _____ DATE _____

1-2 Parentheses and the Order of Operations
UNIT 1

OBJECTIVE: Finding the value of an expression that contains parentheses

Often an expression contains parentheses. To find its value, you first perform any operations inside the parentheses. Remember to follow the correct order of the four basic operations.

EXAMPLE 1 Find the value of $(9 + 3) \times (17 - 8)$.

▸ **Solution**

$(9 + 3) \times (17 - 8)$
  12×9 *First work inside the parentheses.*
    108 *Then multiply.*

EXAMPLE 2 Find the value of $92 - 6(5 + 8)$.

▸ **Solution**

$92 - 6(5 + 8)$
$92 - 6(13)$ *First work inside the parentheses.*
$92 - 78$ *Then multiply. Note that 6(13) means 6×13.*
  14 *Then subtract.*

Find the value of each expression.

1. $54 \div (2 + 4)$ _____
2. $(35 - 6) \times 4$ _____
3. $(12 - 4) \div 2$ _____
4. $(22 + 19) \times 10$ _____
5. $36 \times (12 \div 6)$ _____
6. $45 - (9 + 27)$ _____
7. $(18 - 3) \times (4 + 7)$ _____
8. $(25 - 9) \div (3 + 5)$ _____
9. $38 - (14 - 2) + 9$ _____
10. $9 \times (24 - 16) \div 4$ _____
11. $27 + (3 + 14) \times 6$ _____
12. $60 - (4 \times 8) \div 2$ _____
13. $6(33 - 29)$ _____
14. $(41 + 39)2$ _____
15. $47 + 2(12 - 9)$ _____
16. $90 - 3(8 + 5)$ _____
17. $74 + (17 - 6) \times (6 \div 2)$ _____
18. $(49 - 7) \div (7 - 4) \times 2$ _____
19. $(16 - 2 \times 4) + (64 \div 4 \div 2)$ _____
20. $36 \div (9 \times 2) + (6 + 18 \div 2)$ _____

NAME _____ CLASS _____ DATE _____

1-3 Using Exponents
UNIT 1

OBJECTIVE: Writing expressions in exponential form and finding the value of exponential expressions

You can write some multiplications in a type of "mathematical shorthand" called *exponential form*.

$$\underbrace{3 \times 3 \times 3 \times 3 \times 3 \times 3 \times 3}_{\text{7 identical factors of 3}} = 3^7$$

Exponential Form — 7 is the **exponent**. — 3 is the **base**.

EXAMPLE 1 Write each expression in exponential form.

a. $3 \times 3 \times 3 \times 3$ b. $5 \times 5 \times 7 \times 7 \times 7$ c. 2

▶ Solution

a. $3 \times 3 \times 3 \times 3 = 3^4$ b. $5 \times 5 \times 7 \times 7 \times 7 = 5^2 \times 7^3$ c. $2 = 2^1$

EXAMPLE 2 Find the value of each exponential expression.

a. 5^3 b. $2^4 \times 3^2 \times 7^1$

▶ Solution

a. $5^3 = 5 \times 5 \times 5$ b. $2^4 \times 3^2 \times 7^1 = 2 \times 2 \times 2 \times 2 \times 3 \times 3 \times 7$
$ = 125$ $ = 16 \times 9 \times 7$
                                    $= 1008$

Write each expression in exponential form.

1. $7 \times 7 \times 7 \times 7 \times 7$ _____   2. $2 \times 2 \times 2 \times 2 \times 2 \times 2 \times 2 \times 2$ _____

3. $3 \times 3 \times 5 \times 5 \times 5 \times 5$ _____   4. $5 \times 5 \times 5 \times 7 \times 7 \times 7$ _____

5. $2 \times 2 \times 3 \times 5 \times 5 \times 5$ _____   6. $2 \times 5 \times 5 \times 7 \times 7 \times 7$ _____

Find the value of each exponential expression.

7. 2^3 _____   8. 3^2 _____   9. 5^2 _____   10. 7^3 _____

11. 13^1 _____   12. 7^1 _____   13. 2^7 _____   14. 3^5 _____

15. $2^2 \times 3^4$ _____   16. $2^3 \times 11^2$ _____   17. $2^3 \times 3^2 \times 5^2$ _____

18. $2^3 \times 3^2 \times 7^2$ _____   19. $2^5 \times 3^2 \times 5^1$ _____   20. $2^4 \times 3^1 \times 7^2$ _____

Making Sense of Numbers

NAME _____ CLASS _____ DATE _____

1-4 Exponents and Multiplication
UNIT 1

OBJECTIVE: Using the Product of Powers Rule

In the expression 2^6, 2 is the *base* and 6 is the *exponent*. You read 2^6 as *two to the sixth power*. Its value is $2 \times 2 \times 2 \times 2 \times 2 \times 2 = 64$. The number 64 is called *the sixth power of two*. When you multiply powers of the same base, a pattern emerges.

$$5^3 \times 5^4 = \underbrace{5 \times 5 \times 5}_{3 \text{ factors}} \times \underbrace{5 \times 5 \times 5 \times 5}_{4 \text{ factors}} = 5^7 \quad \rightarrow \quad 5^3 \times 5^4 = 5^{3+4}$$

The Product of Powers Rule
To multiply powers of the same base, add the exponents.

EXAMPLE 1 Write $2^4 \times 2^6$ as a base with a single exponent.

▶ **Solution**

$2^4 \times 2^6 = 2^{4+6} = 2^{10}$ *Add the exponents.*

EXAMPLE 2 Write $5^7 \times 5$ as a base with a single exponent.

▶ **Solution**

$5^7 \times 5 = 5^7 \times 5^1$ *Rewrite 5 as 5^1.*
$\quad\quad\quad = 5^{7+1} = 5^8$ *Add the exponents.*

Write each expression as a base with a single exponent.

1. $3^5 \times 3^4$ _____
2. $2^2 \times 2^3$ _____
3. $11^2 \times 11$ _____

4. $5^4 \times 5^4$ _____
5. $2^2 \times 2^2$ _____
6. $3^5 \times 3 \times 3^2$ _____

7. $2 \times 2^8 \times 2^6$ _____
8. $7 \times 7 \times 7^3$ _____
9. $5 \times 5^2 \times 5$ _____

Tell whether each statement is *true* or *false*.

10. $2^3 \times 5^3 = 7^3$ _____
11. $3^2 \times 3^5 = 3^7$ _____

12. $3^2 \times 3^2 = 9^2$ _____
13. $2^2 \times 2^2 = 4^2$ _____

14. $2 \times 2^3 = 4^3$ _____
15. $5^2 \times 5 = 25^3$ _____

16. $7^4 \times 7^3 = 7^{12}$ _____
17. $11^2 \times 11^2 = 11^4$ _____

1-5 Exponents and the Order of Operations

UNIT 1

OBJECTIVE: Finding the value of an expression that involves whole number operations, parentheses, or powers

Although finding a power of a number indicates multiplication, powers have their own special place in the order of operations.

> **Expanded Order of Operations**
> 1. First do any operations inside parentheses.
> 2. Then find the value of each power.
> 3. Then multiply and divide in order from left to right.
> 4. Then add and subtract in order from left to right.

EXAMPLE Find the value of $67 + 3(6 - 2)^3$.

Solution

$67 + 3(6 - 2)^3$	
$67 + 3(4)^3$	*First work inside the parentheses.*
$67 + 3(64)$	*Then find the value of the power.*
$67 + 192$	*Then multiply. Note that 3(64) means 3 × 64.*
259	*Then add.*

Find the value of each expression.

1. $36 \div 2^2$ _____

2. 7×3^4 _____

3. $21 - 3^2$ _____

4. $(21 - 3)^2$ _____

5. 5×2^3 _____

6. $(5 \times 2)^3$ _____

7. $24 + 4^3 \div 8$ _____

8. $200 - 5^2 \times 3$ _____

9. $84 - (1 + 5)^2$ _____

10. $149 - (8 - 3)^3$ _____

11. $31 + 2(9 - 5)^3$ _____

12. $94 - 3(10 - 8)^4$ _____

13. $153 - (12 - 2^3)$ _____

14. $66 + (4 + 3^2)$ _____

15. $2^3 + 2^2 + 2^4$ _____

16. $3^4 - 3 + 3^2$ _____

17. $122 - (7 + 2)^2 + 37$ _____

18. $5^2 + (11 - 3^2) \div 2$ _____

19. $(3 \times 2^2) - 8 \div (4 \div 2)^2$ _____

20. $(8^2 + 6^2) \div (9 - 7)^2 + 2 \times 2^3$ _____

Making Sense of Numbers

NAME _____ CLASS _____ DATE _____

Using Formulas

OBJECTIVE: Finding an unknown quantity by applying a formula

A formula is a mathematical sentence that describes how two or more quantities are related. If you know the value of all quantities except one, you can use the formula to find the unknown quantity. The following are some basic formulas from geometry.

Some Basic Geometric Formulas

Rectangle with length ℓ and width w
perimeter: $P = 2 \times \ell + 2 \times w$ area: $A = \ell \times w$

Square with one side of length s
perimeter: $P = 4 \times s$ area: $A = s^2$

Cube with one edge of length e
surface area: $S = 6 \times e^2$ volume: $V = e^3$

EXAMPLE The length of a rectangle is 19 and its width is 13. Find the perimeter of this rectangle.

▶ **Solution**

$P = 2 \times \ell + 2 \times w$ Write the rectangle perimeter formula.
$P = 2 \times 19 + 2 \times 13$ Replace ℓ with 19. Replace w with 13.
$P = 38 + 26$ Multiply first.
$P = 64$ Then add.

Find each quantity using one of the formulas given above.

1. the area of a rectangle with length 39 and width 9   _____

2. the perimeter of a square with one side of length 58   _____

3. the perimeter of a rectangle with length 12 and width 7   _____

4. the perimeter of a rectangle with length 38 and width 23   _____

5. the area of a square with one side of length 16   _____

6. the surface area of a cube with one edge of length 12   _____

7. the volume of a cube with one edge of length 10   _____

8. the volume of a cube with one edge of length 21   _____

NAME _____ CLASS _____ DATE _____

2-1 Divisibility of Whole Numbers
UNIT 1

OBJECTIVE: Dividing to determine if one whole number is divisible by another

The whole numbers are 0, 1, 2, 3, . . . (The three dots mean *and so on.*)
One whole number is said to be divisible by a second if the remainder is zero when the first number is divided by the second.

EXAMPLE 1 Find the result of 59 ÷ 8. Is 59 divisible by 8?

Solution

```
    7
 8)59
   56
   ―――
    3   remainder
```

59 ÷ 8 = 7 R3

The remainder is 3.
No, 59 is not divisible by 8.

EXAMPLE 2 Find the result of 112 ÷ 14. Is 112 divisible by 14?

Solution

```
      8
 14)112
    112
    ―――
      0   remainder
```

12 ÷ 14 = 8

The remainder is 0.
Yes, 112 is divisible by 14.

Find the result of each division. Is the first number divisible by the second? Write *Yes* or *No*.

1. 50 ÷ 7 _____ _____
2. 63 ÷ 7 _____ _____
3. 144 ÷ 18 _____ _____
4. 156 ÷ 19 _____ _____
5. 390 ÷ 78 _____ _____
6. 204 ÷ 34 _____ _____
7. 47 ÷ 3 _____ _____
8. 98 ÷ 7 _____ _____
9. 376 ÷ 9 _____ _____
10. 472 ÷ 6 _____ _____
11. 180 ÷ 12 _____ _____
12. 222 ÷ 17 _____ _____
13. 999 ÷ 37 _____ _____
14. 882 ÷ 42 _____ _____
15. 770 ÷ 25 _____ _____
16. 980 ÷ 28 _____ _____
17. 1765 ÷ 7 _____ _____
18. 4875 ÷ 6 _____ _____
19. 4263 ÷ 29 _____ _____
20. 9312 ÷ 16 _____ _____

Making Sense of Numbers   Unit 1 Order of Operations and Number Theory

Tests for Divisibility

OBJECTIVE: Using divisibility tests to determine whether one whole number is divisible by another

In certain cases, you can use a *divisibility test* to determine whether one whole number is divisible by another.

Divisor	Test
2	The last digit is 0, 2, 4, 6, or 8.
3	The sum of the digits is divisible by 3.
4	The number formed by the last two digits is divisible by 4.
5	The last digit is 0 or 5.
8	The number formed by the last three digits is divisible by 8.
9	The sum of the digits is divisible by 9.
10	The last digit is 0.

EXAMPLE Is 1436 divisible by each number?   a. 2   b. 3   c. 4

▶ **Solution**

a. The last digit is 6. Yes, 1436 is divisible by 2.
b. The sum $1 + 4 + 3 + 6$ equals 14, and 14 is not divisible by 3. No, 1436 is not divisible by 3.
c. The number formed by the last two digits is 36, and is divisible by 4. Yes, 1436 is divisible by 4.

Is the first number divisible by the second? Write *Yes* or *No*.

1. 325; 5 _____
2. 325; 10 _____
3. 4000; 10 _____

4. 4000; 5 _____
5. 2397; 3 _____
6. 2397; 9 _____

7. 11,250; 3 _____
8. 11,250; 9 _____
9. 1848; 2 _____

10. 1848; 4 _____
11. 1848; 8 _____
12. 13,482; 2 _____

13. 13,482; 4 _____
14. 13,482; 8 _____
15. 1011; 3 _____

16. 10,483; 2 _____
17. 22,500; 9 _____
18. 3330; 10 _____

19. 8410; 4 _____
20. 5554; 5 _____
21. 44,004; 3 _____

22. 54,080; 8 _____
23. 10,005; 10 _____
24. 3900; 4 _____

NAME _____ CLASS _____ DATE _____

2-3 Factors and Prime Numbers
UNIT 1

OBJECTIVE: Listing all the factors of a whole number and identifying a whole number as prime or composite

When one whole number is divisible by another, the second number is called a **factor** of the first.

EXAMPLE 1 List all the factors of 15.

▶ **Solution**

$15 \div 1 = 15$ $15 \div 3 = 5$ The number 15 is divisible
$15 \div 5 = 3$ $15 \div 15 = 1$ by 1, 3, 5, and 15.

The factors of 15 are 1, 3, 5, and 15.

A **prime number** is a whole number greater than 1 that has exactly two factors, 1 and the number itself. A whole number greater than 1 that has more than two factors is called a **composite number**. The number 1 is neither prime nor composite.

EXAMPLE 2 Identify each number as *prime* or *composite*.   a. 6   b. 7

▶ **Solution**

a. The number 6 has four factors: 1, 2, 3, and 6. It is composite.
b. The number 7 has exactly two factors: 1 and 7. It is prime.

List all the factors of each number.

1. 12 _____   2. 24 _____

3. 60 _____   4. 100 _____

5. 29 _____   6. 57 _____

7. 72 _____   8. 97 _____

Identify each number as *prime* or *composite*.

9. 5 _____   10. 9 _____

11. 25 _____   12. 37 _____

13. 59 _____   14. 79 _____

15. 87 _____   16. 111 _____

Making Sense of Numbers   Unit 1 Order of Operations and Number Theory   **9**

NAME _____ CLASS _____ DATE _____

Writing a Prime Factorization

OBJECTIVE: Writing a composite number as a product of prime factors

Every composite number can be written as a product of prime factors. This product is called the **prime factorization** of the number. You usually write a prime factorization in exponential form, with the factors arranged in order from least to greatest base.

EXAMPLE Write the prime factorization of 60.

Solution

Method 1

Make a *factor tree*. Write products of two factors until all the factors are prime.

$$\begin{array}{c} 60 \\ ③ \times 20 \\ ② \times 10 \\ ② \times ⑤ \end{array}$$

Method 2

Make a *division ladder*. Divide successively by prime numbers until the quotient is prime.

$$\begin{array}{r} 3\overline{)60} \\ 2\overline{)20} \\ 2\overline{)10} \\ 5 \end{array}$$

Using either method, the prime factorization of 60 is $2 \times 2 \times 3 \times 5$. Write this in exponential form as $2^2 \times 3^1 \times 5^1$.

Write the prime factorization of each number.

1. 30 _____
2. 42 _____
3. 12 _____
4. 18 _____
5. 24 _____
6. 36 _____
7. 56 _____
8. 54 _____
9. 32 _____
10. 81 _____
11. 57 _____
12. 85 _____
13. 116 _____
14. 325 _____
15. 132 _____
16. 414 _____
17. 588 _____
18. 680 _____
19. 2100 _____
20. 2640 _____

NAME _____ CLASS _____ DATE _____

2-5 Common Factors and the GCF
UNIT 1

OBJECTIVE: *Finding common factors and the greatest common factor*

A number that is a factor of each member of a set of whole numbers is called a **common factor** of the numbers. The greatest of the common factors is called the **greatest common factor,** or **GCF,** of the numbers.

EXAMPLE 1 List all the common factors of 12 and 18. Find the GCF.

▶ **Solution**

factors of 12: 1, 2, 3, 4, 6   *The common factors are*
factors of 18: 1, 2, 3, 6, 9, 18   *1, 2, 3, and 6.*

The greatest in the list of common factors is 6. So the GCF is 6.

You also can find a GCF by using prime factorization. The GCF is the product of the least powers of any common prime factors.

EXAMPLE 2 Use prime factorization to find the GCF of 36 and 90.

▶ **Solution**

$36 = 2^2 \times 3^2$ *The common prime factors are 2 and 3.*
$90 = 2^1 \times 3^2 \times 5^1$ *The least powers of each are 2^1 and 3^2.*

The product of the least powers is $2^1 \times 3^2 = 18$. So the GCF is 18.

List all the common factors of each set of numbers. Find the GCF.

1. 16, 28   common factors: _____ GCF: _____

2. 48, 72   common factors: _____ GCF: _____

3. 56, 70   common factors: _____ GCF: _____

4. 64, 81   common factors: _____ GCF: _____

Use prime factorization to find the GCF of each set of numbers.

5. 18, 36 _____   6. 45, 60 _____   7. 44, 52 _____

8. 72, 108 _____   9. 60, 126 _____   10. 56, 84 _____

11. 75, 98 _____   12. 45, 112 _____   13. 180, 504 _____

14. 594, 936 _____ 15. 18, 54, 60 _____ 16. 27, 28, 45 _____

Making Sense of Numbers   Unit 1 Order of Operations and Number Theory   **11**

NAME _____ CLASS _____ DATE _____

Multiples of Whole Numbers

OBJECTIVE: Listing multiples of whole numbers and determining whether one whole number is a multiple of another

The counting numbers are 1, 2, 3, 4, . . . (The three dots mean *and so on*.) When a given number is multiplied by a counting number, the product is called a **multiple** of the given number.

EXAMPLE 1 List the first five multiples of 7.

▶ **Solution**

$7 \times 1 = \boxed{7} \quad 7 \times 2 = \boxed{14} \quad 7 \times 3 = \boxed{21} \quad 7 \times 4 = \boxed{28} \quad 7 \times 5 = \boxed{35}$

The first five multiples of 7 are 7, 14, 21, 28, 35.

If one whole number is divisible by another, then the first number is a multiple of the second.

EXAMPLE 2 Is 1488 a multiple of 3?

▶ **Solution**

$1 + 4 + 8 + 8 = 21$ *Apply the divisibility test for 3.*

21 is divisible by 3, so 1488 is divisible by 3.

Yes, 1488 is a multiple of 3.

List the first five multiples of each number.

1. 4 _____
2. 9 _____
3. 12 _____
4. 15 _____
5. 18 _____
6. 23 _____
7. 30 _____
8. 42 _____

Is the first number a multiple of the second? Write *Yes* or *No*.

9. 96; 4 _____
10. 78; 3 _____
11. 117; 9 _____
12. 135; 10 _____
13. 168; 4 _____
14. 265; 3 _____
15. 1052; 5 _____
16. 7065; 8 _____
17. 8451; 9 _____
18. 5254; 4 _____
19. 12,400; 5 _____
20. 26,481; 2 _____

NAME _____ CLASS _____ DATE _____

Common Multiples and the LCM

OBJECTIVE: *Finding common multiples and the least common multiple*

A number that is a multiple of each member of a set of whole numbers is called a **common multiple** of the numbers. The least of the common multiples is called the **least common multiple,** or **LCM,** of the numbers.

EXAMPLE 1 List the first three common multiples of 4 and 6. Find the LCM.

▶ **Solution**

multiples of 4: 4, 8, 12, 16, 20, 24, 28, 32, 36, 40, ...
multiples of 6: 6, 12, 18, 24, 30, 36, 42, ...

The first three common multiples are 12, 24, and 36.
The least of these is 12. So the LCM is 12.

You also can find an LCM by using prime factorization. The LCM is the product of the greatest powers of the prime factors that appear in any of the numbers.

EXAMPLE 2 Use prime factorization to find the LCM of 12 and 42.

▶ **Solution**

$12 = 2^2 \times 3^1$ *The prime factors that appear are 2, 3, and 7.*
$42 = 2^1 \times 3^1 \times 7^1$ *The greatest powers of each are 2^2, 3^1, and 7^1.*

The product of the greatest powers is $2^2 \times 3^1 \times 7^1 = 84$. The LCM is 84.

List the first three common multiples of each set of numbers. Find the LCM.

1. 4, 10   common multiples: _____ LCM: _____

2. 3, 5   common multiples: _____ LCM: _____

3. 6, 8   common multiples: _____ LCM: _____

4. 7, 14   common multiples: _____ LCM: _____

Use prime factorization to find the LCM of each set of numbers.

5. 18, 30 _____   6. 20, 70 _____   7. 12, 28 _____   8. 30, 45 _____

9. 14, 15 _____   10. 21, 55 _____ 11. 42, 66 _____ 12. 42, 60 _____

13. 18, 48 _____ 14. 56, 98 _____ 15. 18, 35, 45 _____ 16. 12, 27, 75 _____

Making Sense of Numbers   Unit 1 Order of Operations and Number Theory   **13**

Unit 2 Fractions

Chapter 3 Fraction Fundamentals
- 3-1 Fractions for Numbers Between 0 and 1 17
- 3-2 Fractions for Numbers 1 and Greater 18
- 3-3 Writing a Mixed Number as a Fraction 19
- 3-4 Writing a Fraction as a Mixed Number or as a Whole Number 20
- 3-5 Modeling Equivalent Fractions 21
- 3-6 Equivalent Fractions: Higher Terms 22
- 3-7 Equivalent Fractions: Lower Terms 23
- 3-8 Lowest Terms of a Fraction 24
- 3-9 Fractions on a Number Line 25
- 3-10 Comparing Fractions: Like Denominators 26
- 3-11 Comparing Fractions: Unlike Denominators 27
- 3-12 Ordering Fractions 28
- 3-13 Estimating Fractions 29
- 3-14 Reading a Customary Ruler 30
- 3-15 Negative and Zero Exponents 31

Chapter 4 Addition of Fractions and Mixed Numbers
- 4-1 Modeling Addition of Fractions 32
- 4-2 Adding Fractions: Like Denominators 33
- 4-3 Adding Fractions: Unlike Denominators 34
- 4-4 Adding Mixed Numbers: Like Denominators 35
- 4-5 Adding Mixed Numbers: Unlike Denominators 36
- 4-6 Estimating Sums Involving Fractions 37
- 4-7 Problems Involving Fraction Addition 38
- 4-8 Problems Involving Mixed Number Addition 39

Chapter 5 Subtraction of Fractions and Mixed Numbers
- 5-1 Modeling a Subtraction of Fractions 40
- 5-2 Subtracting Fractions: Like Denominators 41
- 5-3 Subtracting Fractions: Unlike Denominators 42
- 5-4 Subtracting Mixed Numbers Without Renaming 43
- 5-5 Subtracting Mixed Numbers With Renaming 44
- 5-6 Estimating Differences Involving Fractions 45
- 5-7 Problems Involving Fraction Subtraction 46
- 5-8 Problems Involving Mixed Number Subtraction 47
- 5-9 Problems Involving Either Addition or Subtraction of Fractions or Mixed Numbers 48

Making Sense of Numbers

5-10	Adding and Subtracting With Fractions	49
5-11	Adding and Subtracting With Mixed Numbers	50
5-12	Problems Involving Both Addition and Subtraction of Fractions or Mixed Numbers	51

Chapter 6 Multiplication of Fractions and Mixed Numbers

6-1	Modeling a Multiplication of Fractions	52
6-2	Multiplying Two Fractions	53
6-3	Multiplying a Fraction and a Whole Number	54
6-4	Multiplying Several Fractions	55
6-5	Multiplying With Mixed Numbers	56
6-6	Estimating Products Involving Mixed Numbers	57
6-7	Problems Involving Fraction Multiplication	58
6-8	Problems Involving Mixed Number Multiplication	59
6-9	Problems Involving Addition, Subtraction, or Multiplication of Fractions or Mixed Numbers	60
6-10	Adding, Subtracting, and Multiplying With Fractions	61
6-11	Adding, Subtracting, and Multiplying With Mixed Numbers	62
6-12	Solving Problems Involving Multiplication of Fractions or Mixed Numbers Together With Addition or Subtraction	63
6-13	Renaming a Customary Measure of Length by Multiplying	64
6-14	Renaming a Customary Measure of Weight or Liquid Capacity by Multiplying	65

Chapter 7 Division of Fractions and Mixed Numbers

7-1	Modeling a Division by a Fraction	66
7-2	Reciprocals	67
7-3	Dividing With Fractions	68
7-4	Dividing With Mixed Numbers	69
7-5	Estimating Quotients Involving Fractions and Mixed Numbers	70
7-6	Problems Involving Fraction Division	71
7-7	Problems Involving Mixed Number Division	72
7-8	Problems Involving Addition, Subtraction, Multiplication, or Division of Fractions or Mixed Numbers	73
7-9	Adding, Subtracting, Multiplying, and Dividing With Fractions	74
7-10	Adding, Subtracting, Multiplying, and Dividing With Mixed Numbers	75
7-11	Problems Involving Division of Fractions or Mixed Numbers Together With Addition, Subtraction, or Multiplication	76
7-12	Renaming a Customary Measure by Dividing	77
7-13	Renaming a Customary Measure by Multiplying or Dividing	78
7-14	Exponents and Division	79

NAME _____ CLASS _____ DATE _____

3-1 Fractions for Numbers Between 0 and 1
UNIT 2

OBJECTIVE: Writing a fraction between 0 and 1 to represent a part of a region and to represent a part of a set of figures

A **fraction** represents a part of a whole quantity that has been divided into equal parts. The top number of a fraction is its **numerator,** and the bottom number is its **denominator.**

EXAMPLE 1 The figure at right is divided into equal parts. Write a fraction to represent the shaded region.

▶ **Solution**

number of shaded parts → $\frac{3}{5}$ ← numerator
total number of parts → ← denominator

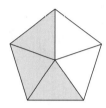

EXAMPLE 2 The figure at right is a set of identical squares. Write a fraction to represent the shaded squares as a part of a set.

▶ **Solution**

number of shaded squares → $\frac{4}{7}$ ← numerator
total number of squares → ← denominator

Write a fraction to represent the shaded region of each figure.

1. _____
2. _____
3. _____

4.  _____
5.  _____
6. 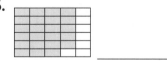 _____

Write a fraction to represent the shaded shapes as a part of a set.

7. _____
8.  _____
9. _____

10.  _____
11. 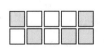 _____
12.  _____

Making Sense of Numbers   Unit 2   Fractions   **17**

3-2 Fractions for Numbers 1 and Greater

OBJECTIVE: Writing a fraction and a whole or mixed number to represent a quantity greater than or equal to 1

Fractions can represent quantities equal to 1 or greater than 1.

EXAMPLE 1 Write a fraction to represent the shaded regions of the figure at right.

▶ **Solution**

Consider each circle as one whole.

$\dfrac{12}{4}$ ← number of shaded parts in figure
← number of equal parts in one circle

A quantity greater than 1 can also be represented by a *mixed number*. A **mixed number** has a whole-number part and a fraction part.

EXAMPLE 2 Write a mixed number to represent the shaded regions of the figure at right.

▶ **Solution**

Two whole circles are shaded. → $2\dfrac{1}{6}$ ← One sixth of the third circle is shaded.

Represent each shaded region as a fraction and as a whole or mixed number.

1.   _____

2.   _____

3.   _____

4.   _____

5. 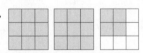 _____

6. 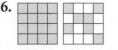 _____

7.  _____

8. 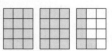 _____

9. 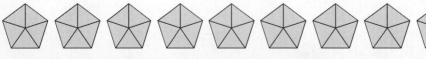 _____

10. 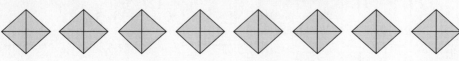 _____

NAME _____ CLASS _____ DATE _____

3-3 UNIT 2 Writing a Mixed Number as a Fraction

OBJECTIVE: Writing a mixed number as a fraction by drawing a model or by using an algorithm

Sometimes you need to write a mixed number as a fraction. One method for doing this is to draw a model.

EXAMPLE 1 Write $2\frac{3}{4}$ as a fraction.

Solution

Draw a model like the one at right. Count the fourths. Eleven-fourths are shaded.

So $2\frac{3}{4} = \frac{11}{4}$.

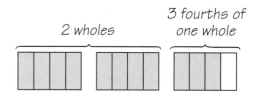

Alternatively, you can use the following procedure to write a mixed number as a fraction.

Writing a Mixed Number as a Fraction

1. Multiply the whole number by the denominator.
2. Add the numerator to the product from Step **1**.
3. Write the sum from Step **2** over the denominator.

EXAMPLE 2 Write $5\frac{2}{3}$ as a fraction.

Solution

$$5\frac{2}{3} = \frac{5 \times 3 + 2}{3} = \frac{15 + 2}{3} = \frac{17}{3}$$

Draw a model of each mixed number. Then write it as a fraction.

1. $4\frac{1}{3}$ _____ 2. $3\frac{5}{8}$ _____

Write each mixed number as a fraction.

3. $1\frac{1}{7}$ _____ 4. $1\frac{5}{11}$ _____ 5. $3\frac{5}{6}$ _____ 6. $4\frac{2}{9}$ _____

7. $6\frac{1}{2}$ _____ 8. $8\frac{8}{9}$ _____ 9. $12\frac{1}{5}$ _____ 10. $15\frac{1}{3}$ _____

Making Sense of Numbers

3-4 Writing a Fraction as a Mixed Number or as a Whole Number

UNIT 2

OBJECTIVE: Writing a fraction as a mixed number or a whole number by drawing a model or by dividing

Sometimes you need to rewrite a fraction as a mixed number or as a whole number. One method for doing this is to draw a model.

EXAMPLE 1 Write $\frac{14}{5}$ as a mixed number.

▶ **Solution**

Draw models for fifths until you arrive at $\frac{14}{5}$.

$\frac{5}{5}$ → $\frac{10}{5}$ → $\frac{14}{5}$ ⎯ 2 wholes ⎯ 4 fifths of one whole

The model shows 2 wholes and 4 fifths of one whole. So $\frac{14}{5} = 2\frac{4}{5}$.

A fraction bar represents a division. So another way to rewrite a fraction as a mixed number or whole number is to divide.

EXAMPLE 2 Write each fraction as a whole or mixed number. a. $\frac{54}{9}$ b. $\frac{83}{8}$

▶ **Solution**

a. $\frac{54}{9} = 54 \div 9 = 6$

b. $\frac{83}{8} = 83 \div 8 = 10$ R3

$= 10\frac{3}{8}$ ← remainder
← denominator

Draw a model of each fraction. Then write it as a whole or mixed number.

1. $\frac{15}{4}$ _____   2. $\frac{11}{2}$ _____

Write each fraction as a whole number or a mixed number.

3. $\frac{14}{9}$ _____   4. $\frac{10}{7}$ _____   5. $\frac{21}{5}$ _____   6. $\frac{28}{3}$ _____

7. $\frac{45}{3}$ _____   8. $\frac{56}{7}$ _____   9. $\frac{95}{6}$ _____   10. $\frac{71}{3}$ _____

20 Unit 2 Fractions   *Making Sense of Numbers*

3-5 Modeling Equivalent Fractions
UNIT 2

OBJECTIVE: *Interpreting and drawing models of equivalent fractions*

Fractions that represent the same amount are called **equivalent fractions**. You can use models to represent equivalent fractions.

EXAMPLE Draw a model to show that $\frac{6}{8} = \frac{3}{4}$.

Solution

Divide a rectangle into eight equal parts. Shade the first six parts.

Divide a congruent rectangle into four equal parts. Shade the first three parts.

The shaded parts are congruent. The conclusion is $\frac{6}{8} = \frac{3}{4}$.

Write the equivalent fractions represented by each model.

1. 2. 3.

4. 5. 6.

Draw a model of each statement in the space provided.

7. $\frac{1}{4} = \frac{2}{8}$ 8. $\frac{2}{6} = \frac{1}{3}$

9. $\frac{2}{5} = \frac{4}{10}$ 10. $\frac{6}{9} = \frac{2}{3}$

11. $\frac{4}{8} = \frac{3}{6}$ 12. $\frac{4}{12} = \frac{3}{9}$

Making Sense of Numbers   Unit 2 Fractions **21**

NAME _____ CLASS _____ DATE _____

3-6 Equivalent Fractions: Higher Terms
UNIT 2

OBJECTIVE: Writing an equivalent fraction with a greater denominator by drawing a model or by multiplying

Fractions that represent the same amount are called **equivalent fractions**. If a fraction is renamed with a denominator that is greater than the given denominator, it is written in *higher terms*.

EXAMPLE Rewrite the statement at right. Replace ? with the number that makes the fractions equivalent. $\frac{2}{3} = \frac{?}{12}$

Solution

Method 1
Draw a model of two thirds.
Split each third into four parts to make twelfths.

$\frac{2}{3}$

$\frac{8}{12}$

Method 2
Multiply both the numerator and denominator by 4.

$\frac{2}{3} = \frac{2 \times 4}{3 \times 4} = \frac{8}{12}$

Using either method, you can write $\frac{2}{3} = \frac{8}{12}$.

Method 2 above uses the following rule for equivalent fractions.

> **Equivalent Fractions: Higher Terms**
>
> To write a given fraction as an equivalent fraction in higher terms, multiply both the numerator and denominator by the same nonzero number.

Rewrite each statement. Replace ? with the number that makes the fractions equivalent.

1. $\frac{1}{4} = \frac{?}{12}$ _____
2. $\frac{1}{5} = \frac{?}{10}$ _____
3. $\frac{2}{3} = \frac{?}{6}$ _____
4. $\frac{3}{4} = \frac{?}{16}$ _____
5. $\frac{7}{3} = \frac{?}{12}$ _____
6. $\frac{9}{5} = \frac{?}{10}$ _____
7. $\frac{3}{7} = \frac{?}{14}$ _____
8. $\frac{5}{6} = \frac{?}{24}$ _____
9. $\frac{4}{7} = \frac{?}{35}$ _____
10. $\frac{9}{8} = \frac{?}{56}$ _____
11. $\frac{13}{9} = \frac{?}{54}$ _____
12. $\frac{15}{6} = \frac{?}{48}$ _____
13. $\frac{6}{7} = \frac{?}{91}$ _____
14. $\frac{11}{8} = \frac{?}{96}$ _____
15. $\frac{17}{12} = \frac{?}{60}$ _____

NAME _____ CLASS _____ DATE _____

3-7 Equivalent Fractions: Lower Terms
UNIT 2

OBJECTIVE: Writing an equivalent fraction with a lesser denominator by drawing a model or by dividing

Fractions that represent the same amount are called **equivalent fractions**. If a fraction is renamed with a denominator that is less than the given denominator, it is written in *lower terms*.

EXAMPLE Rewrite the statement at right. Replace ? with the number that makes the fractions equivalent. $\dfrac{6}{10} = \dfrac{?}{5}$

Solution

Method 1
Draw a model of six-tenths.
Redraw each two-tenths as one-fifth.

$\dfrac{6}{10}$

$\dfrac{3}{5}$

Method 2
Divide both the numerator and denominator by 2.

$\dfrac{6}{10} = \dfrac{6 \div 2}{10 \div 2} = \dfrac{3}{5}$

Using either method, you can write $\dfrac{6}{10} = \dfrac{3}{5}$.

Method 2 above uses the following rule for equivalent fractions.

Equivalent Fractions: Lower Terms

To write a given fraction as an equivalent fraction in lower terms, divide both the numerator and denominator by the same nonzero number.

Rewrite each statement. Replace ? with the number that makes the fractions equivalent.

1. $\dfrac{6}{8} = \dfrac{?}{4}$ _____

2. $\dfrac{4}{12} = \dfrac{?}{3}$ _____

3. $\dfrac{9}{12} = \dfrac{?}{4}$ _____

4. $\dfrac{4}{10} = \dfrac{?}{5}$ _____

5. $\dfrac{20}{16} = \dfrac{?}{4}$ _____

6. $\dfrac{30}{8} = \dfrac{?}{4}$ _____

7. $\dfrac{36}{42} = \dfrac{?}{7}$ _____

8. $\dfrac{81}{45} = \dfrac{?}{5}$ _____

9. $\dfrac{16}{24} = \dfrac{?}{6}$ _____

10. $\dfrac{54}{36} = \dfrac{?}{4}$ _____

11. $\dfrac{32}{28} = \dfrac{?}{14}$ _____

12. $\dfrac{24}{60} = \dfrac{?}{20}$ _____

13. $\dfrac{36}{48} = \dfrac{?}{4}$ _____

14. $\dfrac{110}{55} = \dfrac{?}{5}$ _____

15. $\dfrac{175}{50} = \dfrac{?}{2}$ _____

Making Sense of Numbers

NAME _____ CLASS _____ DATE _____

3-8 Lowest Terms of a Fraction
UNIT 2

OBJECTIVE: *Writing a fraction in lowest terms*

A fraction is in **lowest terms** if its numerator and denominator have no common factor other than 1.

EXAMPLE 1 Write $\frac{48}{54}$ in lowest terms.

▶ **Solution**

Method 1
Divide both the numerator and denominator by common factors until their greatest common factor (GCF) is 1.
$$\frac{48}{54} = \frac{48 \div 2}{54 \div 2} = \frac{24}{27} \rightarrow \frac{24}{27} = \frac{24 \div 3}{27 \div 3} = \frac{8}{9}$$

Method 2
Divide both the numerator and denominator by their GCF.
$$\frac{48}{54} = \frac{48 \div 6}{54 \div 6} = \frac{8}{9} \quad \text{The GCF of 48 and 54 is 6.}$$

You can also use prime factors to write a fraction in lowest terms.

EXAMPLE 2 Write $\frac{96}{84}$ in lowest terms.

▶ **Solution**

Write the prime factorization of the numerator and the denominator. Divide by all common prime factors.

$$\frac{96}{84} = \frac{2^5 \times 3^1}{2^2 \times 3^1 \times 7^1} = \frac{\overset{1}{\cancel{2}} \times \overset{1}{\cancel{2}} \times 2 \times 2 \times 2 \times \overset{1}{\cancel{3}}}{\underset{1}{\cancel{2}} \times \underset{1}{\cancel{2}} \times \underset{1}{\cancel{3}} \times 7} = \frac{8}{7}$$

Write each fraction in lowest terms.

1. $\frac{4}{14}$ _____   2. $\frac{9}{15}$ _____   3. $\frac{6}{48}$ _____   4. $\frac{4}{28}$ _____

5. $\frac{15}{70}$ _____   6. $\frac{35}{60}$ _____   7. $\frac{12}{18}$ _____   8. $\frac{18}{45}$ _____

9. $\frac{36}{8}$ _____   10. $\frac{42}{18}$ _____   11. $\frac{14}{42}$ _____   12. $\frac{18}{72}$ _____

13. $\frac{68}{12}$ _____   14. $\frac{65}{78}$ _____   15. $\frac{34}{51}$ _____   16. $\frac{95}{38}$ _____

17. $\frac{189}{126}$ _____   18. $\frac{132}{198}$ _____   19. $\frac{273}{195}$ _____   20. $\frac{171}{513}$ _____

24 Unit 2 Fractions *Making Sense of Numbers*

NAME _____ CLASS _____ DATE _____

3-9
UNIT 2
Fractions on a Number Line

OBJECTIVE: Writing a fraction to represent a point on a number line

A fraction can represent a point on a number line.

EXAMPLE 1   Write a fraction to represent point *M* at right.

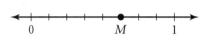

Solution

The distance between 0 and 1 is divided into eight equal parts.
Point *M* is five-eighths of the distance from 0 to 1.
Point *M* is represented by the fraction $\frac{5}{8}$.

EXAMPLE 2   Locate and label point $N\left(1\frac{3}{4}\right)$ on a number line.

Solution

Divide the distance between units into four equal parts.
Point *N* is three-fourths of the distance from 1 to 2.

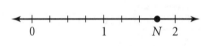

Write a fraction *in lowest terms* to represent each point on the number line below.

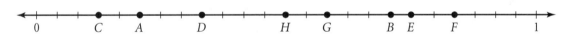

1. A _____   2. B _____   3. C _____   4. D _____

5. E _____   6. F _____   7. G _____   8. H _____

Locate and label each point on the number line at the bottom of the page.

9. $P\left(\frac{7}{8}\right)$ 10. $Q\left(\frac{1}{2}\right)$ 11. $R\left(\frac{2}{8}\right)$ 12. $S\left(1\frac{5}{6}\right)$ 13. $T\left(1\frac{2}{3}\right)$

14. $U\left(\frac{7}{6}\right)$ 15. $V\left(\frac{3}{2}\right)$ 16. $W\left(2\frac{4}{5}\right)$ 17. $X\left(\frac{12}{5}\right)$ 18. $Y\left(\frac{22}{10}\right)$

Making Sense of Numbers   Unit 2 Fractions   **25**

3-10 Comparing Fractions: Like Denominators

OBJECTIVE: Using the symbols $<$, $>$, and $=$ to represent the order of two fractions or mixed numbers with like denominators

When you compare two fractions, you are determining their *order* on a number line. You indicate the order by placing one of the symbols $<$, $>$, or $=$ between the fractions. Here is an example.

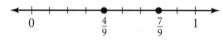

$\frac{4}{9}$ is to the left of $\frac{7}{9}$. → $\frac{4}{9}$ is less than $\frac{7}{9}$. → $\frac{4}{9} < \frac{7}{9}$

$\frac{7}{9}$ is to the right of $\frac{4}{9}$. → $\frac{7}{9}$ is greater than $\frac{4}{9}$. → $\frac{7}{9} > \frac{4}{9}$

It is not necessary to draw a number line every time you compare two fractions. If the fractions have like denominators, you can compare them arithmetically by comparing their numerators.

EXAMPLE Fill in the blank with $<$, $>$, or $=$ to make a true statement: $\frac{19}{8}$ ___?___ $2\frac{5}{8}$

Solution

Method 1
Write $\frac{19}{8}$ as a mixed number.

$\frac{19}{8}$ ___?___ $2\frac{5}{8}$ → $2\frac{3}{8}$ ___?___ $2\frac{5}{8}$

$3 < 5$, so $2\frac{3}{8} < 2\frac{5}{8}$

Method 2
Write $2\frac{5}{8}$ as a fraction.

$\frac{19}{8}$ ___?___ $2\frac{5}{8}$ → $\frac{19}{8}$ ___?___ $\frac{21}{8}$

$19 < 21$, so $\frac{19}{8} < \frac{21}{8}$

Using either method, the conclusion is $\frac{19}{8} < 2\frac{5}{8}$.

Fill in each blank with $<$, $>$, or $=$ to make a true statement.

1. $\frac{8}{11}$ ___ $\frac{3}{11}$
2. $\frac{13}{15}$ ___ $\frac{14}{15}$
3. $5\frac{2}{9}$ ___ $5\frac{4}{9}$
4. $1\frac{17}{20}$ ___ $1\frac{13}{20}$

5. $\frac{11}{5}$ ___ $\frac{14}{5}$
6. $\frac{18}{11}$ ___ $\frac{20}{11}$
7. $6\frac{1}{4}$ ___ $5\frac{3}{4}$
8. $3\frac{9}{10}$ ___ $8\frac{3}{10}$

9. $7\frac{1}{3}$ ___ $\frac{23}{3}$
10. $\frac{45}{8}$ ___ $5\frac{5}{8}$
11. $\frac{29}{7}$ ___ $3\frac{6}{7}$
12. $7\frac{5}{12}$ ___ $\frac{83}{12}$

13. $\frac{44}{3}$ ___ $14\frac{2}{3}$
14. $17\frac{1}{4}$ ___ $\frac{59}{4}$
15. $\frac{65}{7}$ ___ 9
16. 15 ___ $\frac{37}{2}$

17. $16\frac{2}{9}$ ___ $\frac{144}{9}$
18. $\frac{90}{15}$ ___ $6\frac{4}{15}$
19. $19\frac{4}{5}$ ___ $\frac{99}{5}$
20. $\frac{151}{8}$ ___ $18\frac{3}{8}$

NAME _____ CLASS _____ DATE _____

3-11 Comparing Fractions: Unlike Denominators
UNIT 2

OBJECTIVE: Using the symbols <, >, and = to represent the order of two fractions or mixed numbers with unlike denominators

A **common denominator** of a set of fractions is any common multiple of the denominators. The least common multiple (LCM) of the denominators is called the **least common denominator, or LCD,** of the fractions.

EXAMPLE 1 Rewrite $\frac{5}{6}$ and $\frac{3}{4}$ as equivalent fractions using their LCD.

▶ **Solution**

The denominators are 6 and 4. The LCM of 6 and 4 is 12.

$$\frac{5}{6} = \frac{5 \times 2}{6 \times 2} = \frac{10}{12} \qquad \frac{3}{4} = \frac{3 \times 3}{4 \times 3} = \frac{9}{12}$$

You use the LCD to compare fractions with unlike denominators.

EXAMPLE 2 Fill in the blank with <, >, or = to make a true statement: $\frac{4}{9}$ __?__ $\frac{5}{12}$

▶ **Solution**

Write equivalent fractions using the LCD.

$$\frac{4}{9} = \frac{4 \times 4}{9 \times 4} = \frac{16}{36}$$

$$\frac{5}{12} = \frac{5 \times 3}{12 \times 3} = \frac{15}{36}$$

Compare the equivalent fractions.

$$\frac{16}{36} \underline{\ ?\ } \frac{15}{36}$$

$16 > 15$, so $\frac{16}{36} > \frac{15}{36} \rightarrow \frac{4}{9} > \frac{5}{12}$

Rewrite each set of fractions as equivalent fractions using their LCD.

1. $\frac{1}{3}$ and $\frac{4}{5}$ _____

2. $\frac{3}{14}$ and $\frac{1}{2}$ _____

3. $\frac{4}{21}$ and $\frac{5}{6}$ _____

4. $\frac{3}{8}$ and $\frac{5}{36}$ _____

Fill in each blank with <, >, or = to make a true statement.

5. $\frac{2}{5}$ ___ $\frac{3}{7}$

6. $\frac{1}{4}$ ___ $\frac{3}{11}$

7. $\frac{11}{15}$ ___ $\frac{2}{3}$

8. $\frac{9}{28}$ ___ $\frac{2}{7}$

9. $\frac{7}{8}$ ___ $\frac{1}{12}$

10. $\frac{4}{6}$ ___ $\frac{14}{21}$

11. $\frac{13}{8}$ ___ $\frac{17}{10}$

12. $\frac{23}{18}$ ___ $\frac{19}{14}$

13. $3\frac{16}{20}$ ___ $3\frac{4}{5}$

14. $8\frac{5}{6}$ ___ $8\frac{17}{22}$

15. $1\frac{1}{3}$ ___ $\frac{5}{4}$

16. $\frac{13}{7}$ ___ $1\frac{7}{8}$

Making Sense of Numbers

NAME _____ CLASS _____ DATE _____

3-12 Ordering Fractions
UNIT 2

OBJECTIVE: *Arranging a set of fractions in increasing or decreasing order*

Sometimes you must arrange a set of three or more fractions in order from least to greatest or from greatest to least.

EXAMPLE Write in order from least to greatest: $\frac{1}{3}, \frac{2}{5}, \frac{3}{10}$

▶ **Solution**
The LCM of 3, 5, and 10 is 30.

$\frac{1}{3} = \frac{10}{30}, \quad \frac{2}{5} = \frac{12}{30}, \quad \frac{3}{10} = \frac{9}{30}$ *Rewrite the fractions using 30 as the common denominator.*

$9 < 10 < 12$ *Order the numerators from least to greatest.*

$\frac{9}{30} < \frac{10}{30} < \frac{12}{30}$ *Place the fractions in the same order.*

$\frac{3}{10} < \frac{1}{3} < \frac{2}{5}$

Write each set of numbers in order from *least* to *greatest*.

1. $\frac{6}{11}, \frac{2}{11}, \frac{5}{11}$ _____

2. $\frac{9}{20}, \frac{17}{20}, \frac{3}{20}$ _____

3. $\frac{4}{5}, \frac{11}{15}, \frac{13}{15}$ _____

4. $\frac{15}{24}, \frac{13}{24}, \frac{2}{3}$ _____

5. $\frac{5}{6}, \frac{3}{4}, \frac{13}{18}$ _____

6. $\frac{4}{5}, \frac{1}{2}, \frac{5}{7}$ _____

7. $\frac{17}{10}, \frac{7}{4}, \frac{33}{20}$ _____

8. $2\frac{4}{9}, \frac{47}{18}, \frac{31}{12}$ _____

9. $\frac{5}{7}, \frac{3}{4}, \frac{2}{3}, \frac{5}{6}$ _____

10. $\frac{8}{5}, 1\frac{7}{8}, \frac{17}{10}, 1\frac{13}{15}$ _____

Write each set of numbers in order from *greatest* to *least*.

11. $\frac{9}{7}, \frac{5}{7}, \frac{10}{7}$ _____

12. $\frac{19}{5}, 3\frac{2}{5}, \frac{20}{5}, \frac{14}{5}$ _____

13. $\frac{1}{4}, \frac{5}{12}, \frac{2}{9}$ _____

14. $\frac{7}{3}, \frac{23}{10}, \frac{32}{15}$ _____

15. $\frac{1}{3}, \frac{1}{7}, \frac{1}{2}$ _____

16. $\frac{3}{8}, \frac{3}{4}, \frac{3}{2}, \frac{3}{16}$ _____

17. $\frac{1}{2}, \frac{6}{11}, \frac{3}{7}$ _____

18. $\frac{19}{6}, \frac{39}{10}, 3\frac{1}{2}$ _____

19. $\frac{7}{15}, \frac{6}{5}, \frac{1}{8}, \frac{13}{24}$ _____

20. $2\frac{3}{4}, \frac{29}{12}, \frac{53}{21}, 2\frac{5}{14}$ _____

NAME _____ CLASS _____ DATE _____

3-13 Estimating Fractions
UNIT 2

OBJECTIVE: Writing simpler fractions as an estimate of a given fraction, and determining whether a given fraction is closest to 0, $\frac{1}{2}$, or 1

To estimate a fraction, write a simpler fraction that is close in value to it.

EXAMPLE 1 Write a simpler fraction as an estimate. a. $\frac{25}{99}$ b. $\frac{29}{51}$

▶ **Solution**
a. 99 is close to 100, and $\frac{25}{100} = \frac{1}{4}$. So $\frac{25}{99}$ is about $\frac{1}{4}$.
b. $\frac{29}{51}$ is close to $\frac{30}{50}$, and $\frac{30}{50} = \frac{3}{5}$. So $\frac{29}{51}$ is about $\frac{3}{5}$.

You also can estimate a fraction by using some common number sense to determine whether it is closest in value to 0, $\frac{1}{2}$, or 1.

EXAMPLE 2 Is each fraction closest to 0, $\frac{1}{2}$, or 1? a. $\frac{3}{79}$ b. $\frac{44}{87}$ c. $\frac{67}{68}$

▶ **Solution**
a. 3 is small when compared to 79. This means $\frac{3}{79}$ is closest to 0.
b. 87 is nearly twice 44. This means $\frac{44}{87}$ is closest to $\frac{1}{2}$.
c. 67 and 68 are almost equal. This means $\frac{67}{68}$ is closest to 1.

Write a simpler fraction as an estimate of each fraction.

1. $\frac{8}{23}$ _____ 2. $\frac{6}{29}$ _____ 3. $\frac{31}{40}$ _____ 4. $\frac{49}{60}$ _____

5. $\frac{62}{71}$ _____ 6. $\frac{41}{65}$ _____ 7. $\frac{24}{35}$ _____ 8. $\frac{23}{29}$ _____

9. $\frac{11}{78}$ _____ 10. $\frac{39}{161}$ _____ 11. $\frac{99}{59}$ _____ 12. $\frac{141}{79}$ _____

Is each fraction closest to 0, $\frac{1}{2}$, or 1?

13. $\frac{17}{36}$ _____ 14. $\frac{35}{36}$ _____ 15. $\frac{25}{48}$ _____ 16. $\frac{3}{48}$ _____

17. $\frac{71}{75}$ _____ 18. $\frac{41}{79}$ _____ 19. $\frac{15}{32}$ _____ 20. $\frac{88}{95}$ _____

21. $\frac{17}{200}$ _____ 22. $\frac{491}{500}$ _____ 23. $\frac{37}{822}$ _____ 24. $\frac{412}{781}$ _____

Making Sense of Numbers

3-14 Reading a Customary Ruler

UNIT 2

OBJECTIVE: Measuring segments using inches and fractions of an inch

In the United States Customary system of measurement, small lengths are commonly measured in inches and fractions of an inch.

EXAMPLE Find the length of the segment to the nearest eighth of an inch.

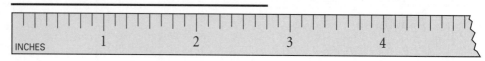

▶ **Solution**

The left end of the segment is at the "zero mark" of the ruler.

The right end is between $2\frac{6}{8}$ and $2\frac{7}{8}$, but closer to $2\frac{6}{8}$.

To the nearest eighth of an inch, the length of the segment is $2\frac{6}{8}$ inches.

Written in lowest terms, this is $2\frac{3}{4}$ inches.

Find the length of each segment to the nearest fourth of an inch.

1. ——————————————————— ———————
2. ——————————— ———————
3. —————————————— ———————
4. ——————— ———————

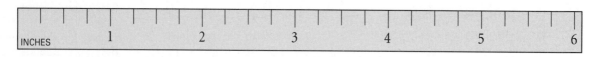

Find the length of each segment to the nearest sixteenth of an inch.

5. ——————————————————— ———————
6. —————————————— ———————
7. ———————— ———————
8. —————————— ———————

30 Unit 2 Fractions

Making Sense of Numbers

NAME _____ CLASS _____ DATE _____

3-15 Negative and Zero Exponents
UNIT 2

OBJECTIVE: Finding the value of exponential expressions involving negative and zero exponents and writing expressions in exponential form

In the past, you have worked with natural number exponents.

The *exponent* is 6.
The *base* is 2.
$$2^6 = \underbrace{2 \times 2 \times 2 \times 2 \times 2 \times 2}_{\text{6 identical factors of 2}}$$

An exponential expression also may involve a *negative* exponent. It is also possible for zero to be an exponent.

Negative and Zero Exponents

If a is a nonzero number and n is a natural number, then:

$$a^{-n} = \frac{1}{a^n} \qquad\qquad a^0 = 1$$

EXAMPLE 1 Find the value of each expression. a. 2^{-6} b. 7^{-1} c. 11^0

Solution

a. $2^{-6} = \dfrac{1}{2^6} = \dfrac{1}{2 \times 2 \times 2 \times 2 \times 2 \times 2}$ b. $7^{-1} = \dfrac{1}{7^1}$ c. $11^0 = 1$

$= \dfrac{1}{64}$ $= \dfrac{1}{7}$

EXAMPLE 2 Write each expression in exponential form. a. $\dfrac{1}{5 \times 5 \times 5}$ b. $\dfrac{1}{2}$

Solution

a. $\dfrac{1}{5 \times 5 \times 5} = \dfrac{1}{5^3} = 5^{-3}$ b. $\dfrac{1}{2} = \dfrac{1}{2^1} = 2^{-1}$

Find the value of each expression.

1. 5^{-2} _____   2. 2^{-3} _____   3. 3^0 _____   4. 11^{-1} _____

5. 2^{-4} _____   6. 3^{-5} _____   7. 5^{-1} _____   8. 13^0 _____

Write each expression in exponential form.

9. $\dfrac{1}{7 \times 7 \times 7 \times 7}$ _____   10. $\dfrac{1}{23 \times 23}$ _____   11. $\dfrac{1}{19}$ _____

12. $\dfrac{1}{2 \times 2 \times 2 \times 2 \times 2}$ _____   13. $\dfrac{1}{3}$ _____   14. $\dfrac{1}{11 \times 11 \times 11}$ _____

Making Sense of Numbers

4-1 Modeling Addition of Fractions

UNIT 2

OBJECTIVE: Interpreting and drawing models of fraction addition

You can use a model to represent an addition of fractions.

EXAMPLE Draw a model of $\frac{3}{8} + \frac{1}{4}$ and write the sum.

Solution

Give the fractions a common denominator. Rewrite $\frac{1}{4}$ as $\frac{2}{8}$.

Divide a rectangle into eight equal parts.

Shade three-eighths with one color.
Shade two-eighths with a different color.
Note that five-eighths are shaded in all.

Therefore, $\frac{3}{8} + \frac{1}{4} = \frac{5}{8}$.

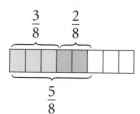

Write the sum that each model represents. Be sure to write all fractions in lowest terms.

1. _____
2. _____
3. _____
4. _____
5. _____
6. _____
7. _____
8. _____

Draw a model of each addition in the space provided. Then write the sum.

9. $\frac{1}{5} + \frac{3}{5}$

   sum: _____

10. $\frac{1}{5} + \frac{7}{10}$

    sum: _____

11. $\frac{1}{4} + \frac{1}{3}$

    sum: _____

12. $\frac{1}{2} + \frac{2}{3}$

    sum: _____

NAME _____ CLASS _____ DATE _____

4-2 Adding Fractions: Like Denominators
UNIT 2

OBJECTIVE: *Finding sums of two or more fractions with like denominators*

To add fractions that have like denominators, you can use the following method.

> **Adding Fractions with Like Denominators**
> 1. Add the numerators.
> 2. Write the sum from Step **1** over the like denominator.
> 3. If necessary, rewrite the result from Step **2** in lowest terms.

EXAMPLE 1 Write each sum in lowest terms. a. $\frac{5}{7} + \frac{1}{7}$ b. $\frac{5}{12} + \frac{1}{12}$

▸ Solution

a. $\frac{5}{7} + \frac{1}{7} = \frac{5+1}{7} = \frac{6}{7}$ 　　b. $\frac{5}{12} + \frac{1}{12} = \frac{5+1}{12} = \frac{6}{12} = \frac{1}{2}$

Sometimes a sum of fractions is a whole number or a mixed number.

EXAMPLE 2 Write each sum in lowest terms. a. $\frac{2}{9} + \frac{7}{9}$ b. $\frac{7}{8} + \frac{3}{8}$

▸ Solution

a. $\frac{2}{9} + \frac{7}{9} = \frac{2+7}{9} = \frac{9}{9} = 1$ 　　b. $\frac{7}{8} + \frac{3}{8} = \frac{7+3}{8} = \frac{10}{8} = \frac{5}{4} = 1\frac{1}{4}$

Write each sum in lowest terms.

1. $\frac{2}{5} + \frac{2}{5}$ _____　　2. $\frac{8}{11} + \frac{1}{11}$ _____　　3. $\frac{1}{8} + \frac{5}{8}$ _____

4. $\frac{3}{10} + \frac{1}{10}$ _____　　5. $\frac{4}{15} + \frac{8}{15}$ _____　　6. $\frac{7}{18} + \frac{5}{18}$ _____

7. $\frac{7}{9} + \frac{4}{9}$ _____　　8. $\frac{2}{15} + \frac{13}{15}$ _____　　9. $\frac{5}{6} + \frac{5}{6}$ _____

10. $\frac{7}{8} + \frac{7}{8}$ _____　　11. $\frac{1}{12} + \frac{11}{12}$ _____　　12. $\frac{5}{12} + \frac{11}{12}$ _____

13. $\frac{2}{9} + \frac{1}{9} + \frac{5}{9}$ _____　　14. $\frac{3}{7} + \frac{1}{7} + \frac{5}{7}$ _____

15. $\frac{13}{15} + \frac{4}{15} + \frac{13}{15}$ _____　　16. $\frac{9}{11} + \frac{5}{11} + \frac{10}{11}$ _____

17. $\frac{7}{9} + \frac{1}{9} + \frac{4}{9}$ _____　　18. $\frac{11}{18} + \frac{5}{18} + \frac{17}{18}$ _____

Making Sense of Numbers

NAME _____ CLASS _____ DATE _____

4-3 UNIT 2 Adding Fractions: Unlike Denominators

OBJECTIVE: Finding sums of two or more fractions with unlike denominators

To add fractions that have unlike denominators, you must first write equivalent fractions that have a common denominator. Then add using the method for fractions with like denominators.

EXAMPLE Write each sum in lowest terms. **a.** $\frac{3}{8} + \frac{1}{2}$ **b.** $\frac{3}{4} + \frac{5}{6}$

Solution

a. The LCM of 8 and 2 is 8. So the least common denominator is 8.

First rewrite $\frac{1}{2}$.   Then add.

$$\frac{1}{2} = \frac{1 \times 4}{2 \times 4} = \frac{4}{8} \qquad \frac{3}{8} + \frac{1}{2} = \frac{3}{8} + \frac{4}{8} = \frac{3 + 4}{8} = \frac{7}{8}$$

b. The LCM of 4 and 6 is 12. So the least common denominator is 12.

First rewrite $\frac{3}{4}$ and $\frac{5}{6}$.   Then add.

$$\frac{3}{4} = \frac{3 \times 3}{4 \times 3} = \frac{9}{12} \qquad \frac{3}{4} + \frac{5}{6} = \frac{9}{12} + \frac{10}{12} = \frac{9 + 10}{12} = \frac{19}{12}$$

$$\frac{5}{6} = \frac{5 \times 2}{6 \times 2} = \frac{10}{12} \qquad\qquad\qquad\qquad\qquad\qquad = 1\frac{7}{12}$$

Write each sum in lowest terms.

1. $\frac{1}{3} + \frac{8}{15}$ _____

2. $\frac{7}{8} + \frac{1}{4}$ _____

3. $\frac{17}{30} + \frac{3}{5}$ _____

4. $\frac{3}{4} + \frac{1}{20}$ _____

5. $\frac{1}{3} + \frac{1}{4}$ _____

6. $\frac{1}{7} + \frac{1}{5}$ _____

7. $\frac{1}{6} + \frac{1}{9}$ _____

8. $\frac{1}{10} + \frac{1}{6}$ _____

9. $\frac{5}{6} + \frac{3}{8}$ _____

10. $\frac{3}{4} + \frac{11}{14}$ _____

11. $\frac{5}{12} + \frac{7}{20}$ _____

12. $\frac{5}{18} + \frac{11}{30}$ _____

13. $\frac{3}{8} + \frac{1}{4} + \frac{7}{8}$ _____

14. $\frac{1}{5} + \frac{3}{5} + \frac{3}{4}$ _____

15. $\frac{7}{8} + \frac{1}{2} + \frac{3}{4}$ _____

16. $\frac{2}{3} + \frac{7}{12} + \frac{5}{6}$ _____

17. $\frac{1}{2} + \frac{1}{3} + \frac{1}{5}$ _____

18. $\frac{1}{6} + \frac{1}{4} + \frac{1}{14}$ _____

19. $\frac{2}{3} + \frac{2}{5} + \frac{5}{6}$ _____

20. $\frac{5}{9} + \frac{8}{15} + \frac{3}{10}$ _____

NAME _____ CLASS _____ DATE _____

4-4 Adding Mixed Numbers: Like Denominators
UNIT 2

OBJECTIVE: *Finding sums of mixed numbers with like denominators*

To add mixed numbers that have like denominators, you can use the following method.

> **Adding Mixed Numbers with Like Denominators**
> 1. Add the fractions.
> 2. Add the whole numbers.
> 3. If necessary, rename the whole number in the sum.
> 4. If necessary, rewrite the sum in lowest terms.

EXAMPLE Write each sum in lowest terms.

a. $4\frac{1}{10} + 2\frac{7}{10}$ b. $2\frac{6}{7} + 1$ c. $3\frac{5}{9} + 2\frac{8}{9}$

▶ **Solution**

a. $4\frac{1}{10}$
   $+ 2\frac{7}{10}$
   $\overline{6\frac{8}{10}}$

b. $2\frac{6}{7}$
   $+ 1$
   $\overline{3\frac{6}{7}}$

c. $3\frac{5}{9}$ Rename
   $+ 2\frac{8}{9}$ the whole
   $\overline{5\frac{13}{9}} = 5 + 1\frac{4}{9} = 6\frac{4}{9}$ number.

Write each sum in lowest terms.

1. $9\frac{3}{5} + 6\frac{1}{5}$ _____
2. $7\frac{2}{9} + 1\frac{2}{9}$ _____
3. $2\frac{1}{8} + 3\frac{5}{8}$ _____
4. $4\frac{1}{6} + 5\frac{1}{6}$ _____
5. $1\frac{3}{10} + 5$ _____
6. $8 + 4\frac{3}{8}$ _____
7. $3\frac{5}{7} + \frac{1}{7}$ _____
8. $\frac{1}{12} + 5\frac{7}{12}$ _____
9. $\frac{3}{4} + 9\frac{1}{4}$ _____
10. $4\frac{13}{20} + \frac{7}{20}$ _____
11. $5\frac{1}{9} + 7\frac{8}{9}$ _____
12. $1\frac{2}{5} + 6\frac{3}{5}$ _____
13. $1\frac{7}{9} + 5\frac{4}{9}$ _____
14. $2\frac{8}{15} + 4\frac{11}{15}$ _____
15. $9\frac{5}{6} + 8\frac{5}{6}$ _____
16. $7\frac{1}{8} + 1\frac{3}{8} + 9\frac{1}{8}$ _____
17. $3\frac{4}{9} + 10\frac{1}{9} + 2\frac{4}{9}$ _____
18. $8\frac{6}{7} + 3\frac{2}{7} + 3\frac{4}{7}$ _____
19. $1\frac{7}{9} + 3\frac{1}{9} + 6\frac{7}{9}$ _____

Making Sense of Numbers

4-5 Adding Mixed Numbers: Unlike Denominators

UNIT 2

OBJECTIVE: Finding sums of mixed numbers with unlike denominators

To add mixed numbers that have unlike denominators, you must first write equivalent mixed numbers that have a common denominator. Then add using the method for mixed numbers with like denominators.

EXAMPLE Write each sum in lowest terms. a. $8\frac{1}{5} + 3\frac{7}{10}$ b. $4\frac{7}{8} + 3\frac{1}{6}$

Solution

a. The LCM of 5 and 10 is 10. So the least common denominator is 10.

$$8\frac{1}{5} \rightarrow 8\frac{2}{10}$$
$$+ 3\frac{7}{10} \rightarrow + 3\frac{7}{10}$$
$$\overline{} \qquad \overline{11\frac{9}{10}}$$

b. The LCM of 8 and 6 is 24. So the least common denominator is 24.

$$4\frac{7}{8} \rightarrow 4\frac{21}{24}$$
$$+ 3\frac{1}{6} \rightarrow + 3\frac{4}{24}$$
$$\overline{} \qquad \overline{7\frac{25}{24}} = 7 + 1\frac{1}{24} = 8\frac{1}{24}$$

Write each sum in lowest terms.

1. $6\frac{2}{3} + 7\frac{1}{6}$ _____
2. $9\frac{3}{8} + 3\frac{1}{2}$ _____
3. $5\frac{1}{3} + 2\frac{5}{12}$ _____
4. $8\frac{3}{14} + 2\frac{1}{2}$ _____
5. $1\frac{3}{4} + 2\frac{1}{10}$ _____
6. $3\frac{1}{6} + 1\frac{4}{15}$ _____
7. $2\frac{1}{4} + \frac{7}{8}$ _____
8. $\frac{11}{18} + 1\frac{7}{9}$ _____
9. $7\frac{1}{2} + \frac{5}{6}$ _____
10. $\frac{7}{12} + 5\frac{2}{3}$ _____
11. $3\frac{1}{2} + \frac{6}{7}$ _____
12. $\frac{2}{3} + 1\frac{4}{5}$ _____
13. $4\frac{8}{9} + \frac{1}{6}$ _____
14. $\frac{7}{9} + 6\frac{4}{15}$ _____
15. $5\frac{3}{4} + 8\frac{5}{6}$ _____
16. $3\frac{5}{8} + 1\frac{7}{10}$ _____
17. $4\frac{19}{20} + 4\frac{1}{12}$ _____
18. $7\frac{11}{15} + 2\frac{11}{12}$ _____
19. $1\frac{1}{4} + 6\frac{1}{8} + 8\frac{1}{4}$ _____
20. $2\frac{2}{3} + 4\frac{1}{6} + 9\frac{2}{3}$ _____
21. $1\frac{4}{5} + 3\frac{2}{5} + \frac{1}{2}$ _____
22. $9\frac{1}{4} + 6\frac{7}{8} + 2\frac{3}{4}$ _____
23. $4\frac{3}{5} + 2\frac{7}{10} + 9\frac{1}{2}$ _____
24. $8\frac{3}{4} + \frac{5}{6} + 2\frac{11}{12}$ _____

NAME _____ CLASS _____ DATE _____

4-6
UNIT 2 Estimating Sums Involving Fractions

OBJECTIVE: Estimating sums of fractions and mixed numbers by rounding and by writing simpler fractions

Often you can estimate a sum of fractions or mixed numbers by rounding to the nearest whole number.

EXAMPLE 1 Estimate the sum $3\frac{1}{2} + 18\frac{5}{6} + 7\frac{1}{18}$ by rounding.

▶ **Solution**

Round $3\frac{1}{2}$ up to 4.

Since $\frac{5}{6}$ is greater than $\frac{1}{2}$, round $18\frac{5}{6}$ up to 19.

Since $\frac{1}{18}$ is less than $\frac{1}{2}$, round $7\frac{1}{18}$ down to 7.

A reasonable estimate is 4 + 19 + 7, or about 30.

Sometimes you can get a better estimate by using simpler fractions.

EXAMPLE 2 Estimate the sum $\frac{19}{30} + 1\frac{7}{12} + 9\frac{7}{18}$ by using simpler fractions.

▶ **Solution**

$\frac{19}{30} \rightarrow \frac{20}{30}$, or $\frac{2}{3}$ $1\frac{7}{12} \rightarrow 1\frac{6}{12}$, or $1\frac{1}{2}$ $9\frac{7}{18} \rightarrow 9\frac{6}{18}$, or $9\frac{1}{3}$

A reasonable estimate is $\frac{2}{3} + 1\frac{1}{2} + 9\frac{1}{3}$, or about $11\frac{1}{2}$.

Estimate each sum by rounding.

1. $8\frac{7}{9} + 6\frac{2}{11}$ _____

2. $2\frac{14}{15} + 1\frac{17}{18}$ _____

3. $7\frac{1}{4} + 4\frac{3}{20}$ _____

4. $10\frac{2}{15} + 1\frac{1}{2}$ _____

5. $7\frac{1}{2} + 1\frac{11}{17}$ _____

6. $5\frac{4}{7} + \frac{9}{20}$ _____

Estimate each sum by using simpler fractions.

7. $\frac{29}{40} + 6\frac{11}{45}$ _____

8. $8\frac{41}{60} + \frac{66}{100}$ _____

9. $1\frac{43}{55} + 9\frac{8}{19}$ _____

10. $4\frac{7}{18} + 6\frac{17}{48}$ _____

11. $5\frac{7}{16} + \frac{49}{99}$ _____

12. $8\frac{7}{27} + \frac{9}{35}$ _____

Making Sense of Numbers

4-7 Problems Involving Fraction Addition

UNIT 2

OBJECTIVE: Solving a real-world problem by finding a sum of fractions

Sometimes you must add two or more fractions to solve a real-world problem.

EXAMPLE Shondra needs $\frac{7}{8}$ yard of felt to make a banner and $\frac{3}{4}$ yard of felt to make a pennant. How much felt does Shondra need in all?

Solution

Strategy You need to find a total, so you must add $\frac{7}{8}$ and $\frac{3}{4}$.

Estimate Round $\frac{7}{8}$ up to 1 and round $\frac{3}{4}$ up to 1.

The total will be about 1 + 1, or 2, but it will be less than 2.

Work Find the sum: $\frac{7}{8} + \frac{3}{4} = \frac{7}{8} + \frac{6}{8} = \frac{7+6}{8} = \frac{13}{8} = 1\frac{5}{8}$

Compare to the estimate: $1\frac{5}{8}$ is close to 2, but less than 2.

Answer Shondra needs $1\frac{5}{8}$ yards of felt altogether.

Solve each problem using the steps *Strategy, Estimate, Work,* and *Answer*.

1. A chef needs $\frac{2}{3}$ cup of flour for one recipe and $\frac{1}{4}$ cup of flour for another. How many cups of flour does the chef need for the two recipes together? _____

2. On the first three days of this week, Tran jogged $\frac{7}{8}$ mile, $\frac{1}{2}$ mile, and $\frac{5}{6}$ mile. How many miles did Tran jog in all on these three days? _____

3. Gina budgets $\frac{1}{3}$ of her monthly salary for rent and $\frac{1}{5}$ of her monthly salary for food. What part of her monthly salary does she budget for rent and food together? _____

4. On five consecutive days last week, the price of one share of a stock increased $\frac{7}{8}$, $\frac{1}{2}$, $\frac{3}{4}$, $\frac{5}{8}$, and $\frac{1}{8}$ of a dollar. What was the total increase in the price of the stock? _____

4-8 Problems Involving Mixed Number Addition

UNIT 2

OBJECTIVE: *Solving a real-world problem by finding a sum of mixed numbers*

Sometimes you must add two or more mixed numbers to solve a real-world problem.

EXAMPLE How much fencing is needed to enclose a triangular garden plot with sides of length $10\frac{5}{6}$ feet, $15\frac{1}{12}$ feet, and $18\frac{1}{2}$ feet?

▶ **Solution**

Strategy You need to find the *perimeter* of the garden plot.
To do this, you must add $10\frac{5}{6}$, $15\frac{1}{12}$ and $18\frac{1}{2}$.

Estimate Round: $10\frac{5}{6}$ up to 11; $15\frac{1}{12}$ down to 15; $18\frac{1}{2}$ up to 19.
The perimeter will be 11 + 15 + 19, or about 45.

Work $10\frac{5}{6} + 15\frac{1}{12} + 18\frac{1}{2} = 10\frac{10}{12} + 15\frac{1}{12} + 18\frac{6}{12} = 43\frac{17}{12} = 43 + 1\frac{5}{12} = 44\frac{5}{12}$

Compare to the estimate: $44\frac{5}{12}$ is close to 45.

Answer It will take $44\frac{5}{12}$ feet of fencing to enclose the garden.

Solve each problem using the steps *Strategy, Estimate, Work,* and *Answer*.

1. The weight of a packing carton is $1\frac{1}{6}$ pounds. The weight of its contents is $21\frac{7}{8}$ pounds. What is the combined weight in pounds of the carton and its contents? _____

2. On Monday, the closing price of a company's stock was $7\frac{7}{8}$ dollars more than the opening price of $46\frac{1}{2}$ dollars. What was the closing price? _____

3. Leah needs $2\frac{1}{4}$ yards of fabric for a jacket and $1\frac{5}{8}$ yards for a matching skirt. How many yards is this in all? _____

4. The measured rainfall in four recent months was $5\frac{3}{4}$ inches, $3\frac{7}{10}$ inches, $\frac{2}{5}$ inch, and $1\frac{1}{2}$ inches. What was the total rainfall in inches for the four months? _____

Making Sense of Numbers   Unit 2 Fractions

NAME _____ CLASS _____ DATE _____

5-1 Modeling a Subtraction of Fractions
UNIT 2

OBJECTIVE: Interpreting and drawing models of fraction subtraction

You can use a model to represent a subtraction of fractions.

EXAMPLE Draw a model of $\frac{5}{6} - \frac{1}{3}$ and write the difference.

Solution

Give the fractions a common denominator. Rewrite $\frac{1}{3}$ as $\frac{2}{6}$.

Divide a rectangle into six equal parts.

Shade five-sixths as shown at right.
Mark an × on two of the shaded sixths.
Note that three-sixths are shaded but
are *not* marked with an ×.

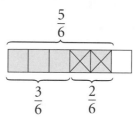

The difference is $\frac{5}{6} - \frac{1}{3} = \frac{3}{6} = \frac{1}{2}$.

Write the difference that each model represents. Be sure to write all fractions in lowest terms.

1. [model] _____   2. [model] _____

3. [model] _____   4. [model] _____

5. [model] _____   6. [model] _____

7. [model] _____   8. [model] _____

Draw a model of each subtraction. Then write the difference.

9. $\frac{4}{5} - \frac{2}{5}$ 10. $\frac{9}{10} - \frac{2}{5}$

difference: _____   difference: _____

11. $\frac{3}{4} - \frac{2}{3}$ 12. $1 - \frac{3}{8}$

difference: _____   difference: _____

40   Unit 2   Fractions   Making Sense of Numbers

NAME _____ CLASS _____ DATE _____

5-2 Subtracting Fractions: Like Denominators
UNIT 2

OBJECTIVE: *Finding differences of two fractions with like denominators*

To subtract fractions that have like denominators, you can use a method similar to that for adding fractions with like denominators.

Subtracting Fractions with Like Denominators

1. Subtract the numerators.
2. Write the difference from Step **1** over the like denominator.
3. If necessary, rewrite the result from Step **2** in lowest terms.

EXAMPLE 1 Write each difference in lowest terms. a. $\dfrac{8}{11} - \dfrac{2}{11}$ b. $\dfrac{9}{10} - \dfrac{3}{10}$

▶ **Solution**

a. $\dfrac{8}{11} - \dfrac{2}{11} = \dfrac{8-2}{11} = \dfrac{6}{11}$ b. $\dfrac{9}{10} - \dfrac{3}{10} = \dfrac{9-3}{10} = \dfrac{6}{10} = \dfrac{3}{5}$

EXAMPLE 2 Find the difference $1 - \dfrac{2}{15}$.

▶ **Solution**

Rewrite 1 as $\dfrac{15}{15}$: $1 - \dfrac{2}{15} = \dfrac{15}{15} - \dfrac{2}{15} = \dfrac{15-2}{15} = \dfrac{13}{15}$

Write each difference in lowest terms.

1. $\dfrac{5}{7} - \dfrac{1}{7}$ _____   2. $\dfrac{12}{13} - \dfrac{4}{13}$ _____   3. $\dfrac{3}{4} - \dfrac{1}{4}$ _____

4. $\dfrac{11}{12} - \dfrac{1}{12}$ _____   5. $\dfrac{17}{18} - \dfrac{3}{18}$ _____   6. $\dfrac{8}{9} - \dfrac{5}{9}$ _____

7. $\dfrac{5}{6} - \dfrac{1}{6}$ _____   8. $\dfrac{7}{8} - \dfrac{1}{8}$ _____   9. $1 - \dfrac{11}{12}$ _____

10. $1 - \dfrac{1}{20}$ _____   11. $1 - \dfrac{5}{14}$ _____   12. $1 - \dfrac{13}{30}$ _____

Find the value of each expression by using the order of operations.

13. $\left(\dfrac{9}{11} - \dfrac{5}{11}\right) - \dfrac{2}{11}$ _____   14. $\dfrac{10}{4} - \left(\dfrac{3}{4} - \dfrac{1}{4}\right)$ _____   15. $\dfrac{8}{9} - \left(\dfrac{7}{9} - \dfrac{2}{9}\right)$ _____

16. $\left(\dfrac{3}{5} - \dfrac{2}{5}\right) - \dfrac{1}{5}$ _____   17. $\left(1 - \dfrac{1}{8}\right) - \dfrac{5}{8}$ _____   18. $1 - \left(1 - \dfrac{3}{10}\right)$ _____

Making Sense of Numbers

NAME _____ CLASS _____ DATE _____

5-3
UNIT 2

Subtracting Fractions: Unlike Denominators

OBJECTIVE: Finding differences of two fractions with unlike denominators

To subtract fractions that have unlike denominators, you must first write equivalent fractions that have a common denominator. Then subtract using the method for like denominators.

EXAMPLE Write each difference in lowest terms. a. $\dfrac{23}{30} - \dfrac{2}{5}$ b. $\dfrac{5}{6} - \dfrac{3}{14}$

▶ **Solution**

a. The LCM of 30 and 5 is 30.
   So the least common denominator is 30.

   First rewrite $\dfrac{2}{5}$. Then subtract.

   $\dfrac{2}{5} = \dfrac{2 \times 6}{5 \times 6} = \dfrac{12}{30}$ $\dfrac{23}{30} - \dfrac{2}{5} = \dfrac{23}{30} - \dfrac{12}{30} = \dfrac{23-12}{30} = \dfrac{11}{30}$

b. The LCM of 6 and 14 is 42.
   So the least common denominator is 42.

   First rewrite $\dfrac{5}{6}$ and $\dfrac{3}{14}$.   Then subtract.

   $\dfrac{5}{6} = \dfrac{5 \times 7}{6 \times 7} = \dfrac{35}{42}$ $\dfrac{5}{6} - \dfrac{3}{14} = \dfrac{35}{42} - \dfrac{9}{42} = \dfrac{35-9}{42} = \dfrac{26}{42}$

   $\dfrac{3}{14} = \dfrac{3 \times 3}{14 \times 3} = \dfrac{9}{42}$ $= \dfrac{13}{21}$

Write each difference in lowest terms.

1. $\dfrac{5}{8} - \dfrac{1}{2}$ _____

2. $\dfrac{3}{5} - \dfrac{7}{15}$ _____

3. $\dfrac{11}{12} - \dfrac{2}{3}$ _____

4. $\dfrac{31}{36} - \dfrac{3}{4}$ _____

5. $\dfrac{1}{3} - \dfrac{1}{8}$ _____

6. $\dfrac{1}{2} - \dfrac{1}{9}$ _____

7. $\dfrac{1}{6} - \dfrac{1}{10}$ _____

8. $\dfrac{1}{8} - \dfrac{1}{12}$ _____

9. $\dfrac{4}{5} - \dfrac{1}{4}$ _____

10. $\dfrac{9}{14} - \dfrac{1}{3}$ _____

11. $\dfrac{3}{4} - \dfrac{1}{6}$ _____

12. $\dfrac{7}{10} - \dfrac{3}{8}$ _____

Find the value of each expression by using the order of operations.

13. $\left(\dfrac{7}{8} - \dfrac{1}{2}\right) - \dfrac{1}{8}$ _____

14. $\dfrac{7}{8} - \left(\dfrac{1}{2} - \dfrac{1}{8}\right)$ _____

15. $\dfrac{11}{12} - \left(\dfrac{1}{3} - \dfrac{1}{6}\right)$ _____

16. $\left(\dfrac{17}{18} - \dfrac{2}{3}\right) - \dfrac{1}{6}$ _____

17. $\dfrac{14}{15} - \left(\dfrac{1}{5} + \dfrac{1}{3}\right)$ _____

18. $\left(\dfrac{9}{10} - \dfrac{1}{2}\right) - \dfrac{1}{3}$ _____

5-4 Subtracting Mixed Numbers Without Renaming

UNIT 2

OBJECTIVE: Finding differences of mixed numbers without renaming the whole-number part

To subtract mixed numbers, you use the following general method.

> **Subtracting Mixed Numbers without Renaming**
> 1. If necessary, write equivalent mixed numbers that have a common denominator.
> 2. Subtract the fractions.
> 3. Subtract the whole numbers.
> 4. If necessary, rewrite the difference in lowest terms.

EXAMPLE Write each difference in lowest terms. a. $5\frac{7}{8} - 3\frac{1}{8}$ b. $5\frac{3}{4} - 1\frac{1}{3}$

Solution

a.
$$5\frac{7}{8}$$
$$-3\frac{1}{8}$$
$$\overline{2\frac{6}{8}} = 2\frac{3}{4} \quad \text{Rewrite the difference in lowest terms.}$$

b.
$$5\frac{3}{4} \rightarrow 5\frac{9}{12}$$
$$-1\frac{1}{3} \rightarrow -1\frac{4}{12}$$
$$\overline{4\frac{5}{12}}$$
Write equivalent mixed numbers with common denominators.

Write each difference in lowest terms.

1. $6\frac{11}{15} - 5\frac{4}{15}$ _____
2. $12\frac{7}{9} - 4\frac{2}{9}$ _____
3. $7\frac{9}{11} - \frac{3}{11}$ _____
4. $9\frac{6}{7} - \frac{1}{7}$ _____
5. $5\frac{7}{8} - 2$ _____
6. $14\frac{1}{2} - 10$ _____
7. $8\frac{4}{5} - 8\frac{1}{5}$ _____
8. $1\frac{14}{15} - 1\frac{7}{15}$ _____
9. $6\frac{9}{10} - 3\frac{1}{10}$ _____
10. $15\frac{8}{9} - 4\frac{2}{9}$ _____
11. $1\frac{5}{8} - \frac{3}{8}$ _____
12. $18\frac{11}{12} - \frac{1}{12}$ _____
13. $5\frac{7}{10} - 3\frac{2}{5}$ _____
14. $11\frac{2}{3} - 2\frac{7}{12}$ _____
15. $5\frac{1}{6} - 1\frac{1}{18}$ _____
16. $7\frac{19}{20} - 6\frac{3}{4}$ _____
17. $10\frac{13}{18} - \frac{2}{9}$ _____
18. $9\frac{1}{3} - \frac{1}{12}$ _____

Making Sense of Numbers — Unit 2 Fractions **43**

5-5 Subtracting Mixed Numbers With Renaming

UNIT 2

OBJECTIVE: Finding differences of mixed numbers when it is necessary to rename the whole-number part

Sometimes you need to rename before you can subtract with mixed numbers.

EXAMPLE Find each difference. a. $15\frac{2}{7} - 9\frac{6}{7}$ b. $12 - 4\frac{3}{8}$

Solution

a. You cannot subtract $\frac{2}{7} - \frac{6}{7}$, so rename $15\frac{2}{7}$ as follows.

$$15\frac{2}{7} = 14 + 1\frac{2}{7} = 14 + \frac{9}{7} = 14\frac{9}{7}$$

$$15\frac{2}{7} \rightarrow 14\frac{9}{7}$$
$$-9\frac{6}{7} \rightarrow -9\frac{6}{7}$$
$$\overline{} \overline{5\frac{3}{7}}$$

b. Rename 12 as a mixed number.

$$12 = 11 + 1 = 11 + \frac{8}{8} = 11\frac{8}{8}$$

$$12 \rightarrow 11\frac{8}{8}$$
$$-4\frac{3}{8} \rightarrow -4\frac{3}{8}$$
$$\overline{} \overline{7\frac{5}{8}}$$

Write each difference in lowest terms.

1. $10\frac{1}{5} - 3\frac{2}{5}$ _____
2. $4\frac{5}{11} - 1\frac{9}{11}$ _____
3. $5\frac{1}{9} - \frac{8}{9}$ _____

4. $13\frac{1}{3} - \frac{2}{3}$ _____
5. $1\frac{4}{15} - \frac{8}{15}$ _____
6. $3\frac{5}{7} - 2\frac{6}{7}$ _____

7. $16 - 2\frac{1}{6}$ _____
8. $22 - 15\frac{7}{10}$ _____
9. $12 - \frac{7}{8}$ _____

10. $3 - \frac{5}{12}$ _____
11. $12\frac{1}{9} - 4\frac{4}{9}$ _____
12. $5\frac{3}{16} - 1\frac{11}{16}$ _____

13. $4\frac{2}{3} - 2\frac{7}{9}$ _____
14. $10\frac{1}{14} - 1\frac{6}{7}$ _____
15. $8\frac{1}{2} - 6\frac{5}{6}$ _____

16. $15\frac{3}{10} - 9\frac{4}{5}$ _____
17. $16\frac{1}{12} - \frac{3}{4}$ _____
18. $11\frac{1}{4} - \frac{13}{20}$ _____

19. $8\frac{1}{5} - 1\frac{2}{3}$ _____
20. $12\frac{1}{2} - 5\frac{4}{7}$ _____
21. $21\frac{1}{9} - 7\frac{5}{6}$ _____

22. $9\frac{1}{6} - 1\frac{3}{4}$ _____
23. $23\frac{1}{10} - 22\frac{1}{8}$ _____
24. $3\frac{2}{27} - 2\frac{7}{18}$ _____

NAME _____ CLASS _____ DATE _____

5-6 Estimating Differences Involving Fractions
UNIT 2

OBJECTIVE: Estimating differences of fractions and mixed numbers by rounding one or both numbers

When you are subtracting with fractions, making an estimate of the difference can help you decide if your answer is reasonable. You can estimate by adjusting one or both of the numbers involved.

EXAMPLE Estimate each difference. a. $11\frac{17}{18} - 4\frac{1}{3}$ b. $10\frac{1}{16} - \frac{25}{96}$

▶ **Solution**

a. $11\frac{17}{18}$ is very close to 12, so round it up.

$$11\frac{17}{18} - 4\frac{1}{3} \rightarrow \text{about } 12 - 4\frac{1}{3} \rightarrow \text{about } 7\frac{2}{3}$$

b. $10\frac{1}{16}$ is very close to 10, so round it down.

$\frac{25}{96}$ is very close to $\frac{1}{4}$, so use $\frac{1}{4}$ as a simpler fraction.

$$10\frac{1}{16} - \frac{25}{96} \rightarrow \text{about } 10 - \frac{1}{4} \rightarrow \text{about } 9\frac{3}{4}$$

Estimate each difference by rounding just one number.

1. $5\frac{1}{3} - \frac{35}{36}$ _____   2. $8\frac{1}{2} - \frac{1}{16}$ _____

3. $7\frac{3}{4} - 5\frac{1}{28}$ _____   4. $14\frac{5}{8} - 2\frac{19}{20}$ _____

5. $6\frac{3}{100} - \frac{1}{2}$ _____   6. $10\frac{1}{48} - \frac{1}{3}$ _____

7. $9\frac{23}{24} - 2\frac{1}{2}$ _____   8. $5\frac{14}{15} - 1\frac{2}{3}$ _____

Estimate each difference by rounding both numbers.

9. $21\frac{44}{45} - 13\frac{1}{90}$ _____   10. $15\frac{1}{25} - 1\frac{49}{50}$ _____

11. $8\frac{11}{12} - 3\frac{41}{42}$ _____   12. $28\frac{2}{51} - 17\frac{2}{103}$ _____

13. $14\frac{11}{34} - 2\frac{1}{68}$ _____   14. $8\frac{18}{35} - 1\frac{69}{70}$ _____

Making Sense of Numbers   Unit 2 Fractions **45**

NAME _____ CLASS _____ DATE _____

5-7
UNIT 2

Problems Involving Fraction Subtraction

OBJECTIVE: Solving a real-world problem by finding a difference of fractions

Sometimes you must subtract two fractions to solve a real-world problem.

EXAMPLE A car's gas tank was $\frac{9}{10}$ full at the start of a trip and $\frac{1}{4}$ full at the end of the trip. No gas was added during the trip. What fractional part of a full tank of gas was used on the trip?

▶ **Solution**

Strategy You need to find the difference between the amount at the start of the trip and the amount at the end, so you subtract $\frac{9}{10} - \frac{1}{4}$.

Estimate Round $\frac{9}{10}$ up to 1. The difference will be about $1 - \frac{1}{4}$, or $\frac{3}{4}$.

Work Find the difference: $\frac{9}{10} - \frac{1}{4} = \frac{18}{20} - \frac{5}{20} = \frac{18-5}{20} = \frac{13}{20}$

Compare to the estimate: 13 is close to 15, and $\frac{15}{20} = \frac{3}{4}$.

Answer The amount of gas used on the trip was $\frac{13}{20}$ of a full tank.

Solve each problem using the steps *Strategy, Estimate, Work,* and *Answer*.

1. A board with a thickness of $\frac{3}{4}$ inch must be shaved down to a thickness of $\frac{5}{16}$ inch. How many inches must be shaved from the thickness of the board? _____

2. Archie has $\frac{1}{4}$ cup of milk. He needs $\frac{2}{3}$ cup of milk to make a recipe. How much more milk does he need in order to make the recipe? _____

3. Jamaal budgets $\frac{3}{20}$ of his salary for savings and $\frac{1}{12}$ of his salary for entertainment. How much more does he budget for savings than for entertainment? _____

4. Bree jogged four-fifths of a mile, then walked seven-eighths of a mile. Did she jog or walk farther? How many miles farther? _____

46 Unit 2 Fractions *Making Sense of Numbers*

NAME _____ CLASS _____ DATE _____

5-8 Problems Involving Mixed Number Subtraction
UNIT 2

OBJECTIVE: Solving a real-world problem by finding a difference of fractions

Sometimes you must subtract two mixed numbers in order to solve a real-world problem.

EXAMPLE Joe bought stock in a company for $35\frac{7}{8}$ dollars per share. He later sold the stock for $42\frac{1}{4}$ dollars per share. How much did he earn on each share of stock?

Solution

Strategy You need to find the amount of increase, so subtract $42\frac{1}{4} - 35\frac{7}{8}$.

Round $42\frac{1}{4}$ down to 42 and round $35\frac{7}{8}$ up to 36.

Estimate The increase will be about $42 - 36$, or 6.

Work Find the difference: $42\frac{1}{4} - 35\frac{7}{8} = 42\frac{2}{8} - 35\frac{7}{8} = 41\frac{10}{8} - 35\frac{7}{8} = 6\frac{3}{8}$

Compare to the estimate: $6\frac{3}{8}$ is close to 6.

Answer Joe earned $6\frac{3}{8}$ dollars on each share of stock.

Solve each problem using the steps *Strategy, Estimate, Work,* and *Answer.*

1. The length of a piece of fabric is $7\frac{1}{4}$ yards. How many yards will be left if $2\frac{2}{3}$ yards are used? _____

2. Newer models of personal computers store data on disks that are $3\frac{1}{2}$ inches wide. Older models used disks that were $5\frac{1}{4}$ inches wide. How many inches wider was this? _____

3. A quart of milk contains four cups. How many cups will be left after $1\frac{3}{4}$ cups are used in a recipe? _____

4. A disc jockey's schedule for thirty minutes of air time must include seven and one-half minutes of commercials. How many minutes remain for other programming? _____

Making Sense of Numbers

NAME _____ CLASS _____ DATE _____

Problems Involving Either Addition or Subtraction of Fractions or Mixed Numbers

OBJECTIVE: Solving a real-world problem by finding either a sum or difference of fractions or mixed numbers

An important part of devising your problem solving strategy is choosing the correct mathematical operation. When solving a problem requires either addition or subtraction, use the following guidelines to make the correct choice.

Choosing Addition or Subtraction

Use *addition*:   to find how many in all
to find the result after an increase

Use *subtraction*:   to find how much (many) more or less
to find the result after a decrease
to find the remaining part of a whole

Solve.

1. To make a 2-pound loaf of wheat bread, Paulo needs $1\frac{1}{4}$ cups of wheat flour and $2\frac{3}{4}$ cups of white flour.

   a. How many more cups of white flour does he need than wheat flour? _____

   b. How many cups of flour does he need altogether? _____

2. One day last week, the low price of a certain stock was $29\frac{1}{2}$ dollars and the high price was $31\frac{3}{8}$ dollars. What was the difference between the high and low prices? _____

3. A bag of nuts should weigh $5\frac{1}{4}$ ounces. Its actual weight is $5\frac{5}{32}$ ounces. Is this more or less than $5\frac{1}{4}$ ounces? How many ounces more or less? _____

4. The lengths of the four walls of Jennifer's room are $12\frac{1}{3}$ feet, $14\frac{1}{4}$ feet, $12\frac{1}{3}$ feet, and $14\frac{1}{4}$ feet. What is the perimeter of Jennifer's room? _____

48   Unit 2   Fractions   *Making Sense of Numbers*

NAME _____ CLASS _____ DATE _____

5-10 Adding and Subtracting With Fractions
UNIT 2

OBJECTIVE: Finding the value of an expression that involves fraction addition and subtraction

An expression that contains fractions may involve both addition and subtraction. To find its value, you must follow the order of operations. That is, first do any operations within parentheses. Then add and subtract in order from left to right.

EXAMPLE Find the value of each expression. a. $\frac{9}{10} - \left(\frac{3}{10} + \frac{1}{10}\right)$ b. $\frac{7}{8} - \frac{1}{2} + \frac{3}{4}$

Solution

a. First do the addition inside the parentheses.
$$\frac{9}{10} - \left(\frac{3}{10} + \frac{1}{10}\right)$$
$$\frac{9}{10} - \frac{4}{10}$$
$$\frac{5}{10}$$
$$\frac{1}{2}$$

b. Start by rewriting the fractions with a common denominator.
$$\frac{7}{8} - \frac{1}{2} + \frac{3}{4}$$
$$\frac{7}{8} - \frac{4}{8} + \frac{6}{8} \quad \text{Now subtract.}$$
$$\frac{3}{8} + \frac{6}{8} \quad \text{Then add.}$$
$$\frac{9}{8} = 1\frac{1}{8}$$

Find the value of each expression in lowest terms.

1. $\frac{4}{5} - \left(\frac{1}{5} + \frac{2}{5}\right)$ _____

2. $\frac{1}{12} + \frac{7}{12} - \frac{5}{12}$ _____

3. $\left(\frac{11}{15} - \frac{2}{15}\right) + \frac{1}{15}$ _____

4. $\frac{5}{6} - \left(\frac{1}{3} + \frac{1}{6}\right)$ _____

5. $\frac{7}{10} + \left(\frac{4}{5} - \frac{3}{10}\right)$ _____

6. $\frac{8}{9} + \frac{2}{9} - \frac{1}{2}$ _____

7. $\frac{7}{8} - \frac{5}{8} + \frac{3}{16}$ _____

8. $\frac{11}{12} - \frac{2}{3} + \frac{1}{4}$ _____

9. $\frac{7}{10} + \frac{3}{5} - \frac{1}{2}$ _____

10. $\frac{17}{18} - \left(\frac{1}{3} + \frac{4}{9}\right)$ _____

11. $\left(\frac{3}{10} + \frac{5}{6}\right) - \frac{1}{3}$ _____

12. $\left(\frac{1}{9} + \frac{5}{9}\right) - \left(\frac{4}{9} - \frac{1}{9}\right)$ _____

13. $\left(\frac{7}{8} - \frac{3}{4}\right) + \left(\frac{1}{2} - \frac{3}{8}\right)$ _____

14. $\frac{11}{12} - \left(\frac{2}{3} - \frac{1}{4}\right) + \frac{5}{6}$ _____

Making Sense of Numbers

NAME _____ CLASS _____ DATE _____

Adding and Subtracting With Mixed Numbers

OBJECTIVE: Finding the value of an expression that involves mixed number addition and subtraction

An expression that contains mixed numbers may involve both addition and subtraction. To find its value, remember to follow the order of operations. That is, first do any operations within parentheses. Then add and subtract in order from left to right.

EXAMPLE Find the value of $4\frac{1}{9} - \left(1\frac{2}{9} + 1\frac{5}{9}\right)$.

Solution

First do the addition inside parentheses. Then subtract.

Method 1

$4\frac{1}{9} - \left(1\frac{2}{9} + 1\frac{5}{9}\right)$

$4\frac{1}{9} - 2\frac{7}{9}$ Add the mixed numbers in parentheses.

$3\frac{10}{9} - 2\frac{7}{9}$

$1\frac{3}{9} = 1\frac{1}{3}$

Method 2

$4\frac{1}{9} - \left(1\frac{2}{9} + 1\frac{5}{9}\right)$

$\frac{37}{9} - \left(\frac{11}{9} + \frac{14}{9}\right)$ Write each mixed number as a fraction and then add.

$\frac{37}{9} - \frac{25}{9}$

$\frac{12}{9} = 1\frac{3}{9} = 1\frac{1}{3}$

Find the value of each expression in lowest terms.

1. $7\frac{4}{5} - \left(2\frac{2}{5} + 4\frac{1}{5}\right)$ _____

2. $2\frac{1}{6} + \left(3\frac{5}{6} - 1\frac{1}{6}\right)$ _____

3. $4\frac{1}{3} - 1\frac{2}{3} + 5\frac{2}{3}$ _____

4. $2\frac{1}{4} + 1\frac{1}{4} - 1\frac{3}{4}$ _____

5. $\left(5\frac{1}{9} - 3\frac{2}{9}\right) + 1\frac{7}{9}$ _____

6. $\left(3\frac{1}{8} + 1\frac{1}{8}\right) - 2\frac{5}{8}$ _____

7. $3\frac{1}{2} + 2\frac{3}{4} - 4\frac{3}{4}$ _____

8. $2\frac{1}{5} - 1\frac{3}{10} + 2\frac{4}{5}$ _____

9. $4\frac{1}{2} - \left(1\frac{1}{2} + 2\frac{1}{6}\right)$ _____

10. $\left(2\frac{1}{3} + 1\frac{1}{12}\right) - 1\frac{2}{3}$ _____

11. $1\frac{1}{8} + 2\frac{1}{2} - 1\frac{3}{4}$ _____

12. $3\frac{1}{2} - 1\frac{1}{3} + 1\frac{5}{6}$ _____

NAME _____ CLASS _____ DATE _____

5-12
UNIT 2

Problems Involving Both Addition and Subtraction of Fractions or Mixed Numbers

OBJECTIVE: Solving a real-world problem by finding sums and differences of fractions and mixed numbers

In many cases, the solution of a problem will require both addition and subtraction of fractions or mixed numbers.

EXAMPLE Lin budgeted $\frac{1}{3}$ of her salary for rent, $\frac{1}{5}$ for food, and $\frac{1}{4}$ for transportation. What part of her salary was left for other expenses?

Solution

Strategy You need to find the sum already budgeted, then subtract from 1.

Estimate $\frac{1}{3}$ is a little more than $\frac{1}{4}$, and $\frac{1}{5}$ is a little less than $\frac{1}{4}$.

So Lin has budgeted about $\frac{1}{4} + \frac{1}{4} + \frac{1}{4}$, or $\frac{3}{4}$. About $\frac{1}{4}$ is left.

Work Find the sum: $\frac{1}{3} + \frac{1}{4} + \frac{1}{5} = \frac{20}{60} + \frac{15}{60} + \frac{12}{60} = \frac{47}{60}$ *60 is the LCD of 3, 4, and 5.*

Subtract from 1: $1 - \frac{47}{60} = \frac{13}{60}$

Compare to the estimate: 13 is close to 15, and $\frac{15}{60} = \frac{1}{4}$.

Answer There was $\frac{13}{60}$ of Lin's salary remaining for other expenses.

Solve each problem using the steps *Strategy, Estimate, Work,* and *Answer*.

1. Two pieces were cut from a board that was $6\frac{1}{2}$ feet long. One was $1\frac{5}{6}$ feet long and the other was $1\frac{1}{4}$ feet long. What was the length in feet of the remaining piece? _____

2. The opening price of a company's stock one day was $32\frac{3}{4}$ dollars. The price fell $9\frac{7}{8}$ dollars by noon, then rose $15\frac{1}{2}$ dollars before closing. What was the closing price? _____

3. Harry had a bag that contained $7\frac{1}{2}$ cups of flour. He used $4\frac{1}{4}$ cups, $1\frac{1}{3}$ cups, and $\frac{3}{4}$ cup of this flour in three recipes. How many cups of flour were left? _____

Making Sense of Numbers   Unit 2 Fractions **51**

NAME _____ CLASS _____ DATE _____

6-1 Modeling a Multiplication of Fractions
UNIT 2

OBJECTIVE: Interpreting and drawing models of fraction multiplication

You can use a model to represent a multiplication of fractions.

EXAMPLE Draw a model of $\frac{1}{4} \times \frac{2}{3}$ and write the product.

▶ **Solution**

Divide a rectangle into four equal parts along its width. Shade one-fourth with one color.

Divide the rectangle into three equal parts along its length. Shade two-thirds with another color.

The rectangle is now divided into twelve equal parts. Two-twelfths are shaded with both colors.

The product is $\frac{1}{4} \times \frac{2}{3} = \frac{2}{12} = \frac{1}{6}$.

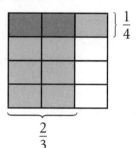

Write the product that each model represents. Be sure to write all fractions in lowest terms.

1.

2.

3.

_____   _____   _____

4.

5.

6.

_____   _____   _____

Draw a model of each multiplication. Then write the product.

7. $\frac{1}{2} \times \frac{1}{3}$

8. $\frac{1}{3} \times \frac{2}{5}$

product: _____   product: _____

9. $\frac{3}{4} \times \frac{1}{3}$

10. $\frac{7}{8} \times \frac{4}{5}$

product: _____   product: _____

52 Unit 2 Fractions   *Making Sense of Numbers*

NAME _____ CLASS _____ DATE _____

6-2 Multiplying Two Fractions
UNIT 2

OBJECTIVE: Finding the product of two fractions

To multiply two fractions, you can use the following method.

> **Multiplying Fractions**
> 1. Multiply the numerators.
> 2. Multiply the denominators.
> 3. If possible, divide both numerator and denominator by a common factor. This will give you the final product in lowest terms.

EXAMPLE Write each product in lowest terms. a. $\frac{1}{4} \times \frac{5}{6}$ b. $\frac{4}{11} \times \frac{3}{4}$ c. $\frac{5}{9} \times \frac{6}{7}$

Solution

a. $\frac{1}{4} \times \frac{5}{6} = \frac{1 \times 5}{4 \times 6} = \frac{5}{24}$

b. $\frac{4}{11} \times \frac{3}{4} = \frac{\cancel{4}^1}{11} \times \frac{3}{\cancel{4}_1} = \frac{1 \times 3}{11 \times 1} = \frac{3}{11}$ *Divide each 4 by 4.*

c. $\frac{5}{9} \times \frac{6}{7} = \frac{5}{\cancel{9}_3} \times \frac{\cancel{6}^2}{7} = \frac{5 \times 2}{3 \times 7} = \frac{10}{21}$ *Divide 6 and 9 by 3.*

Write each product in lowest terms.

1. $\frac{1}{3} \times \frac{1}{2}$ _____   2. $\frac{1}{8} \times \frac{1}{3}$ _____   3. $\frac{2}{5} \times \frac{3}{11}$ _____

4. $\frac{4}{7} \times \frac{2}{3}$ _____   5. $\frac{5}{9} \times \frac{4}{5}$ _____   6. $\frac{3}{7} \times \frac{7}{8}$ _____

7. $\frac{1}{6} \times \frac{2}{3}$ _____   8. $\frac{3}{4} \times \frac{1}{12}$ _____   9. $\frac{9}{10} \times \frac{1}{6}$ _____

10. $\frac{1}{15} \times \frac{6}{7}$ _____   11. $\frac{4}{11} \times \frac{5}{6}$ _____   12. $\frac{7}{15} \times \frac{9}{10}$ _____

13. $\frac{2}{9} \times \frac{3}{8}$ _____   14. $\frac{5}{18} \times \frac{3}{20}$ _____   15. $\frac{3}{7} \times \frac{14}{15}$ _____

16. $\frac{25}{36} \times \frac{4}{5}$ _____   17. $\frac{4}{15} \times \frac{21}{32}$ _____   18. $\frac{15}{28} \times \frac{8}{25}$ _____

19. $\frac{27}{32} \times \frac{20}{21}$ _____   20. $\frac{8}{5} \times \frac{25}{16}$ _____   21. $\frac{16}{9} \times \frac{15}{14}$ _____

Making Sense of Numbers   Unit 2 Fractions **53**

NAME _____ CLASS _____ DATE _____

6-3 UNIT 2 Multiplying a Fraction and a Whole Number

OBJECTIVE: Finding and estimating products of fractions and whole numbers

To multiply a fraction and a whole number, write the whole number as a fraction with a denominator of 1. Then follow the procedure for multiplying two fractions.

EXAMPLE 1 Write the product $15 \times \frac{5}{6}$ in lowest terms.

Solution

$$15 \times \frac{5}{6} = \frac{15}{1} \times \frac{5}{6} = \frac{\overset{5}{\cancel{15}}}{1} \times \frac{5}{\underset{2}{\cancel{6}}} = \frac{5 \times 5}{1 \times 2} = \frac{25}{2} = 12\frac{1}{2}$$

Divide 15 and 6 by 3.

You can estimate a product of a fraction and a whole number by rounding.

EXAMPLE 2 Estimate each product. a. $\frac{3}{11} \times 80$ b. $47 \times \frac{20}{29}$

Solution

a. $\frac{3}{11} \times 80$
   ↓   ↓   Replace
   $\frac{1}{4} \times 80$ $\frac{3}{11}$ with $\frac{1}{4}$.
   ⏟
   about 20

b. $47 \times \frac{20}{29}$ Replace 47 with 48
   ↓   ↓   and
   $48 \times \frac{2}{3}$ replace
   ⏟ $\frac{20}{29}$ with $\frac{2}{3}$.
   about 32

Write each product in lowest terms.

1. $\frac{1}{5} \times 40$ _____
2. $42 \times \frac{1}{7}$ _____
3. $15 \times \frac{2}{3}$ _____
4. $\frac{3}{8} \times 48$ _____

5. $\frac{1}{6} \times 20$ _____
6. $30 \times \frac{1}{4}$ _____
7. $\frac{5}{9} \times 21$ _____
8. $24 \times \frac{9}{14}$ _____

Estimate each product.

9. $\frac{1}{3} \times 22$ _____
10. $30 \times \frac{1}{8}$ _____
11. $\frac{2}{5} \times 19$ _____

12. $55 \times \frac{7}{9}$ _____
13. $\frac{4}{17} \times 28$ _____
14. $54 \times \frac{11}{67}$ _____

15. $35 \times \frac{21}{51}$ _____
16. $\frac{45}{67} \times 36$ _____
17. $\frac{12}{25} \times 61$ _____

NAME _____ CLASS _____ DATE _____

6-4 Multiplying Several Fractions
UNIT 2

OBJECTIVE: *Finding products of three or more fractions*

When a product involves three or more fractions, you follow the same procedure you use with two fractions.

EXAMPLE Write the product $\frac{1}{3} \times \frac{10}{11} \times \frac{3}{4}$ in lowest terms.

▶ **Solution**

Method 1
Multiply the numerators.
Multiply the denominators.
Simplify the result.

$$\frac{1}{3} \times \frac{10}{11} \times \frac{3}{4} = \frac{1 \times 10 \times 3}{3 \times 11 \times 4}$$

$$= \frac{30}{132}$$

$$= \frac{5}{22}$$

Method 2
Divide numerator and denominator pairs by any common factors. Then multiply.

$$\frac{1}{3} \times \frac{10}{11} \times \frac{3}{4} = \frac{1}{\cancel{3}_1} \times \frac{\cancel{10}^5}{11} \times \frac{\cancel{3}^1}{\cancel{4}_2}$$

$$= \frac{1 \times 5 \times 1}{1 \times 11 \times 2}$$

$$= \frac{5}{22}$$

Write each product in lowest terms.

1. $\frac{1}{2} \times \frac{3}{5} \times \frac{2}{3}$ _____

2. $\frac{4}{5} \times \frac{5}{7} \times \frac{1}{4}$ _____

3. $\frac{3}{4} \times \frac{1}{7} \times \frac{7}{9}$ _____

4. $\frac{5}{8} \times \frac{1}{3} \times \frac{4}{5}$ _____

5. $\frac{2}{3} \times \frac{1}{8} \times \frac{6}{7}$ _____

6. $\frac{6}{11} \times \frac{2}{9} \times \frac{1}{4}$ _____

7. $\frac{3}{5} \times \frac{1}{9} \times \frac{15}{16}$ _____

8. $\frac{2}{3} \times \frac{1}{8} \times \frac{12}{13}$ _____

9. $\frac{4}{7} \times \frac{14}{15} \times \frac{5}{6}$ _____

10. $\frac{3}{8} \times \frac{11}{12} \times \frac{10}{11}$ _____

11. $\frac{1}{4} \times \frac{5}{8} \times \frac{4}{5} \times \frac{8}{9}$ _____

12. $\frac{5}{7} \times \frac{1}{2} \times \frac{2}{5} \times \frac{7}{8}$ _____

13. $\frac{3}{8} \times \frac{7}{9} \times \frac{6}{7} \times \frac{3}{5}$ _____

14. $\frac{2}{3} \times \frac{5}{9} \times \frac{5}{6} \times \frac{9}{10}$ _____

15. $\frac{4}{7} \times \frac{6}{7} \times \frac{5}{8} \times \frac{14}{15}$ _____

16. $\frac{8}{9} \times \frac{5}{12} \times \frac{3}{10} \times \frac{4}{5}$ _____

17. $\frac{1}{3} \times \frac{5}{9} \times \frac{9}{10} \times 24$ _____

18. $\frac{3}{8} \times \frac{1}{6} \times 36 \times \frac{2}{9}$ _____

Making Sense of Numbers

6-5 Multiplying With Mixed Numbers
UNIT 2

OBJECTIVE: Finding products that involve mixed numbers

To multiply with mixed numbers, use the following method.

> **Multiplying With Mixed Numbers**
> 1. Write each mixed number and whole number as a fraction.
> 2. Multiply the fractions.
> 3. If necessary, rewrite the result from Step **2** in lowest terms.

EXAMPLE Write each product in lowest terms. a. $\frac{1}{3} \times 4\frac{1}{8}$ b. $3\frac{1}{2} \times 5\frac{1}{3}$

Solution

a. $\frac{1}{3} \times 4\frac{1}{8} = \frac{1}{3} \times \frac{33}{8}$

$= \frac{1 \times \cancel{33}^{11}}{\cancel{3}_{1} \times 8}$

$= \frac{1 \times 11}{1 \times 8}$

$= \frac{11}{8} = 1\frac{3}{8}$

b. $3\frac{1}{2} \times 5\frac{1}{3} = \frac{7}{2} \times \frac{16}{3}$

$= \frac{7}{\cancel{2}_{1}} \times \frac{\cancel{16}^{8}}{3}$

$= \frac{7 \times 8}{1 \times 3}$

$= \frac{56}{3} = 18\frac{2}{3}$

Write each product in lowest terms.

1. $\frac{1}{2} \times 1\frac{1}{2}$ _____
2. $2\frac{1}{2} \times \frac{1}{3}$ _____
3. $4\frac{1}{2} \times \frac{1}{4}$ _____

4. $\frac{3}{5} \times 3\frac{1}{2}$ _____
5. $5\frac{1}{3} \times \frac{1}{4}$ _____
6. $\frac{4}{5} \times 3\frac{1}{3}$ _____

7. $\frac{2}{3} \times 4\frac{1}{2}$ _____
8. $2\frac{2}{3} \times \frac{3}{4}$ _____
9. $12 \times 2\frac{1}{3}$ _____

10. $20 \times 2\frac{2}{5}$ _____
11. $14 \times 2\frac{1}{4}$ _____
12. $2\frac{5}{6} \times 16$ _____

13. $2\frac{1}{3} \times 3\frac{1}{2}$ _____
14. $1\frac{3}{4} \times 2\frac{1}{3}$ _____
15. $1\frac{2}{3} \times 2\frac{1}{4}$ _____

16. $3\frac{1}{2} \times \frac{6}{7} \times 9\frac{1}{3}$ _____
17. $4\frac{4}{5} \times 8\frac{1}{3} \times \frac{5}{6}$ _____

18. $7\frac{1}{2} \times 8 \times 2\frac{2}{5}$ _____
19. $1\frac{7}{9} \times 3\frac{3}{4} \times 6$ _____

NAME _____ CLASS _____ DATE _____

6-6 Estimating Products Involving Mixed Numbers
UNIT 2

OBJECTIVE: *Estimating products involving mixed numbers by rounding*

You can estimate a product involving mixed numbers by rounding one or more of the numbers.

EXAMPLE Estimate each product. a. $5\frac{1}{2} \times 1\frac{1}{9} \times 3\frac{11}{12}$ b. $\frac{1}{5} \times 13\frac{1}{20}$

Solution

a. Round $5\frac{1}{2}$ up to 6. Round $1\frac{1}{9}$ down to 1. Round $3\frac{11}{12}$ up to 4.

$5\frac{1}{2} \times 1\frac{1}{9} \times 3\frac{11}{12}$ → about $6 \times 1 \times 4$ → about 24

b. $13\frac{1}{20}$ is close to 15, making the multiplication with $\frac{1}{5}$ easier.

$\frac{1}{5} \times 13\frac{1}{20}$ → about $\frac{1}{5} \times 15$ → about 3

Estimate each product by rounding.

1. $7\frac{2}{11} \times 4\frac{3}{20}$ _____

2. $1\frac{5}{9} \times 16\frac{8}{15}$ _____

3. $9\frac{1}{2} \times 4\frac{14}{15}$ _____

4. $11\frac{2}{99} \times 3\frac{1}{2}$ _____

5. $6\frac{1}{50} \times \frac{17}{18}$ _____

6. $\frac{99}{100} \times 22\frac{7}{12}$ _____

7. $14\frac{24}{25} \times 2\frac{1}{3} \times \frac{19}{20}$ _____

8. $3\frac{2}{5} \times 4\frac{5}{8} \times 10\frac{1}{2}$ _____

Estimate each product by rounding.

9. $\frac{1}{3} \times 11\frac{4}{9}$ _____

10. $21\frac{3}{16} \times \frac{1}{4}$ _____

11. $33\frac{7}{18} \times \frac{4}{5}$ _____

12. $\frac{5}{6} \times 46\frac{5}{14}$ _____

13. $\frac{11}{23} \times 52$ _____

14. $32 \times \frac{5}{19}$ _____

15. $40 \times \frac{36}{49}$ _____

16. $\frac{65}{99} \times 21$ _____

17. $\frac{4}{25} \times 17\frac{2}{15}$ _____

18. $103\frac{1}{25} \times \frac{39}{79}$ _____

Making Sense of Numbers   Unit 2 Fractions   **57**

NAME _____ CLASS _____ DATE _____

Problems Involving Fraction Multiplication

OBJECTIVE: Solving a real-world problem by finding a product involving fractions

Sometimes you must find a product involving one or more fractions to solve a real-world problem.

EXAMPLE	The price of a television is $189. The television is now on sale for two-thirds of the price. What is the sale price?
	Solution
Strategy	You need to find two-thirds of $189. So you must multiply $\frac{2}{3} \times 189$. 189 is close to 180, making the multiplication with $\frac{2}{3}$ easier.
Estimate	The product will be about $\frac{2}{3} \times 180$, or 120, but it will be a little more than 120 because 189 was rounded down to 180.
Work	Find the product: $\frac{2}{3} \times 189 = \frac{2}{3} \times \frac{189}{1} = \frac{2}{\cancel{3}} \times \frac{\cancel{189}^{63}}{1} = \frac{2 \times 63}{1 \times 1} = 126$ Compare to the estimate: 126 is close to 120, but more than 120.
Answer	The sale price of the television is $126.

Solve each problem using the steps *Strategy, Estimate, Work,* and *Answer.*

1. David withdrew $\frac{1}{4}$ of the money in his savings account. He spent $\frac{1}{2}$ of the amount he withdrew on clothes. What fractional part of his savings did David spend on clothes? _____

2. A recipe calls for $\frac{3}{4}$ cup of honey. Mai is making $\frac{1}{3}$ of the recipe. How many cups of honey does she need? _____

3. This year's budget for the Midville schools is $360,000. The school committee voted to spend two-fifths of it on building renovations. What amount of money is this? _____

4. A farmer wants to plant three-fourths of a field with lettuce. Two-thirds of that area will be planted with romaine lettuce. What fractional part of the entire field will be planted with romaine lettuce? _____

5. Any amendment to the Constitution of the United States of America must be ratified by three-fourths of the fifty states. How many states is this? _____

NAME _____ CLASS _____ DATE _____

Problems Involving Mixed Number Multiplication

OBJECTIVE: Solving a real-world problem by finding a product involving mixed numbers

Sometimes the process of solving a real-world problem requires you to multiply with mixed numbers.

EXAMPLE The scale of a map is 1 inch = $2\frac{1}{4}$ miles. What actual number of miles is represented by five inches on this map?

Solution

Strategy You know the distance for each inch, so you multiply to find the distance for multiple inches. Find the product $5 \times 2\frac{1}{4}$.

Estimate Round $2\frac{1}{4}$ down to 2. The distance will be about 5×2, or 10, but a little more than 10 because $2\frac{1}{4}$ was rounded down to 2.

Work Find the product: $5 \times 2\frac{1}{4} = \frac{5}{1} \times \frac{9}{4} = \frac{45}{4} = 11\frac{1}{4}$

Compare to the estimate: $11\frac{1}{4}$ is close to 10, but a little more.

Answer The actual distance represented by five inches is $11\frac{1}{4}$ miles.

Solve each problem using the steps *Strategy, Estimate, Work,* and *Answer*.

1. Refer to the map described above. What actual number of miles is represented by $6\frac{1}{2}$ inches on the map? _____

2. Vida bicycled $1\frac{2}{3}$ hours at an average speed of $7\frac{1}{2}$ miles per hour. What is the total distance that she bicycled? _____

3. Helmer needs to mail five packages. Each package weighs $1\frac{3}{4}$ pounds. What will be the total weight of the five packages? _____

4. A recipe calls for $2\frac{3}{4}$ cups of flour. Jan wants to triple the recipe. How many cups of flour will she need? _____

Making Sense of Numbers   Unit 2   Fractions   **59**

NAME _____ CLASS _____ DATE _____

Problems Involving Addition, Subtraction, or Multiplication of Fractions or Mixed Numbers

OBJECTIVE: *Solving a real-world problem by finding a sum, difference, or product involving fractions or mixed numbers*

An important part of your problem solving strategy is choosing the correct mathematical operation. The following guidelines for choosing multiplication might help you make the correct choice.

> **Choosing Multiplication**
>
> Use multiplication:
> to find "how much in all" when you know "how much in each"
> to double an amount, triple an amount, and so on

Solve each problem by using addition, subtraction, or multiplication.

1. Mark worked $3\frac{1}{2}$ hours bagging groceries at $6 per hour and $5\frac{1}{4}$ hours baby-sitting at $4 per hour.

    a. How many hours did he work in all? _____

    b. How many more hours did he work at baby-sitting than bagging groceries? _____

    c. How much did he earn from bagging groceries? _____

    d. How much did he earn from baby-sitting? _____

2. Risa has to make four costumes for the school play. Each costume requires $2\frac{1}{3}$ yards of fabric. How many yards of fabric does she need in all? _____

3. Sean has four cups of flour. He is making a recipe that requires $2\frac{1}{3}$ cups of flour. How many cups of flour will remain after he makes the recipe? _____

4. A design is $\frac{7}{8}$ inch long and $1\frac{7}{16}$ inches wide. Janette plans to make a copy of the design at three times this size. What will be the length and width of her copy? _____

60   Unit 2   Fractions   *Making Sense of Numbers*

NAME _____ CLASS _____ DATE _____

6-10 Adding, Subtracting, and Multiplying With Fractions
UNIT 2

OBJECTIVE: Finding the value of an expression that involves a combination of addition, subtraction, and multiplication of fractions

An expression that contains fractions may involve a combination of the operations of addition, subtraction, and multiplication. To find its value, you must follow the order of operations.

EXAMPLE Find the value of each expression.   a. $\frac{1}{4} \times \left(\frac{1}{5} + \frac{3}{5}\right)$ b. $\frac{5}{9} - \left(\frac{1}{3}\right)^2$

Solution

a. First do the operation inside the parentheses.

$$\frac{1}{4} \times \left(\frac{1}{5} + \frac{3}{5}\right)$$

$$\frac{1}{4} \times \frac{4}{5}$$

$$\frac{1 \times \cancel{4}^1}{\cancel{4}_1 \times 5} \quad \text{Divide by 4.}$$

$$\frac{1 \times 1}{1 \times 5} = \frac{1}{5}$$

b. First find the value of the power.

$$\frac{5}{9} - \left(\frac{1}{3}\right)^2$$

$$\frac{5}{9} - \left(\frac{1}{3} \times \frac{1}{3}\right)$$

$$\frac{5}{9} - \frac{1}{9}$$

$$\frac{4}{9}$$

Find the value of each expression in lowest terms.

1. $\frac{11}{16} - \frac{3}{8} \times \frac{1}{2}$ _____

2. $\frac{8}{9} + \frac{1}{3} \times \frac{2}{3}$ _____

3. $\frac{2}{3} \times \left(\frac{4}{7} - \frac{1}{7}\right)$ _____

4. $\frac{5}{6} \times \left(\frac{2}{5} + \frac{4}{5}\right)$ _____

5. $\frac{3}{10} + \frac{2}{3} \times \frac{1}{4}$ _____

6. $\frac{14}{15} \times \left(\frac{7}{8} - \frac{2}{3}\right)$ _____

7. $\frac{3}{16} + \left(\frac{1}{4}\right)^2$ _____

8. $\frac{7}{9} - \left(\frac{2}{3}\right)^2$ _____

9. $\left(\frac{4}{5}\right)^2 + \frac{7}{10}$ _____

10. $1 - \left(\frac{3}{7}\right)^2$ _____

11. $\frac{5}{6} \times \left(\frac{3}{5} - \frac{1}{5}\right)^2$ _____

12. $\left(\frac{1}{4} + \frac{1}{2}\right)^2 \times \frac{14}{15}$ _____

Making Sense of Numbers   Unit 2 Fractions   **61**

NAME _____ CLASS _____ DATE _____

6-11 Adding, Subtracting, and Multiplying With Mixed Numbers
UNIT 2

OBJECTIVE: Finding the value of an expression that involves a combination of addition, subtraction, and multiplication of mixed numbers

An expression that contains mixed numbers may involve a combination of addition, subtraction, and multiplication. To find its value, remember to follow the order of operations.

EXAMPLE Find the value of $1\frac{4}{5} \times \left(3\frac{5}{6} - 3\frac{1}{2}\right)^2$.

Solution

$1\frac{4}{5} \times \left(3\frac{5}{6} - 3\frac{1}{2}\right)^2$

$\frac{9}{5} \times \left(\frac{23}{6} - \frac{7}{2}\right)^2$ Write the mixed numbers as fractions.

$\frac{9}{5} \times \left(\frac{23}{6} - \frac{21}{6}\right)^2$ Rewrite $\frac{7}{2}$ as $\frac{21}{6}$.

$\frac{9}{5} \times \left(\frac{2}{6}\right)^2$ Subtract inside the parentheses.

$\frac{9}{5} \times \left(\frac{1}{3}\right)^2$ Simplify $\frac{2}{6}$.

$\frac{9}{5} \times \frac{1}{9}$ Calculate the power.

$\frac{9 \times 1}{5 \times 9} = \frac{9}{45} = \frac{1}{5}$ Multiply. Then simplify the result.

Write the value of each expression in lowest terms.

1. $1\frac{1}{3} + 1\frac{1}{3} \times 1\frac{1}{3}$ _____

2. $3\frac{1}{2} \times 2\frac{3}{4} - 7\frac{3}{4}$ _____

3. $2\frac{2}{3} \times \left(1\frac{1}{4} + 2\frac{1}{2}\right)$ _____

4. $\left(1\frac{1}{8} - \frac{5}{6}\right) \times 1\frac{5}{7}$ _____

5. $3\frac{1}{4} - \left(1\frac{1}{2}\right)^2$ _____

6. $\left(1\frac{1}{4}\right)^2 + 1\frac{1}{16}$ _____

7. $\left(2\frac{2}{3}\right)^2 \times 1\frac{7}{8}$ _____

8. $2\frac{2}{5} \times \left(1\frac{2}{3}\right)^2$ _____

9. $\left(4\frac{1}{8} - 3\frac{7}{8}\right)^2 \times 7\frac{1}{5}$ _____

10. $2\frac{4}{7} \times \left(4 - 2\frac{1}{4}\right)^2$ _____

Unit 2   Fractions   *Making Sense of Numbers*

NAME _____ CLASS _____ DATE _____

6-12 Problems Involving Multiplication of Fractions or Mixed Numbers Together With Addition or Subtraction
UNIT 2

OBJECTIVE: Solving a real-world problem by finding a product of fractions or mixed numbers as well as a sum or difference

Solving a problem may require multiple steps involving addition, subtraction, or multiplication of fractions or mixed numbers.

EXAMPLE How many feet of ribbon will remain on a 15-foot roll after cutting off four pieces of ribbon that are each $2\frac{3}{4}$ feet long?

▶ **Solution**

Strategy Multiply to find the length of the 4 pieces. Then subtract from 15.

Estimate Round $2\frac{3}{4}$ up to 3. The amount cut off will be about 4×3, or 12. So the amount remaining will be about $15 - 12$, or 3.

Work Find the product: $4 \times 2\frac{3}{4} = \frac{4}{1} \times \frac{11}{4} = \frac{4 \times 11}{1 \times 4} = \frac{44}{4} = 11$

Subtract from 15: $15 - 11 = 4$

Compare to the estimate: 4 is reasonably close to 3.

Answer The amount of ribbon remaining on the roll will be 4 feet.

Solve each problem using the steps *Strategy*, *Estimate*, *Work*, and *Answer*.

1. A gas tank can hold 25 gallons. The gauge shows that it is $\frac{1}{4}$ full. How many gallons are needed to fill the tank? _____

2. Leah has to make six small costumes that each require $3\frac{1}{8}$ yards of fabric and two large costumes that each require $3\frac{3}{4}$ yards. How many yards does she need in all? _____

3. A formula for the perimeter, P, of a rectangle with length ℓ and width w is $P = 2 \times (\ell + w)$. What is the perimeter in feet of a rectangle with length $3\frac{2}{3}$ feet and width $2\frac{1}{4}$ feet? _____

NAME _____ CLASS _____ DATE _____

6-13 Renaming a Customary Measure of Length by Multiplying
UNIT 2

OBJECTIVE: Using multiplication to rename a customary measure of length

The following are the commonly used customary units of length.

Customary Units of Length	
1 foot = 12 inches	1 mile = 5280 feet
1 yard = 3 feet = 36 inches	1 mile = 1760 yards

To rename a measure, you may need to multiply with fractions.

EXAMPLE Fill in the blank to make a true statement: $3\frac{2}{3}$ feet = _____ inches

Solution

Multiply $3\frac{2}{3}$ by 12: $3\frac{2}{3} \times 12$ *Multiply by 12 because 1 foot = 12 inches.*

$= \frac{11}{\underset{1}{\cancel{3}}} \times \frac{\overset{4}{\cancel{12}}}{1}$ *Divide by 3.*

$= \frac{11 \times 4}{1 \times 1} = \frac{44}{1} = 44$

Therefore, $3\frac{2}{3}$ feet = 44 inches.

Fill in each blank with the number that makes a true statement.

1. 9 feet = _____ inches
2. $2\frac{1}{4}$ feet = _____ inches
3. 6 yards = _____ inches
4. $4\frac{2}{3}$ yards = _____ inches
5. 12 yards = _____ feet
6. $5\frac{1}{3}$ yards = _____ feet
7. 2 miles = _____ feet
8. $2\frac{1}{3}$ miles = _____ feet
9. 5 miles = _____ yards
10. $1\frac{3}{4}$ miles = _____ yards
11. $2\frac{1}{8}$ feet = _____ inches
12. $3\frac{1}{4}$ yards = _____ feet
13. $1\frac{3}{10}$ yards = _____ inches
14. $9\frac{5}{6}$ yards = _____ feet

64 Unit 2 Fractions *Making Sense of Numbers*

6-14 Renaming a Customary Measure of Weight or Liquid Capacity by Multiplying

UNIT 2

OBJECTIVE: Using multiplication to rename a customary measure of weight or liquid capacity

The following are the commonly used customary units of weight and liquid capacity.

Customary Units of Weight and Liquid Capacity

1 pound = 16 ounces
1 ton = 2000 pounds

1 cup = 8 fluid ounces
1 pint = 2 cups
1 quart = 2 pints
1 gallon = 4 quarts

EXAMPLE Fill in the blank to make a true statement: $5\frac{3}{4}$ pints = _____ cups

Solution

Multiply $5\frac{3}{4}$ by 2: $5\frac{3}{4} \times 2$ *Multiply by 2 because 1 pint = 2 cups.*

$$= \frac{23}{\cancel{4}_2} \times \frac{\cancel{2}^1}{1} \quad \text{Divide by 2.}$$

$$= \frac{23 \times 1}{2 \times 1} = \frac{23}{2} = 11\frac{1}{2}$$

Therefore, $5\frac{3}{4}$ pints = $11\frac{1}{2}$ cups.

Fill in each blank with the number that makes a true statement.

1. 3 pounds = _____ ounces

2. $7\frac{3}{4}$ pounds = _____ ounces

3. $5\frac{1}{2}$ tons = _____ pounds

4. $\frac{1}{6}$ ton = _____ pounds

5. 6 quarts = _____ pints

6. $4\frac{1}{4}$ cups = _____ fluid ounces

7. $6\frac{3}{4}$ pints = _____ cups

8. $3\frac{2}{3}$ gallons = _____ quarts

9. 3 quarts = _____ cups

10. 7 gallons = _____ pints

11. $2\frac{1}{2}$ pints = _____ fluid ounces

12. $5\frac{1}{4}$ quarts = _____ cups

Making Sense of Numbers

NAME _____ CLASS _____ DATE _____

7-1 Modeling a Division by a Fraction
UNIT 2

OBJECTIVE: Interpreting and drawing models of division by a fraction

You can use a model to represent division by a fraction.

EXAMPLE Quotient is the result of a division. Draw a model of $3 \div \frac{1}{4}$ and write the quotient.

Solution

Draw three congruent circles.
Divide each into four equal parts.
There are twelve parts in all.

Therefore, there are twelve $\frac{1}{4}$'s in 3, so $3 \div \frac{1}{4} = 12$.

In each exercise, refer to the model at left. Fill in the blanks to write each quotient.

1. There are _____ $\frac{1}{3}$'s in 2, so _____.

2. There are _____ $\frac{1}{5}$'s in 4, so _____.

3. There are _____ $\frac{1}{6}$'s in $3\frac{5}{6}$, so _____.

4. There are _____ $\frac{1}{4}$'s in $2\frac{1}{2}$, so _____.

5. There are _____ $\frac{2}{3}$'s in 4, so _____.

6. There are _____ $\frac{3}{5}$'s in $2\frac{2}{5}$, so _____.

Draw a model of each division. Then write the quotient.

7. $2 \div \frac{1}{8}$

8. $3\frac{3}{4} \div \frac{1}{4}$

quotient: _____

quotient: _____

7-2 Reciprocals

OBJECTIVE: *Finding the reciprocal of a given number*

Two numbers whose product is 1 are called **reciprocals** of each other. The following are some examples of reciprocals.

$$5 \times \frac{1}{5} = 1 \qquad \frac{3}{7} \times \frac{7}{3} = 1 \qquad 8\frac{1}{2} \times \frac{2}{17} = 1$$

Every number except zero has exactly one reciprocal. Zero has no reciprocal. To find the reciprocal of a number, write it in fraction form and interchange the numerator and denominator.

EXAMPLE Write the reciprocal of each number. a. $\frac{2}{11}$ b. 8 c. $3\frac{2}{5}$

Solution

a. $\frac{2}{11} \times \frac{11}{2}$
The reciprocal of $\frac{2}{11}$ is $\frac{11}{2}$.

b. $8 = \frac{8}{1} \times \frac{1}{8}$
The reciprocal of 8 is $\frac{1}{8}$.

c. $3\frac{2}{5} = \frac{17}{5} \times \frac{5}{17}$
The reciprocal of $3\frac{2}{5}$ is $\frac{5}{17}$.

Write the reciprocal of each number as a whole number or as a fraction in lowest terms. If there is no reciprocal, write *none*.

1. $\frac{5}{9}$ _____
2. $\frac{14}{3}$ _____
3. 12 _____
4. 50 _____

5. $\frac{1}{9}$ _____
6. $\frac{1}{200}$ _____
7. 0 _____
8. 1 _____

9. $1\frac{1}{7}$ _____
10. $3\frac{1}{15}$ _____
11. $4\frac{5}{6}$ _____
12. $8\frac{11}{12}$ _____

Tell whether the numbers in each pair are reciprocals of each other. Write *Yes* or *No*.

13. 16, $\frac{1}{16}$ _____
14. $\frac{6}{7}, \frac{7}{6}$ _____
15. $5\frac{1}{4}, 4\frac{1}{5}$ _____

16. $1\frac{1}{10}, \frac{10}{11}$ _____
17. 14, $\frac{14}{1}$ _____
18. 0, 1 _____

Fill in each blank with the number that makes the statement true.

19. $\frac{1}{17} \times 17 =$ _____
20. $\frac{1}{4} \times$ _____ $= 1$
21. $23 \times$ _____ $= 1$

22. _____ $\times \frac{8}{5} = 1$
23. $5\frac{3}{7} \times \frac{7}{38} =$ _____
24. $\frac{3}{19} \times$ _____ $= 1$

25. _____ $\times 7\frac{2}{3} = 1$
26. $1 \times$ _____ $= 1$
27. $13 \times$ _____ $= 1$

Making Sense of Numbers

7-3 Dividing With Fractions

UNIT 2

OBJECTIVE: *Finding quotients involving fractions*

In the division $\frac{2}{3} \div \frac{6}{7}$, $\frac{2}{3}$ is the *dividend*, $\frac{6}{7}$ is the *divisor*, and the result of this division is called a *quotient*. To divide by a fraction, you can use the following rule.

Dividing by a Fraction
1. Multiply the dividend by the reciprocal of the divisor.
2. If necessary, rewrite the result from Step **1** in lowest terms.

EXAMPLE 1 Write the quotient $\frac{2}{3} \div \frac{6}{7}$ in lowest terms.

Solution

$$\frac{2}{3} \div \frac{6}{7} = \frac{2}{3} \times \frac{7}{6} = \frac{\overset{1}{2} \times 7}{3 \times \underset{3}{6}} = \frac{1 \times 7}{3 \times 3} = \frac{7}{9}$$

When a division involves a whole number, write the whole number as a fraction with denominator 1.

EXAMPLE 2 Write each quotient in lowest terms.   a. $\frac{1}{5} \div 3$ b. $6 \div \frac{8}{9}$

Solution

a. $\frac{1}{5} \div 3 = \frac{1}{5} \div \frac{3}{1} = \frac{1}{5} \times \frac{1}{3} = \frac{1 \times 1}{5 \times 3} = \frac{1}{15}$

b. $6 \div \frac{8}{9} = \frac{6}{1} \div \frac{8}{9} = \frac{\overset{3}{6}}{1} \times \frac{9}{\underset{4}{8}} = \frac{3 \times 9}{1 \times 4} = \frac{27}{4} = 6\frac{3}{4}$

Write each quotient in lowest terms.

1. $\frac{2}{7} \div \frac{3}{5}$ _____
2. $\frac{3}{5} \div \frac{2}{9}$ _____
3. $\frac{4}{7} \div \frac{2}{7}$ _____
4. $\frac{2}{7} \div \frac{4}{7}$ _____

5. $\frac{2}{9} \div \frac{2}{3}$ _____
6. $\frac{2}{3} \div \frac{2}{9}$ _____
7. $\frac{1}{5} \div \frac{1}{3}$ _____
8. $\frac{1}{4} \div \frac{1}{7}$ _____

9. $\frac{15}{16} \div \frac{3}{8}$ _____
10. $\frac{24}{25} \div \frac{4}{5}$ _____
11. $\frac{4}{9} \div \frac{8}{15}$ _____
12. $\frac{9}{10} \div \frac{12}{25}$ _____

13. $\frac{1}{4} \div 2$ _____
14. $\frac{1}{6} \div 6$ _____
15. $\frac{3}{5} \div 2$ _____
16. $\frac{5}{7} \div 7$ _____

17. $\frac{3}{4} \div 9$ _____
18. $\frac{2}{9} \div 4$ _____
19. $6 \div \frac{1}{2}$ _____
20. $8 \div \frac{3}{4}$ _____

7-4 Dividing With Mixed Numbers

UNIT 2

OBJECTIVE: Finding quotients involving mixed numbers

To divide with mixed numbers, use the following method.

Dividing With Mixed Numbers

1. Write each mixed number and whole number as a fraction.
2. Divide the fractions.
3. If necessary, rewrite the result from Step **2** in lowest terms.

EXAMPLE Write each quotient in lowest terms. a. $4\frac{3}{8} \div 7$ b. $3\frac{1}{3} \div 2\frac{7}{9}$

Solution

a. $4\frac{3}{8} \div 7 = \frac{35}{8} \div \frac{7}{1}$ b. $3\frac{1}{3} \div 2\frac{7}{9} = \frac{10}{3} \div \frac{25}{9}$

$= \frac{35}{8} \times \frac{1}{7}$ $= \frac{10}{3} \times \frac{9}{25}$

$= \frac{\overset{5}{\cancel{35}} \times 1}{8 \times \underset{1}{\cancel{7}}}$ $= \frac{\overset{2}{\cancel{10}}}{\underset{1}{\cancel{3}}} \times \frac{\overset{3}{\cancel{9}}}{\underset{5}{\cancel{25}}}$

$= \frac{5 \times 1}{8 \times 1} = \frac{5}{8}$ $= \frac{2 \times 3}{1 \times 5} = \frac{6}{5} = 1\frac{1}{5}$

Write each quotient in lowest terms.

1. $1\frac{2}{3} \div 2$ _____ 2. $4\frac{3}{4} \div 3$ _____ 3. $5\frac{1}{3} \div 4$ _____

4. $3\frac{3}{5} \div 9$ _____ 5. $3\frac{4}{7} \div \frac{1}{7}$ _____ 6. $8\frac{2}{5} \div \frac{1}{5}$ _____

7. $2\frac{5}{8} \div \frac{3}{8}$ _____ 8. $3\frac{8}{9} \div \frac{7}{9}$ _____ 9. $7\frac{1}{2} \div \frac{3}{4}$ _____

10. $6\frac{2}{3} \div \frac{5}{6}$ _____ 11. $3\frac{1}{2} \div \frac{3}{4}$ _____ 12. $1\frac{1}{3} \div \frac{8}{15}$ _____

13. $7 \div 1\frac{3}{4}$ _____ 14. $10 \div 1\frac{2}{3}$ _____ 15. $8 \div 1\frac{1}{2}$ _____

16. $9 \div 1\frac{1}{9}$ _____ 17. $12 \div 2\frac{2}{3}$ _____ 18. $16 \div 1\frac{1}{5}$ _____

19. $\frac{1}{4} \div 1\frac{4}{5}$ _____ 20. $\frac{5}{7} \div 2\frac{1}{3}$ _____ 21. $\frac{4}{5} \div 1\frac{1}{5}$ _____

Making Sense of Numbers

7-5 Estimating Quotients Involving Fractions and Mixed Numbers

OBJECTIVE: Estimating quotients involving fractions and mixed numbers by rounding

You can estimate a quotient involving fractions or mixed numbers by rounding the dividend, the divisor, or both.

EXAMPLE Estimate each quotient. a. $46\frac{7}{10} \div 5$ b. $11\frac{3}{8} \div 3\frac{1}{6}$ c. $7\frac{5}{6} \div \frac{7}{29}$

Solution

a. Note that $46\frac{7}{10}$ is close to 45, and 45 is divisible by 5.

$$46\frac{7}{10} \div 5 \rightarrow \text{about } 45 \div 5 \rightarrow \text{about } 9$$

b. First round the divisor, $3\frac{1}{6}$, to 3.

Now note that $11\frac{3}{8}$ is close to 12, and 12 is divisible by 3.

$$11\frac{3}{8} \div 3\frac{1}{6} \rightarrow \text{about } 12 \div 3 \rightarrow \text{about } 4$$

c. First note that 29 is close to 28, so $\frac{7}{29}$ is close to $\frac{7}{28} = \frac{1}{4}$.

Now round $7\frac{5}{6}$ to 8.

$$7\frac{5}{6} \div \frac{7}{29} \rightarrow \text{about } 8 \div \frac{1}{4} \rightarrow \text{about } 8 \times 4 \rightarrow \text{about } 32$$

Estimate each quotient.

1. $54\frac{3}{20} \div 8$ _____

2. $37\frac{1}{16} \div 3$ _____

3. $63 \div 7\frac{4}{5}$ _____

4. $15 \div 4\frac{8}{9}$ _____

5. $46 \div 8\frac{14}{15}$ _____

6. $65 \div 6\frac{1}{100}$ _____

7. $17\frac{1}{3} \div 4\frac{1}{3}$ _____

8. $46\frac{1}{2} \div 7\frac{7}{9}$ _____

9. $38\frac{3}{7} \div 2\frac{19}{20}$ _____

10. $59\frac{3}{50} \div 4\frac{1}{12}$ _____

11. $25 \div \frac{23}{47}$ _____

12. $73 \div \frac{29}{30}$ _____

NAME _____ CLASS _____ DATE _____

7-6
UNIT 2

Problems Involving Fraction Division

OBJECTIVE: *Solving a problem by finding a quotient involving fractions*

Sometimes the process of solving a real-world problem requires you to find a quotient involving one or more fractions.

EXAMPLE	A lot that covers $\frac{7}{8}$-acre of land is to be split into small parcels. Each parcel will contain $\frac{1}{16}$-acre. How many small parcels will there be?

Solution

Strategy — You need to find how many $\frac{1}{16}$-acre parcels are in the $\frac{7}{8}$-acre lot. So you must divide $\frac{7}{8} \div \frac{1}{16}$.

Estimate — $\frac{7}{8}$ is close to 1. The quotient will be about $1 \div \frac{1}{16}$, or 16, but it will be a little less because $\frac{7}{8}$ was rounded up to 1.

Work — Find the quotient: $\frac{7}{8} \div \frac{1}{16} = \frac{7}{8} \times \frac{16}{1} = \frac{7}{8} \times \frac{\overset{2}{\cancel{16}}}{1} = \frac{7 \times 2}{1 \times 1} = \frac{14}{1} = 14$

Compare to the estimate: 14 is close to 16, but less than 16.

Answer — There will be 14 parcels of land.

Solve each problem using the steps *Strategy, Estimate, Work,* and *Answer.*

1. How many $\frac{2}{3}$-yard pieces of fabric can be cut from a bolt that contains 36 yards of fabric? _____

2. A grocer buys peanuts in 4-pound cans and sells them in $\frac{3}{4}$-pound bags. How many bags of peanuts can the grocer make from each can? _____

3. A bag of pretzels that weighs $\frac{3}{4}$ pound is to be shared equally by four people. How many pounds of pretzels will be in each share? _____

4. A disc jockey schedules air time in quarter-hour periods. How many periods must be scheduled in the six hours between 11:00 P.M. and 5:00 A.M.? _____

Making Sense of Numbers

NAME _____ CLASS _____ DATE _____

7-7 Problems Involving Mixed Number Division
UNIT 2

OBJECTIVE: Solving a real-world problem by finding a quotient involving mixed numbers

Sometimes the process of solving a real-world problem requires you to divide with mixed numbers.

EXAMPLE	Meagan worked $2\frac{3}{4}$ hours on Saturday and received a check for $22. What was Meagan's rate of pay per hour?

▶ **Solution**

Strategy — You know *total dollars* and *total hours,* so you divide dollars by hours to find *dollars per hour.* Find the quotient $22 \div 2\frac{3}{4}$.

Estimate — Round $2\frac{3}{4}$ up to 3. Note that 22 is close to 21, and 21 is divisible by 3. The number of dollars per hour will be about $21 \div 3$, or 7.

Work — Find the quotient: $22 \div 2\frac{3}{4} = \frac{22}{1} \div \frac{11}{4} = \frac{\cancel{22}^{2}}{1} \times \frac{4}{\cancel{11}_{1}} = \frac{2 \times 4}{1 \times 1} = \frac{8}{1} = 8$

Compare to the estimate: 8 is close to 7.

Answer — Meagan's rate of pay was $8 per hour.

Solve each problem using the steps *Strategy, Estimate, Work,* and *Answer.*

1. Sam is planning to use a $2\frac{1}{4}$-gallon jug to fill a 36-gallon barrel with water. How many times must he fill the jug? _____

2. One batch of cookies requires $2\frac{1}{3}$ cups of flour. Callie has $10\frac{1}{2}$ cups of flour. How many batches of cookies can she make? _____

3. It takes $2\frac{1}{3}$ feet of ribbon to make a bow. How many bows can you make from a 35-foot roll of ribbon? _____

4. The width of one strip of wallpaper is $1\frac{3}{4}$ feet. How many strips will be needed to cover a wall that is $10\frac{1}{2}$ feet wide? _____

5. A garden border is $18\frac{2}{3}$ feet long. Tim must separate it into six equal parts. What will be the length of each part? _____

72   Unit 2   Fractions   *Making Sense of Numbers*

NAME _____ CLASS _____ DATE _____

Problems Involving Addition, Subtraction, Multiplication, or Division of Fractions or Mixed Numbers

OBJECTIVE: *Solving a real-world problem by finding a sum, difference, product, or quotient involving fractions or mixed numbers*

An important part of your problem solving strategy is choosing the correct mathematical operation. The following guidelines for choosing division might help you make the correct choice.

Choosing Division

Use division when you know a total and you need to find:
the number of parts of a given total
the amount in each of several equal parts

Solve by using addition, subtraction, multiplication, or division.

1. It takes $4\frac{1}{2}$ pounds of grapes to make one pound of raisins.

   a. How many pounds of raisins can be made from 100 pounds of grapes? _____

   b. How many pounds of grapes are needed to make 100 pounds of raisins? _____

2. José walked $3\frac{2}{3}$ miles yesterday and 5 miles today. How many more miles did he walk today than yesterday? _____

3. How much fencing is needed to enclose a triangular garden plot with sides of length $6\frac{1}{8}$ feet, $5\frac{1}{2}$ feet, and $8\frac{1}{4}$ feet? _____

4. Meredith drove $3\frac{1}{2}$ hours at an average speed of 54 miles per hour. How many miles did she drive in all? _____

5. Twelve pounds of oranges are being shipped in a crate that weighs $2\frac{3}{16}$ pounds. What is the weight in pounds of the oranges and crate together? _____

Making Sense of Numbers   Unit 2   Fractions   **73**

7-9 Adding, Subtracting, Multiplying, and Dividing With Fractions

UNIT 2

OBJECTIVE: Finding the value of an expression that involves a combination of addition, subtraction, multiplication, and division of fractions

An expression that contains fractions may involve a combination of the operations of addition, subtraction, multiplication, and division. To find its value, you must follow the order of operations.

EXAMPLE Find the value of each expression. a. $\frac{3}{5} + \frac{2}{3} \div \frac{5}{6}$ b. $\frac{1}{2} \div \frac{2}{7} \times \frac{1}{3}$

Solution

a. First divide, then add.

$\frac{3}{5} + \frac{2}{3} \div \frac{5}{6}$

$\frac{3}{5} + \frac{2}{3} \times \frac{6}{5}$ Multiply by the reciprocal of $\frac{5}{6}$.

$\frac{3}{5} + \frac{12}{15}$

$\frac{3}{5} + \frac{4}{5} = \frac{3+4}{5} = \frac{7}{5} = 1\frac{2}{5}$

b. Multiply and divide in order from left to right.

$\frac{1}{2} \div \frac{2}{7} \times \frac{1}{3}$

$\frac{1}{2} \times \frac{7}{2} \times \frac{1}{3}$ Multiply by the reciprocal of $\frac{2}{7}$.

$\frac{7}{4} \times \frac{1}{3}$

$\frac{7}{12}$

Find the value of each expression in lowest terms.

1. $\frac{5}{6} - \frac{1}{3} \div \frac{1}{2}$ _____

2. $\frac{3}{4} + \frac{1}{8} \div \frac{2}{5}$ _____

3. $\frac{2}{9} \div \frac{2}{3} + \frac{3}{4}$ _____

4. $\frac{7}{8} \div \frac{1}{4} - \frac{4}{5}$ _____

5. $\frac{6}{7} \div \frac{1}{2} \times \frac{14}{15}$ _____

6. $\frac{1}{10} \div \frac{2}{5} \times \frac{8}{9}$ _____

7. $\frac{7}{12} \div \left(\frac{5}{6} \times \frac{3}{10}\right)$ _____

8. $\frac{8}{15} \times \left(\frac{3}{8} \div \frac{1}{6}\right)$ _____

9. $\left(\frac{1}{2}\right)^2 \div \frac{4}{9}$ _____

10. $\frac{9}{10} \div \left(\frac{2}{5}\right)^2$ _____

11. $\frac{1}{6} + \frac{1}{2} \div \frac{5}{6} - \frac{2}{5}$ _____

12. $\frac{11}{12} - \frac{3}{4} \div \frac{2}{3} \times \frac{2}{9}$ _____

13. $\frac{3}{4} \div \frac{4}{9} - \frac{7}{8} \times \frac{6}{7}$ _____

14. $\frac{2}{9} \times \frac{3}{10} + \frac{1}{2} \div \frac{5}{8}$ _____

15. $\frac{1}{2} \div \left(\frac{1}{4} + \frac{1}{6}\right) \times \frac{3}{20}$ _____

16. $\frac{4}{11} \times \left(\frac{1}{8} + \frac{1}{3}\right) \div \frac{5}{9}$ _____

17. $\left(\frac{3}{4} - \frac{3}{8}\right) \div \left(\frac{2}{5} + \frac{1}{2}\right)$ _____

18. $\left(\frac{1}{3} + \frac{5}{6}\right) \div \left(\frac{5}{6} - \frac{1}{2}\right)^2$ _____

NAME _____ CLASS _____ DATE _____

7-10
UNIT 2

Adding, Subtracting, Multiplying, and Dividing With Mixed Numbers

OBJECTIVE: Finding the value of an expression that involves a combination of addition, subtraction, multiplication, and division of mixed numbers

An expression that contains mixed numbers may involve a combination of addition, subtraction, multiplication, and division. To find its value, remember to follow the order of operations.

EXAMPLE Find the value of $2\frac{1}{4} \div \left(1\frac{5}{8} - 1\frac{1}{4}\right)$.

Solution

$2\frac{1}{4} \div \left(1\frac{5}{8} - 1\frac{1}{4}\right)$

$\frac{9}{4} \div \left(\frac{13}{8} - \frac{5}{4}\right)$ Write the mixed numbers as fractions.

$\frac{9}{4} \div \left(\frac{13}{8} - \frac{10}{8}\right)$ Rewrite $\frac{5}{4}$ as $\frac{10}{8}$.

$\frac{9}{4} \div \frac{3}{8}$ Subtract inside the parentheses.

$\frac{9}{4} \times \frac{8}{3}$ Rewrite the division as a multiplication.

$\frac{\cancel{9}^3}{\cancel{4}_1} \times \frac{\cancel{8}^2}{\cancel{3}_1}$ Divide 9 and 3 by 3 and 4 and 8 by 2.

$\frac{3 \times 2}{1 \times 1} = \frac{6}{1} = 6$

Find the value of each expression in lowest terms.

1. $1\frac{1}{4} + 3\frac{3}{4} \div \frac{5}{6}$ _____

2. $2\frac{2}{3} - 1\frac{1}{8} \div 2\frac{1}{4}$ _____

3. $6\frac{1}{4} \div 1\frac{7}{8} - 1\frac{3}{4}$ _____

4. $5\frac{1}{3} \div \frac{4}{5} + 3\frac{1}{2}$ _____

5. $1\frac{5}{9} \times 1\frac{5}{7} \div 4\frac{2}{3}$ _____

6. $4\frac{1}{2} \div 2\frac{2}{5} \times 1\frac{1}{6}$ _____

7. $2\frac{1}{10} \div \left(\frac{5}{6} \times 1\frac{4}{5}\right)$ _____

8. $1\frac{5}{9} \times \left(4\frac{2}{7} \div 7\frac{1}{2}\right)$ _____

9. $4\frac{2}{3} \div 3\frac{1}{2} + 1\frac{3}{5} \times 1\frac{1}{8}$ _____

10. $3\frac{1}{8} \times 1\frac{1}{5} - 2\frac{2}{9} \div 3\frac{1}{3}$ _____

Making Sense of Numbers   Unit 2 Fractions

NAME _____ CLASS _____ DATE _____

Problems Involving Division of Fractions or Mixed Numbers Together With Addition, Subtraction, or Multiplication

OBJECTIVE: Solving a real-world problem by finding a quotient of fractions or mixed numbers as well as a sum, difference, or product

Solving a problem may require multiple steps involving division of fractions or mixed numbers as well as other operations.

EXAMPLE Two sacks of dried peas weighing $2\frac{3}{4}$ pounds and $1\frac{5}{8}$ pounds are to be divided into five storage bags. What amount will be in each bag?

Solution

Strategy Add to find the total number of pounds. Then divide by 5.

Estimate Round $2\frac{3}{4}$ up to 3. Round $1\frac{5}{8}$ up to 2. The total is about $3 + 2$, or 5. So the amount in each storage bag will be about $5 \div 5$, or 1.

Work Find the total: $2\frac{3}{4} + 1\frac{5}{8} = 2\frac{6}{8} + 1\frac{5}{8} = 3\frac{11}{8} = 3 + 1\frac{3}{8} = 4\frac{3}{8}$

Divide by 5: $4\frac{3}{8} \div 5 = \frac{35}{8} \div \frac{5}{1} = \frac{35}{8} \times \frac{1}{5} = \frac{\overset{7}{\cancel{35}} \times 1}{8 \times \underset{1}{\cancel{5}}} = \frac{7 \times 1}{8 \times 1} = \frac{7}{8}$

Compare to the estimate: $\frac{7}{8}$ is reasonably close to 1.

Answer There will be $\frac{7}{8}$ pound of dried peas in each bag.

Solve each problem using the steps *Strategy, Estimate, Work,* and *Answer.*

1. Darnelle worked $5\frac{1}{2}$ hours on Monday and $6\frac{3}{4}$ hours on Tuesday. He received a check for $147 for the two days of work. What was his rate of pay per hour? _____

2. Karl walked $2\frac{1}{2}$ miles in $\frac{1}{2}$ hour, and then 1 mile in $\frac{1}{3}$ hour. What was his average rate of walking in miles per hour? _____

3. Angie needs $2\frac{1}{4}$ cups of flour for each cake and $1\frac{1}{2}$ cups of flour for each batch of cookies that she makes. She has 6 cups of flour. How many batches of cookies can she make if she makes one cake? if she makes two cakes? _____

NAME _____ CLASS _____ DATE _____

7-12
UNIT 2

Renaming a Customary Measure by Dividing

OBJECTIVE: Using division to rename a given customary measure

When renaming a customary measure, you may need to divide with fractions.

EXAMPLE Fill in the blank to make a true statement: $16\frac{1}{2}$ inches = __?__ feet

Solution

Divide $16\frac{1}{2}$ by 12: $16\frac{1}{2} \div 12$ *Divide by 12 because 12 inches = 1 foot.*

$$= \frac{33}{2} \div \frac{12}{1}$$

$$= \frac{\overset{11}{\cancel{33}}}{2} \times \frac{1}{\underset{4}{\cancel{12}}} = \frac{11 \times 1}{2 \times 4} = \frac{11}{8} = 1\frac{1}{8}$$

Therefore, $16\frac{1}{2}$ inches = $1\frac{1}{8}$ feet.

Fill in each blank to make a true statement.

1. 60 feet = _____ yards

2. $4\frac{1}{2}$ feet = _____ yards

3. 144 inches = _____ yards

4. $85\frac{1}{2}$ inches = _____ yards

5. 63 inches = _____ feet

6. $14\frac{2}{3}$ inches = _____ feet

7. 660 feet = _____ miles

8. 6600 feet = _____ miles

9. 80 ounces = _____ pounds

10. $58\frac{2}{3}$ ounces = _____ pounds

11. 1200 pounds = _____ tons

12. 3750 pounds = _____ tons

13. 10 pints = _____ quarts

14. $22\frac{1}{2}$ pints = _____ quarts

15. 64 fluid ounces = _____ cups

16. $9\frac{1}{3}$ fluid ounces = _____ cups

17. 19 cups = _____ pints

18. $2\frac{3}{4}$ cups = _____ pints

19. 22 quarts = _____ gallons

20. $5\frac{1}{3}$ quarts = _____ gallons

Making Sense of Numbers

7-13 Renaming a Customary Measure by Multiplying or Dividing

UNIT 2

OBJECTIVE: Using either multiplication or division to rename a given customary measure

When renaming a customary unit of measure, you must decide whether to multiply or divide. You can use the following general guidelines to help you decide.

> **Renaming Units of Measure**
> Multiply to rename a larger unit in terms of a smaller unit.
> Divide to rename a smaller unit in terms of a larger unit.

EXAMPLE Fill in each blank to make a true statement.

a. 15 quarts = __?__ pints   b. 15 quarts = __?__ gallons

Solution

a. A quart is larger than a pint, so you multiply.

1 quart = 2 pints

× 2

15 quarts = 30 pints

b. A quart is smaller than a gallon, so you divide.

4 quarts = 1 gallon

÷ 4

15 quarts = $3\frac{3}{4}$ gallons

Fill in each blank to make a true statement.

1. $13\frac{1}{2}$ feet = _____ yards

2. $13\frac{1}{2}$ feet = _____ inches

3. 10 pounds = _____ ounces

4. 10 pounds = _____ tons

5. $4\frac{1}{2}$ cups = _____ fluid ounces

6. $4\frac{1}{2}$ cups = _____ pints

7. 52 inches = _____ feet

8. 11 quarts = _____ gallons

9. $3\frac{7}{8}$ pounds = _____ ounces

10. $19\frac{1}{2}$ inches = _____ feet

11. $12\frac{1}{2}$ quarts = _____ gallons

12. $21\frac{1}{3}$ ounces = _____ pounds

NAME _____ CLASS _____ DATE _____

7-14 Exponents and Division
UNIT 2

OBJECTIVE: Using positive, negative, and zero exponents to divide powers

You can use the methods you learned for dividing fractions to help you divide powers of the same base.

EXAMPLE Write each quotient as the given base with a single exponent.

a. $\dfrac{5^6}{5^2}$ b. $\dfrac{7^3}{7^3}$ c. $\dfrac{3^4}{3^5}$

Solution

a. $\dfrac{5^6}{5^2} = \dfrac{\cancel{5} \times \cancel{5} \times 5 \times 5 \times 5 \times 5}{\cancel{5} \times \cancel{5}} = 5 \times 5 \times 5 \times 5 = 5^4$ $5^4 = 5^{6-2}$

b. $\dfrac{7^3}{7^3} = \dfrac{\cancel{7} \times \cancel{7} \times \cancel{7}}{\cancel{7} \times \cancel{7} \times \cancel{7}} = \dfrac{1}{1} = 1 = 7^0$ $7^0 = 7^{3-3}$

c. $\dfrac{3^4}{3^5} = \dfrac{\cancel{3} \times \cancel{3} \times \cancel{3} \times \cancel{3}}{\cancel{3} \times \cancel{3} \times \cancel{3} \times \cancel{3} \times 3} = \dfrac{1}{3} = \dfrac{1}{3^1} = 3^{-1}$ $3^{-1} = 3^{4-5}$

Write each quotient as the given base with a single exponent.

1. $\dfrac{2^9}{2^3}$ _____ 2. $\dfrac{7^8}{7^5}$ _____ 3. $\dfrac{11^2}{11^5}$ _____ 4. $\dfrac{5^4}{5^{10}}$ _____

5. $\dfrac{2^8}{2^7}$ _____ 6. $\dfrac{5^7}{5^6}$ _____ 7. $\dfrac{13^4}{13^5}$ _____ 8. $\dfrac{7^5}{7^6}$ _____

9. $\dfrac{3^5}{3}$ _____ 10. $\dfrac{19^7}{19}$ _____ 11. $\dfrac{5}{5^8}$ _____ 12. $\dfrac{2}{2^4}$ _____

13. $\dfrac{17^2}{17}$ _____ 14. $\dfrac{5}{5^2}$ _____ 15. $\dfrac{2^9}{2^9}$ _____ 16. $\dfrac{11^5}{11^5}$ _____

17. $\dfrac{3^{16}}{3^8}$ _____ 18. $\dfrac{7}{7^{13}}$ _____ 19. $\dfrac{11^{15}}{11^{16}}$ _____ 20. $\dfrac{13^{10}}{13^{10}}$ _____

Tell whether each statement is *true* or *false*.

21. $\dfrac{7^4}{5^4} = 2^4$ _____ 22. $\dfrac{11^{10}}{11^2} = 11^8$ _____ 23. $\dfrac{17^4}{17^2} = 17^2$ _____

24. $\dfrac{3^{10}}{3^5} = 3^2$ _____ 25. $\dfrac{2^{10}}{2^{10}} = 2^1$ _____ 26. $\dfrac{5^{12}}{5} = 5^{12}$ _____

Making Sense of Numbers   Unit 2 Fractions **79**

Unit 3 Decimals

Chapter 8 Decimal Fundamentals
- **8-1** Understanding Decimals and Place Value 83
- **8-2** Locating Decimals on a Number Line 84
- **8-3** Rounding Decimals. 85
- **8-4** Comparing and Ordering Decimals 86
- **8-5** Writing a Terminating Decimal as a Fraction 87
- **8-6** Writing a Fraction as a Terminating Decimal 88
- **8-7** Writing a Fraction as a Repeating Decimal. 89
- **8-8** Reading a Metric Ruler 90

Chapter 9 Addition and Subtraction of Decimals
- **9-1** Adding Decimals 91
- **9-2** Estimating Decimal Sums. 92
- **9-3** Solving Problems Involving Decimal Addition 93
- **9-4** Adding Decimals and Fractions 94
- **9-5** Subtracting Decimals 95
- **9-6** Estimating Decimal Differences 96
- **9-7** Solving Problems Involving Decimal Subtraction 97
- **9-8** Subtracting Decimals and Fractions 98
- **9-9** Adding and Subtracting With Decimals 99
- **9-10** Solving Profit Problems 100

Chapter 10 Multiplication of Decimals
- **10-1** Multiplying a Decimal by a Power of 10 101
- **10-2** Multiplying Decimals. 102
- **10-3** Finding a Power of a Decimal. 103
- **10-4** Estimating Decimal Products 104
- **10-5** Solving Problems Involving Decimal Multiplication 105
- **10-6** Multiplying Decimals and Fractions. 106
- **10-7** Adding, Subtracting, and Multiplying With Decimals 107
- **10-8** Changing to a Smaller Unit of Metric Measure 108
- **10-9** Writing Numbers in Scientific Notation 109

Chapter 11 Division of Decimals
- **11-1** Dividing a Decimal by a Power of 10 110
- **11-2** Dividing Decimals 111
- **11-3** Decimals, Division, and Zeros 112
- **11-4** Estimating Decimal Quotients 113

Making Sense of Numbers

11-5	Solving Problems Involving Decimal Division	114
11-6	Interpreting the Quotient	115
11-7	Dividing Decimals and Fractions	116
11-8	Adding, Subtracting, Multiplying, and Dividing With Decimals	117
11-9	Changing to a Larger Unit of Metric Measure	118
11-10	Writing Numbers Between 0 and 1 in Scientific Notation	119

NAME _____ CLASS _____ DATE _____

Understanding Decimals and Place Value

OBJECTIVE: *Reading and writing decimals*

A *decimal* is a number with a decimal point. The decimal point separates the whole-number part of the decimal from that part of the number less than 1. Various decimal places to the left and to the right of the decimal point are named below.

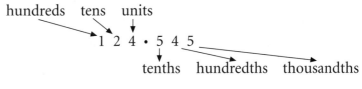

EXAMPLE 1 Give the value of the underlined digit in 347.6<u>5</u>3.

▶ **Solution**

The digit 5 is in the hundredths place. The value of 5 is 0.05.

You may need to write a decimal in words.

EXAMPLE 2 Write 54.33 in words.

▶ **Solution**

54 . 33

fifty-four and thirty-three hundredths

Give the value of the underlined digit in each decimal.

1. 3<u>4</u>5.67 _____
2. 12.00<u>5</u> _____
3. 13,444.<u>1</u>8 _____

4. <u>1</u>38.444 _____
5. 10.5<u>5</u>6 _____
6. 1200.4<u>9</u> _____

7. 15.335<u>6</u> _____
8. 1067.<u>2</u> _____
9. 554.99<u>4</u> _____

Write each decimal in words.

10. 12.95 _____

11. 236.66 _____

12. 33.645 _____

13. 78.992 _____

14. 63.405 _____

Making Sense of Numbers   Unit 3   Decimals   **83**

8-2 Locating Decimals on a Number Line

UNIT 3

OBJECTIVE: Graphing and reading decimals on a number line

You can locate a decimal on a number line by putting a dot at a tick mark on a ruler-like picture.

EXAMPLE 1 Graph 1.4 on a number line.

▶ **Solution**

Draw a line and divide the space between two consecutive whole numbers into ten equal segments. Locate 1.4 four ticks to the right of 1.

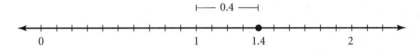

Given a number line and a point marked on it, you can use a decimal to represent the point.

EXAMPLE 2 Write a decimal to represent the point marked on this number line.

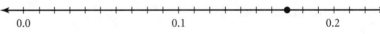

▶ **Solution**

The point is at the seventh tick to the right of 0.1.
The point represents 0.17.

Graph each decimal on the number line at right.

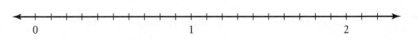

1. 0.1
2. 0.5
3. 1.8
4. 2.0

Graph each decimal on the number line at right.

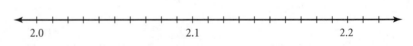

5. 2.02
6. 2.03
7. 2.07
8. 2.15

Write the decimal corresponding to each point on the number line.

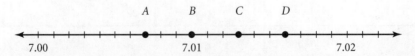

9. A _____
10. C _____
11. B _____
12. D _____

84 Unit 3 Decimals *Making Sense of Numbers*

NAME _____ CLASS _____ DATE _____

Rounding Decimals

OBJECTIVE: Rounding decimals

When you round a decimal, you replace the given decimal with a number that terminates at the specified decimal place.

EXAMPLE Round each decimal to the specified decimal place.
a. 24.567 to the nearest hundredth
b. 18.42 to the nearest tenth
c. 93.5 to the nearest whole number

▶ **Solution**

a. Identify the digit in the hundredths place. Look at the digit to its right.

                — This is the hundredths place.
    24.56⑦ ← Since the digit in the thousandths
                  place is more than 5, replace 6 with 7.

Thus, 24.567 rounded to the nearest hundredth is 24.57.

b. Identify the digit in the tenths place. Look at the digit to its right.

                — This is the tenths place.
    18.4② ← Since the digit in the hundredths
                  place is less than 5, leave 4 as 4.

Thus, 18.42 rounded to the nearest tenth is 18.4.

c. Identify the digit in the units place. Look at the digit to its right.

                — This is the units place.
    93.⑤ ← Since the digit in the tenths
                place is 5, replace 3 with 4.

Thus, 93.5 rounded to the nearest whole number is 94.

Round each decimal to the specified decimal place.

1. 123.451; nearest hundredth _____

2. 123.45; nearest tenth _____

3. 0.333; nearest tenth _____

4. 0.543; nearest hundredth _____

5. 19.95; nearest whole number _____

6. 8.09; nearest whole number _____

7. 3.141; nearest hundredth _____

8. 1.414; nearest tenth _____

9. 0.0045; nearest thousandth _____

10. 0.056; nearest tenth _____

11. 18.001; nearest whole number _____

12. 3.89; nearest whole number _____

Making Sense of Numbers

NAME _____ CLASS _____ DATE _____

8-4 Comparing and Ordering Decimals
UNIT 3

OBJECTIVE: Comparing two decimals and ordering a list of decimals

Two decimals are *equivalent* if they are equal. The decimals at right are equivalent.

36.75 and 36.750

If two decimals are not equal, then one of them is greater than the other and one of them is less than the other.

EXAMPLE 1

Compare. Replace each ___?___ with >, <, or =.

a. 23.5 ___?___ 22.78   b. 13.4 ___?___ 13.40

Solution

a. 2[3].5
   2[2].7 8
       → 3 > 2
Therefore, 23.5 > 22.78.

b. 1 3 . 4 [0]
   1 3 . 4 [0]   *invisible 0*
Therefore, 13.4 = 13.40.

You order a list of decimals when you write them in order from least to greatest or greatest to least.

EXAMPLE 2

Write 3.07, 3.70, and 0.37 in order from least to greatest.

Solution

3.[0]7   *This is the second smallest number.*
3.[7]0   *This is the largest number.*
[0].37   *This is the smallest number.*

From least to greatest: 0.37, 3.07, and 3.70.

Compare. Write >, <, or =.

1. 18.4 _____ 18.3   2. 18.06 _____ 18.6   3. 7.6 _____ 6.7

4. 99.95 _____ 100   5. 11.66 _____ 11.6   6. 0.566 _____ 1.5666

7. 7.98 _____ 8.00   8. 13.000 _____ 12.999   9. 19.040 _____ 19.0400

Write each list in order from least to greatest.

10. 11.1, 1.11, 111, and 111.1 _____

11. 2.3, 2.03, 44.1, 3.20, 4.5, and 32.00 _____

12. 0.3, 0.003, 0.004, 0.14, 1.1, 0.55, and 0.15 _____

86 Unit 3 Decimals   *Making Sense of Numbers*

NAME _____ CLASS _____ DATE _____

8-5 Writing a Terminating Decimal as a Fraction
UNIT 3

OBJECTIVE: Writing a terminating decimal as a fraction or a mixed number

A *terminating decimal* is a decimal that has a finite number of nonzero digits to the right of the decimal point. For example, 12.345 is a terminating decimal. Terminating decimals can be written as fractions.

EXAMPLE 1 Write each decimal as a fraction in lowest terms.
a. 0.7 b. 0.45

▶ **Solution**
a. $0.7 = \frac{7}{10}$ b. $0.45 = \frac{45}{100} = \frac{9}{20}$ *Divide numerator and denominator by 5.*

If a terminating decimal is greater than 1, then you can write the decimal as a mixed number.

EXAMPLE 2 Write each decimal as a mixed number with the fraction part in lowest terms.
a. 3.75 b. 7.125

▶ **Solution**
a. $3.75 = 3\frac{75}{100} = 3\frac{3}{4}$ *Divide numerator and denominator by 25.*

b. $7.125 = 7\frac{125}{1000} = 7\frac{1}{8}$ *Divide numerator and denominator by 125.*

Write each decimal as a fraction in lowest terms or as a mixed number with the fraction part in lowest terms.

1. 0.1 _____   2. 0.6 _____   3. 0.90 _____   4. 0.4 _____

5. 0.04 _____ 6. 0.25 _____ 7. 0.33 _____ 8. 0.78 _____

9. 0.002 _____ 10. 0.100 _____ 11. 0.125 _____ 12. 0.375 _____

13. 1.5 _____ 14. 1.7 _____ 15. 10.4 _____ 16. 99.9 _____

17. 13.65 _____ 18. 10.250 _____ 19. 11.01 _____ 20. 35.76 _____

21. 1.007 _____ 22. 4.555 _____ 23. 8.750 _____ 24. 6.222 _____

Making Sense of Numbers

NAME _____ CLASS _____ DATE _____

Writing a Fraction as a Terminating Decimal

OBJECTIVE: Writing a fraction or a mixed number as a terminating decimal

When you divide the numerator of a fraction by its denominator, you will get a decimal. A *terminating decimal* has a finite number of nonzero digits to the right of the decimal point.

EXAMPLE 1 Write each fraction as a decimal.

a. $\dfrac{11}{8}$ b. $\dfrac{9}{12}$

Solution

a.
```
    1.375
 8)11.000
    8
    ─
    30
    24
    ──
    60
    56
    ──
    40
    40
    ──
     0
```

b. $\dfrac{9}{12} = \dfrac{3}{4}$

Divide 3 by 4.

```
   0.75
 4)3.00
   2 8
   ───
    20
    20
   ───
     0
```

EXAMPLE 2 Write $2\dfrac{1}{4}$ as a decimal.

Solution

Divide 1 by 4. The division is shown at right.
Notice that the division terminates at the hundredths place.

Then add 2 to 0.25. Thus, $2\dfrac{1}{4} = 2.25$.

```
   0.25
 4)1.00
   8
   ──
   20
   20
   ──
    0
```

Write each fraction or mixed number as a decimal.

1. $\dfrac{1}{5}$ _____ 2. $\dfrac{18}{24}$ _____ 3. $\dfrac{8}{10}$ _____ 4. $\dfrac{12}{20}$ _____

5. $\dfrac{3}{8}$ _____ 6. $\dfrac{12}{16}$ _____ 7. $\dfrac{7}{25}$ _____ 8. $\dfrac{24}{25}$ _____

9. $7\dfrac{3}{4}$ _____ 10. $18\dfrac{7}{10}$ _____ 11. $5\dfrac{4}{5}$ _____ 12. $4\dfrac{5}{8}$ _____

13. $4\dfrac{17}{20}$ _____ 14. $7\dfrac{3}{40}$ _____ 15. $100\dfrac{9}{80}$ _____ 16. $18\dfrac{17}{32}$ _____

NAME _____ CLASS _____ DATE _____

8-7 Writing a Fraction as a Repeating Decimal
UNIT 3

OBJECTIVE: Writing a fraction as a repeating decimal

When you divide the numerator of a fraction by its denominator, you will get a decimal. That decimal will be a terminating decimal or a repeating decimal.

A *terminating decimal* has a finite number of nonzero digits to the right of the decimal point. A *repeating decimal* is one in which one or more digits form a repeating pattern.

The decimal $3.\overline{45}$ is a repeating decimal. The bar over the digits 4 and 5 indicates that these digits repeat indefinitely in a pattern.

EXAMPLE Write $\frac{7}{12}$ as a decimal.

▶ **Solution**

Divide 7 by 12. Notice in the division at right that the division continues in a patterned way. The digit 3 will occur over and over again.

Thus, $\frac{7}{12} = 0.583\ldots = 0.58\overline{3}$

```
       0.583...
    12)7.000
       6 0
       ─────
       1 00
         96
       ─────
         40  ◀─┐
         36    │ Repeating
       ─────   │ begins
         40  ◀─┘
         36
       ─────
         ...
```

Write each fraction or mixed number as a repeating decimal.

1. $\frac{1}{3}$ _____
2. $\frac{2}{3}$ _____
3. $\frac{1}{6}$ _____
4. $\frac{5}{6}$ _____

5. $\frac{1}{9}$ _____
6. $\frac{5}{9}$ _____
7. $\frac{1}{11}$ _____
8. $\frac{3}{11}$ _____

9. $\frac{2}{7}$ _____
10. $\frac{6}{7}$ _____
11. $\frac{4}{15}$ _____
12. $\frac{3}{7}$ _____

13. $\frac{1}{12}$ _____
14. $\frac{11}{12}$ _____
15. $\frac{1}{15}$ _____
16. $\frac{1}{18}$ _____

17. $4\frac{1}{3}$ _____
18. $5\frac{4}{9}$ _____
19. $1\frac{7}{11}$ _____
20. $7\frac{2}{3}$ _____

21. $9\frac{1}{6}$ _____
22. $3\frac{6}{7}$ _____
23. $11\frac{1}{6}$ _____
24. $10\frac{9}{11}$ _____

25. $9\frac{1}{11}$ _____
26. $11\frac{3}{7}$ _____
27. $10\frac{1}{18}$ _____
28. $6\frac{5}{12}$ _____

Making Sense of Numbers

8-8 Reading a Metric Ruler

UNIT 3

OBJECTIVE: Reading a distance on a metric ruler

Shown below is a *metric ruler* marked in *centimeters* and in *millimeters*. The distance between two consecutive long ticks is 1 centimeter. The distance between two short ticks is 1 millimeter.

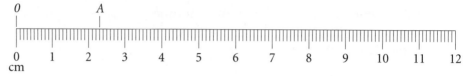

In the metric system, 1 centimeter is 10 millimeters and 1 millimeter is 0.1 centimeter.

EXAMPLE Find the distance between points O and A, OA, on the ruler above:

a. in centimeters (cm)   b. in millimeters (mm)

▶ **Solution**

Point A is at the third short tick to the right of the long tick indicating 2 centimeters.

a. The distance OA is 2.3 centimeters, abbreviated 2.3 cm.
b. The distance OA is 23 millimeters, abbreviated 23 mm.

Refer to the ruler below. Find the distance in centimeters and in millimeters between O and the point indicated by each letter.

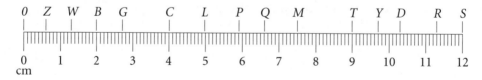

1. B _____   2. D _____

3. L _____   4. M _____

5. Y _____   6. Z _____

7. C _____   8. G _____

9. P _____   10. Q _____

11. S _____   12. R _____

13. W _____   14. T _____

90 Unit 3 Decimals   *Making Sense of Numbers*

NAME _____ CLASS _____ DATE _____

9-1 Adding Decimals
UNIT 3

OBJECTIVE: Adding decimals

You add decimals by using what you know about decimals together with what you know about adding whole numbers.

Recall that all whole numbers are decimals with an invisible decimal point.
$$23 = 23.0$$

Recall that you can place 0's at the far right of a decimal and get an equivalent decimal.
$$15.7 = 15.70 \qquad 15.7 = 15.700$$

Adding Decimals

1. Arrange the decimals so that decimal points align. Add zeros as needed to make equivalent decimals. Then place the decimal point in the sum.
2. Add as with whole numbers.

EXAMPLE   Add: $23 + 15.75 + 14.6$

▶ **Solution**

1. Arrange the decimals.

```
  23. 00    Add two zeros.
  15. 75
+ 14. 60    Add one zero.
 ─────
    .       Place the decimal
            point in the sum.
```

2. Add as with whole numbers.

```
  ¹2¹3. 00
   15. 75
 + 14. 60
 ────────
   53. 35
```

Therefore, $23 + 15.75 + 14.6 = 53.35$.

Add.

1. $11.4 + 20.3$ _____

2. $7.5 + 8.5$ _____

3. $21.6 + 21.8$ _____

4. $11 + 54.8$ _____

5. $19.5 + 24.84$ _____

6. $9.3 + 12.78$ _____

7. $42 + 34.95 + 18.5$ _____

8. $18.1 + 13.2 + 19.65$ _____

9. $13.4 + 28 + 19.5$ _____

10. $94.95 + 89.9 + 17.49$ _____

11. $7.8 + 17 + 11.98 + 27.79$ _____

12. $28.19 + 12 + 45.15 + 17.40$ _____

13. $10 + 18 + 37.3 + 43.1$ _____

14. $100.45 + 32 + 18.9 + 18.3$ _____

Making Sense of Numbers

NAME _____ CLASS _____ DATE _____

9-2 Estimating Decimal Sums
UNIT 3

OBJECTIVE: Using whole numbers to estimate sums of decimals

To estimate the sum of two decimals, you can find the sum of whole numbers that are close to the given decimals.

EXAMPLE 1 Use rounding to estimate the total cost of items costing $0.89, $6.19, and $11.95.

▶ **Solution**

1. Round each separate cost to the nearest whole number.
   0.89 → 1   6.19 → 6   11.95 → 12
2. Add the whole-number estimates.   1 + 6 + 12 = 19
   The total purchase is about $19.

In some problems, you may need to use an *overestimate*. An overestimate of a decimal is the next whole number greater than the given decimal.

EXAMPLE 2 Is $20 enough to purchase the items from Example 1?

▶ **Solution**

1. Estimate each decimal using an overestimate.
   0.89 → 1   6.19 → 7   11.95 → 12
2. Add the overestimates.   1 + 7 + 12 = 20
   Since the sum of the overestimates is 20, you can buy the items with $20.

Use rounding to the nearest whole number to estimate each sum.

1. 12.05 + 112.45 _____   2. 19.59 + 16.3 _____   3. 91.01 + 9.02 _____

4. 23.6 + 19.8 _____   5. 0.09 + 18.98 _____   6. 1.09 + 1.01 _____

7. 1.6 + 11.98 + 75.5 + 18.8 _____   8. 7.4 + 10.08 + 15.5 + 15.5 _____

Find an overestimate for the total purchase. Is $50 enough for each total purchase?

9. $19.95, $5.19, $4.98, and $11.05 _____

10. $5.90, $9.98, $11.42, $0.89, $2.18, and $9.98 _____

11. $15.10, $9.95, $12.25, $1.89, $5.18, and $0.98 _____

92 Unit 3 Decimals   *Making Sense of Numbers*

9-3 Solving Problems Involving Decimal Addition

OBJECTIVE: Using addition of decimals to solve real-world problems

EXAMPLE 1 Find the total distance that a bicyclist travels given these individual distances in miles.

Mon.	Tues.	Wed.	Thurs.	Fri.
24	25.6	27.2	28	30.5

▶ **Solution**

Since you are looking for the total distance, add decimals.
$$24 + 25.6 + 27.2 + 28 + 30.5 = 135.3$$
In all, the bicyclist travels 135.3 miles.

EXAMPLE 2 Four pipes are used to fill a tank. The table at right shows the number of gallons pumped into the tank by each pipe. How many gallons will the tank have?

A	B	C	D
1055.42	1266.45	1355.66	1425.00

▶ **Solution**

Find the total of all gallons supplied.
$$1055.42 + 1266.45 + 1355.66 + 1425.00 = 5102.53$$
5102.53 gallons are pumped into the tank.

Solve each problem.

1. A depositor made deposits of $43.50, $114.50, $650.33, and $1560.68 into a bank account. How much was the total deposit?

2. A depositor made withdrawals of $47.20, $44.60, $850.55, and $1350.20 from a bank account. How much was the total withdrawal?

3. An excavator removed 210.5 cubic yards, 212.6 cubic yards, and 218.25 cubic yards of dirt. How much was removed altogether?

4. Four students raised $250.25, $180.75, $190.00, and $540 for a school fund raising event. How much did they raise altogether?

5. A recycler collected 10.2 tons, 11.5 tons, 14.65 tons, and 13.8 tons of old newspapers. How many tons of paper were collected altogether?

Making Sense of Numbers

NAME _____ CLASS _____ DATE _____

9-4 Adding Decimals and Fractions
UNIT 3

OBJECTIVE: *Finding a sum involving both decimals and fractions*

To add a decimal and a fraction, write both numbers as decimals or both numbers as fractions.

EXAMPLE 1 Add: $3.6 + \frac{4}{5} + 4.85$

Solution

Since two of the numbers in the sum are decimals and one of the numbers is a fraction, change the fraction to a decimal, and then add.

$\frac{4}{5} = 0.8$

$$3.6 + \frac{4}{5} + 4.85 = 3.6 + 0.8 + 4.85 = 9.25$$

Therefore, $3.6 + \frac{4}{5} + 4.85 = 9.25$.

EXAMPLE 2 Add: $10.3 + 4\frac{2}{3}$

Solution

Since $\frac{2}{3}$ is represented by a repeating decimal, change 10.3 to a mixed number, and then add.

$10.3 = 10\frac{3}{10}$

$$10.3 + 4\frac{2}{3} = 10\frac{3}{10} + 4\frac{2}{3} = 14\frac{29}{30}$$

Therefore, $10.3 + 4\frac{2}{3} = 14\frac{29}{30}$.

Add.

1. $3 + 1\frac{1}{2}$ _____
2. $5.5 + 3\frac{1}{2}$ _____
3. $5.4 + 4\frac{3}{5}$ _____

4. $10.7 + 8\frac{1}{5}$ _____
5. $10\frac{3}{4} + 20.86$ _____
6. $7\frac{1}{4} + 17.04$ _____

7. $4.5 + 3\frac{1}{3}$ _____
8. $1\frac{2}{3} + 9.1$ _____
9. $4\frac{2}{7} + 0.5$ _____

10. $10.8 + 3\frac{3}{4} + 8.34$ _____
11. $3\frac{2}{5} + 8.14 + 7.33$ _____

12. $1.111 + 4\frac{1}{8} + 0.6$ _____
13. $1.5 + 3.5 + 5\frac{1}{3}$ _____

14. $7.1 + 0.9 + 1\frac{2}{3}$ _____
15. $\frac{1}{2} + 1\frac{1}{2} + 3\frac{2}{3}$ _____

94 Unit 3 Decimals *Making Sense of Numbers*

NAME _____ CLASS _____ DATE _____

9-5 Subtracting Decimals
UNIT 3

OBJECTIVE: *Finding the difference when one decimal is subtracted from another*

You subtract one decimal from another by using what you know about decimals together with what you know about subtracting whole numbers.

> **Subtracting Decimals**
>
> 1. Arrange the decimals so that decimal points align. Then place the decimal point in the difference. Add zeros as needed to make equivalent decimals.
> 2. Subtract as with whole numbers.

EXAMPLE 1 Subtract: $10 - 4.04$

▶ **Solution**

Align decimal points.

```
  10. 00     Add two zeros.
-  4. 04
  _____     Place the decimal
       .     point in the difference.
```

Subtract as with whole numbers.

```
  10. 00
-  4. 04
  _____
   5. 96
```

Therefore, $10 - 4.04 = 5.96$.

EXAMPLE 2 Subtract: $98.24 - 74.39$

▶ **Solution**

Align decimal points.

```
  98. 24
- 74. 39
  _____     Place the decimal
       .     point in the difference.
```

Subtract as with whole numbers.

```
  9 8. 2 4
- 7 4. 3 9
  _____
  2 3. 8 5
```

Therefore, $98.24 - 74.39 = 23.85$.

Subtract.

1. $12 - 8.7$ _____

2. $20 - 19.9$ _____

3. $100 - 99.95$ _____

4. $18 - 0.1$ _____

5. $14.22 - 12.66$ _____

6. $8.38 - 4.3$ _____

7. $18.1 - 16.41$ _____

8. $13.88 - 12.5$ _____

9. $10.89 - 9.89$ _____

10. $11.3 - 11.28$ _____

11. $96.3 - 96.03$ _____

12. $16.7 - 12.6$ _____

Making Sense of Numbers

9-6 Estimating Decimal Differences

UNIT 3

OBJECTIVE: Using whole numbers or decimals rounded to a specified decimal place to estimate differences of decimals

By rounding decimals to whole numbers, you can find an estimate of a difference of decimals.

EXAMPLE 1 Estimate 15.2 − 7.8 by using whole numbers.

▶ **Solution**

1. Round each number in the difference to the nearest whole number.
   15.2 → 15   7.8 → 8
2. Subtract the whole-number estimates.   15 − 8 = 7
   The difference is about 7.

For larger numbers, you can make estimates by using decimals rounded to a certain decimal place.

EXAMPLE 2 Estimate 347.35 − 268.95 by using decimals rounded to the nearest ten.

▶ **Solution**

1. Estimate each decimal by rounding to the nearest ten.
   347.35 → 350   268.95 → 270
2. Subtract estimates found in Step **1**.   350 − 270 = 80
   The difference 347.35 − 268.95 is about 80.

Estimate each difference by using whole numbers.

1. 10.2 − 9.8 _____   2. 16.1 − 6.1 _____   3. 24.9 − 14.9 _____

4. 9.9 − 1.8 _____   5. 100 − 84.8 _____   6. 60 − 15.1 _____

7. 54.33 − 40.08 _____   8. 4.98 − 4.08 _____   9. 10 − 0.8 _____

10. 140 − 0.1 _____   11. 18.6 − 6.41 _____   12. 32 − 23.2 _____

Estimate each difference by rounding to the nearest ten.

13. 483 − 480 _____   14. 1256 − 984 _____   15. 655.3 − 567.8 _____

16. 163.98 − 23.7 _____   17. 2387 − 103.1 _____   18. 8653.2 − 8650 _____

19. 71.908 − 22.074 _____   20. 3457 − 114.3 _____   21. 7651.1 − 7440 _____

Solving Problems Involving Decimal Subtraction

OBJECTIVE: Using subtraction of decimals to solve real-world problems

Given two readings or displays, you can find the change from the smaller reading to the greater reading by using subtraction.

EXAMPLE 1 A motorist noted the odometer readings at right. How many miles was the motorist's trip?

Start	65622.8
End	65483.7

Solution

The difference calculated at right shows the length of the motorist's trip. In all, the motorist drove 139.1 miles.

```
  65,622.8
- 65,483.7
─────────
     139.1
```

Subtraction is also used to find how much of a quantity remains after a certain amount is removed.

EXAMPLE 2 How much flour remains after removing 24.5 pounds of flour from a storage container that originally contained 102.3 pounds?

Solution

Subtract the amount taken from the amount in the container. The amount remaining is 77.8 pounds of flour.

```
  102.3   original amount
-  24.5   amount removed
───────
   77.8   amount remaining
```

Solve each problem.

1. Given readings of 236.6 miles and 289.1 miles on a bicycle odometer, how many miles did the cyclist travel? _____

2. From a tank with 750 gallons of water, 620.5 gallons are removed. How many gallons remain in the tank? _____

3. On a cold morning, the temperature changed from 23.6°F to 18.5°F. By how many degrees did the temperature fall? _____

4. From an account having $12,347.83, a depositor withdrew $845.79. How much money remains in the account? _____

5. From a board 16.375 feet long, a carpenter cut a board 12.125 feet long. How much of the original board remains? _____

Making Sense of Numbers

NAME _____ CLASS _____ DATE _____

9-8 Subtracting Decimals and Fractions
UNIT 3

OBJECTIVE: *Finding a difference involving both decimals and fractions*

Given a difference involving a decimal and a fraction or mixed number, first write both numbers as decimals or as fractions.

EXAMPLE 1 Subtract: $17.54 - 11\frac{1}{5}$

▶ **Solution**

Write $\frac{1}{5}$ as a decimal. Then subtract decimals. $\frac{1}{5} = 0.2$

$$17.54 - 11\frac{1}{5} = 17.54 - 11.2 = 6.34$$

Therefore, $17.54 - 11\frac{1}{5} = 6.34$.

EXAMPLE 2 Subtract: $8.5 - 3\frac{2}{3}$

▶ **Solution**

Write 8.5 as a mixed number. Subtract mixed numbers. $0.5 = \frac{1}{2}$

$$8.5 - 3\frac{2}{3} = 8\frac{1}{2} - 3\frac{2}{3} = 8\frac{3}{6} - 3\frac{4}{6} = 4\frac{5}{6}$$

Therefore, $8.5 - 3\frac{2}{3} = 4\frac{5}{6}$.

Subtract.

1. $16.22 - 10\frac{1}{2}$ _____
2. $13.8 - 9\frac{3}{4}$ _____
3. $18.9 - 8\frac{3}{5}$ _____

4. $9\frac{1}{4} - 9.02$ _____
5. $99\frac{4}{5} - 98$ _____
6. $15\frac{1}{8} - 13$ _____

7. $10\frac{3}{8} - 8.333$ _____
8. $80\frac{4}{5} - 80.799$ _____
9. $17\frac{5}{8} - 16.625$ _____

10. $10.5 - 9\frac{1}{3}$ _____
11. $9.75 - 3\frac{1}{3}$ _____
12. $27.25 - 11\frac{2}{3}$ _____

13. $20.5 - 11\frac{3}{7}$ _____
14. $19.5 - 9\frac{1}{7}$ _____
15. $30.75 - 18\frac{2}{3}$ _____

16. $1.375 - \frac{3}{8}$ _____
17. $4.25 - 3\frac{5}{8}$ _____
18. $9.8 - 8\frac{4}{5}$ _____

19. $1.4 - \frac{1}{3}$ _____
20. $6.2 - 5\frac{2}{3}$ _____
21. $11.3 - 10\frac{1}{9}$ _____

NAME _____ CLASS _____ DATE _____

9-9 Adding and Subtracting with Decimals
UNIT 3

OBJECTIVE: Finding the value of an expression involving both addition and subtraction of decimals

To find the value of an expression involving both addition and subtraction, follow the order of operations.

EXAMPLE 1 Evaluate $43.24 + 18.11 - 50.89$.

Solution
$43.24 + 18.11 - 50.89 = 61.35 - 50.89$ Add 43.24 and 18.11.
$\qquad\qquad\qquad\qquad\quad = 10.46$ Subtract 50.89 from 61.35.
Thus, $43.24 + 18.11 - 50.89 = 10.46$.

EXAMPLE 2 Evaluate $132.5 - (45.98 + 23.76)$.

Solution
$132.5 - (45.98 + 23.76) = 132.5 - 69.74$ Add 45.98 and 23.76.
$\qquad\qquad\qquad\qquad\quad = 62.76$ Subtract 69.74 from 132.5.
Thus, $132.5 - (45.98 + 23.76) = 62.76$.

Evaluate each expression.

1. $16.2 + 18.1 - 7.1$ _____

2. $100 - (33.22 + 55.1)$ _____

3. $13.2 - (0.5 + 9.4)$ _____

4. $1200 - (1000 + 45.8)$ _____

5. $18.45 - 10.88 + 18$ _____

6. $127.41 - 100 + 17.99$ _____

7. $1.45 - 1.08 - 0.18$ _____

8. $0.45 - 0.11 - 0.18$ _____

9. $70.16 - (60.5 - 50.9)$ _____

10. $112 - (80.1 - 79.3)$ _____

11. $92.17 + 19 - (41.4 + 30.3)$ _____

12. $10 + 50.56 - (49 - 30.7)$ _____

13. $130 - 89 - (57.3 - 56)$ _____

14. $88.1 - 78.22 - (0.7 - 0.6)$ _____

15. $38.2 - (18.1 + 17.3 - 3.3)$ _____

16. $57.1 - (19.1 - 12.4 + 3.6)$ _____

17. $\$22.40 + \$18.44 + \$400.98 - (\$15.00 + \$25.88 + \$22.05 + \$55.69)$ _____

18. $\$34.66 + \$19.03 + \$510.89 - (\$25.00 + \$34.77 + \$52.06 + \$51.22)$ _____

Making Sense of Numbers

9-10 Solving Profit Problems

OBJECTIVE: Finding profit after calculating income and expenses

After income is earned and expenses are paid, a successful business will have a *profit*, the difference when expenses are subtracted from income.

EXAMPLE A small business has income and expenses as shown below. Find the profit of that business.

income	expenses
$200.68	$188.50
$869.90	$655.44
$65.22	$98.45

▶ **Solution**

Add income amounts.
  $200.68 + 869.90 + 65.22 = 1135.80$
Add expense amounts.
  $188.50 + 655.44 + 98.45 = 942.39$
Subtract expenses from income.
  $1135.80 - 942.39 = 193.41$
The profit for this business is $193.41.

Find the profit given income and expenses.

	income	expenses	
1.	$238.95, $297.55	$400.50, $37.88	
2.	$1366.75, $497.55	$473.60, $147.50	
3.	$77.33, $600.00	$510.40, $66.68	
4.	$1800.95, $777.95	$777.95, $1135.88	
5.	$1100.00, $195.11	$95.11, $1100.00	
6.	$538.15, $297.44	$538.15, $297.44	
7.	$22,333.95, $1600.55	$22,333.95, $1600.55	
8.	$87.39, $640.05, $222.49	$91.42, $538.05, $202.49	
9.	$920.39, $222.75, $322.18	$900.42, $133.65, $302.18	
10.	$888.19, $312.15, $600.48	$888.19, $312.15, $500.48	

10-1 Multiplying a Decimal by a Power of 10

UNIT 3

OBJECTIVE: Multiplying a decimal by a power of 10

A power of 10 is any product of 10 with itself a finite number of times. Each of the products below is a power of 10.

$$10 \cdot 10 = 10^2 \quad (10 \text{ squared})$$
$$10 \cdot 10 \cdot 10 = 10^3 \quad (10 \text{ cubed})$$

The exponent of 10 indicates the power of 10, or the number of times 10 is a factor in the product.

To multiply a decimal by a power of 10, move the decimal point to the right as many places as indicated by the number of zeros or the exponent in the power of 10.

EXAMPLE

Multiply: a. 624.345×100 b. 120.6×10^4

Solution

a. Locate the decimal point.

6 2 4 . 3 4 5
2 places right

So, $624.345 \times 100 = 62,434.5$.

b. Locate the decimal point. Add three zeros.

1 2 0 . 6 0 0 0
4 places right

So, $120.6 \times 10^4 = 1,206,000$.

Multiply.

1. 12.225×10^2 _____

2. 100.75×10^2 _____

3. 88.55×10^2 _____

4. 85.6×10^2 _____

5. 35.25×10^3 _____

6. 103.46×10^3 _____

7. 0.435×10^3 _____

8. 0.84×10^3 _____

9. 0.01×10^3 _____

10. 0.03×10^3 _____

11. 0.007×10^3 _____

12. 0.005×10^3 _____

13. 1.006×10^3 _____

14. 1.001×10^3 _____

15. 0.0001×10^3 _____

16. $12,338.4 \times 10^1$ _____

17. $17,229.05 \times 10^1$ _____

18. $88,888.25 \times 10^2$ _____

19. 7500.08×10^3 _____

Making Sense of Numbers

10-2 Multiplying Decimals

UNIT 3

OBJECTIVE: *Finding the product of two decimals*

Multiplying two decimals is similar to multiplying whole numbers. The following examples will show you where to place the decimal point in the product.

EXAMPLE 1 Multiply: 6.33 × 7

▶ **Solution**

```
  6.33     two decimal places
×    7
 44.31     two decimal places
```

Thus, 6.33 × 7 = 44.31.

If both decimals have digits to the right of the decimal point, the product will have as many decimal places as the sum of the numbers of places in the given decimals.

EXAMPLE 2 Multiply: 4.25 × 3.6

▶ **Solution**

```
  4.25    two decimal places
× 3.6     one decimal place
  255
 1275
15.300    three decimal places
```

Therefore, 4.25 × 3.6 = 15.300, or simply 15.3.

Multiply.

1. 12 × 8.5 _____

2. 6.3 × 9 _____

3. 12 × 3.6 _____

4. 125 × 4.8 _____

5. 124 × 3.1 _____

6. 256 × 8.4 _____

7. 1.5 × 2.5 _____

8. 3.5 × 3.5 _____

9. 4.4 × 3.2 _____

10. 7.2 × 0.6 _____

11. 0.3 × 11.6 _____

12. 0.7 × 0.8 _____

13. 17.2 × 3.65 _____

14. 1.72 × 9.7 _____

15. 8.68 × 1.7 _____

16. 0.24 × 0.48 _____

17. 0.65 × 0.65 _____

18. 12.35 × 5.34 _____

NAME _____ CLASS _____ DATE _____

10-3 Finding a Power of a Decimal
UNIT 3

OBJECTIVE: Finding a decimal product given as an exponential expression

Recall that multiplication of a number, x, by itself can be written as $x \cdot x$, or x^2. The expression x^2 is called an *exponential expression* with base x and exponent 2.

EXAMPLE 1 Find each product. a. 2.5^2 b. 0.4^2

▶ **Solution**

a. $2.5^2 = 2.5 \times 2.5 = 6.25$ b. $0.4^2 = 0.4 \times 0.4 = 0.16$

Recall also that multiplication of a number, x, by itself three times can be written as $x \cdot x \cdot x$, or x^3. The expression x^3 is called an exponential expression with base x and exponent 3.

EXAMPLE 2 Find each product. a. 3.2^3 b. 0.2^3

▶ **Solution**

a. $3.2^3 = 3.2 \times 3.2 \times 3.2$ *one decimal place each*
$= (3.2 \times 3.2) \times 3.2$
$= 10.24 \times 3.2$
$= 32.768$ *three decimal places*

b. $0.2^3 = 0.2 \times 0.2 \times 0.2$ *one decimal place each*
$= (0.2 \times 0.2) \times 0.2$
$= 0.04 \times 0.2$
$= 0.008$ *three decimal places*

Find each product.

1. 1.5^2 _____   2. 1.3^2 _____   3. 1.2^2 _____

4. 7.2^2 _____   5. 10.2^2 _____   6. 22.1^2 _____

7. 0.7^2 _____   8. 0.8^2 _____   9. 0.1^2 _____

10. 1.25^2 _____   11. 4.03^2 _____   12. 7.05^2 _____

13. 1.2^3 _____   14. 2.3^3 _____   15. 4.5^3 _____

16. 10.1^3 _____   17. 15.6^3 _____   18. 20.4^3 _____

19. 0.3^3 _____   20. 0.5^3 _____   21. 0.1^3 _____

Making Sense of Numbers

NAME _____ CLASS _____ DATE _____

10-4 Estimating Decimal Products
UNIT 3

OBJECTIVE: Using whole numbers to estimate products of decimals

To estimate the product of two decimals, you can find the product of whole numbers that are close to the given decimals.

EXAMPLE 1 Estimate the cost of 9 shirts if each shirt costs $18.95.

▶ **Solution**

The cost of each shirt is about $19. The product 9 × 19 is an estimate of the total cost.

$$9 \times 19 = 171$$

An estimate of the cost is $171.00.

EXAMPLE 2 Use whole numbers to estimate 15.2 × 9.8.

▶ **Solution**

1. Estimate each decimal using a whole number.
   15.2 is about 15   9.8 is about 10
2. Multiply whole numbers.
   15 × 10 = 150
   An estimate of 15.2 × 9.8 is 150.

If a product involves a decimal between 0 and 1, an estimate of the decimal might be 0 or 1.

0.02 × 65 → 0 × 65 → 0   0.98 × 65 → 1 × 65 → 65

Use whole numbers to estimate each cost.

1. four tires each costing $69.89 _____

2. seven school books each costing $35.25 _____

3. seventy-five tickets each costing $6.75 _____

Use whole numbers to estimate each product.

4. 17.6 × 3.2 _____   5. 25.1 × 4.8 _____   6. 98.3 × 9.8 _____

7. 77.9 × 4.5 _____   8. 107.5 × 4.5 _____   9. 249.95 × 1.2 _____

10. 999.9 × 1.9 _____   11. 1200.3 × 5.4 _____ 12. 26.3 × 0.8 _____

13. 77.85 × 0.6 _____   14. 5.8 × 0.01 _____   15. 23.3 × 0.025 _____

NAME _____ CLASS _____ DATE _____

Solving Problems Involving Decimal Multiplication

OBJECTIVE: Using decimal multiplication to solve real-world problems

Recall that the area of a rectangle is found by multiplying length and width. Recall also that the area of a square is found by multiplying the length of one side by itself.

EXAMPLE 1 Find each area.
a. rectangle with length 20.4 feet and width 18.5 feet
b. square whose sides are all 15.6 meters long

▶ Solution
a. Multiply: 20.4 × 18.5   20.4 × 18.5 = 377.4
   The area of the rectangle is 377.4 square feet.
b. Multiply: 15.6 × 15.6   15.6 × 15.6 = 243.36
   The area of the square is 243.36 square meters.

A worker who earns a fixed amount of money per hour of work earns a *wage*.

EXAMPLE 2 If Sharon works 36 hours in a certain week and earns $10.45 per hour, what are her total wages for that week?

▶ Solution
Multiply: 36 × 10.45   36 × 10.45 = 376.2
Sharon's total wages are $376.20 for that week.

Find each area.

1. rectangle: length 25.2 meters and width 30.5 meters _____

2. rectangle: length 30.6 feet and width 60.4 feet _____

3. square: length 18.6 meters and width 18.6 meters _____

Find total wages.

4. 25.5 hours at $18.25 per hour _____   5. 40 hours at $14.60 per hour _____

6. 30 hours at $11.80 per hour _____   7. 38.6 hours at $8.75 per hour _____

8. 40 hours at $54.50 per hour _____   9. 38 hours at $28.80 per hour _____

Making Sense of Numbers   Unit 3 Decimals **105**

10-6 Multiplying Decimals and Fractions

UNIT 3

OBJECTIVE: *Finding the product of a decimal and a fraction or mixed number*

Multiplication of a decimal and a mixed number or fraction often occurs when making a purchase.

EXAMPLE 1 Find the cost of $1\frac{1}{2}$ pounds of catfish costing $5.80 per pound.

Solution

Method 1: Write the mixed number as a fraction. Then multiply.

$$1\frac{1}{2} \times 5.8 = \frac{3}{2} \times 5.8 = 3 \times 2.9 = 8.7$$

Method 2: Write the mixed number as a decimal. Then multiply.

$$1\frac{1}{2} \times 5.8 = 1.5 \times 5.8 = 8.7$$

By either method, the cost is $8.70.

Sometimes it may be more convenient to change a decimal to a fraction or mixed number before multiplying.

EXAMPLE 2 Multiply: $2\frac{2}{3} \times 6.75$

Solution

Since $\frac{2}{3}$ is represented by the repeating decimal $0.\overline{6}$, change 6.75 to a mixed number. Then multiply.

$$2\frac{2}{3} \times 6.75 = 2\frac{2}{3} \times 6\frac{3}{4}$$
$$= \frac{8}{3} \times \frac{27}{4}$$
$$= 18$$

Therefore, $2\frac{2}{3} \times 6.75 = 18$.

Solve by multiplying.

1. Find the cost of $2\frac{1}{2}$ pounds of coffee costing $7.99 per pound. _____

2. Find the cost of $14\frac{3}{4}$ gallons of gasoline costing $1.55 per gallon. _____

Multiply.

3. $3\frac{1}{3} \times 3.5$ _____ 4. $7\frac{1}{3} \times 3.25$ _____ 5. $7\frac{2}{3} \times 1.75$ _____

6. $6\frac{2}{7} \times 8.4$ _____ 7. $1\frac{4}{7} \times 10.6$ _____ 8. $1\frac{5}{11} \times 2.75$ _____

9. $3\frac{4}{7} \times 9.6$ _____ 10. $5\frac{5}{6} \times 8.5$ _____ 11. $4\frac{1}{6} \times 4.75$ _____

NAME _____ CLASS _____ DATE _____

10-7
UNIT 3

Adding, Subtracting, and Multiplying with Decimals

OBJECTIVE: *Finding the value of an expression involving addition, subtraction, and multiplication with decimals*

To evaluate an expression involving multiple operations, follow the order of operations.

EXAMPLE 1 Evaluate $2.5(1.3 + 6.4) - 10.65$.

▶ **Solution**

$2.5(1.3 + 6.4) - 10.65 = 2.5(7.7) - 10.65$ *Work inside parentheses.*
$ = 19.25 - 10.65$ *Multiply.*
$ = 8.6$ *Subtract.*

Therefore, $2.5(1.3 + 6.4) - 10.65 = 8.6$.

EXAMPLE 2 Evaluate $5.5(3.3 + 3.6) - 1.6(7.5 - 6.8)^2$.

▶ **Solution**

$5.5(3.3 + 3.6) - 1.6(7.5 - 6.8)^2 = 5.5(6.9) - 1.6(0.7)^2$
$ = 37.95 - 1.6(0.49)$
$ = 37.166$

Therefore, $5.5(3.3 + 3.6) - 1.6(7.5 - 6.8)^2 = 37.166$.

Evaluate.

1. $3(2.5) + 4(6.2)$ _____

2. $3.5(4) - 3.4(2)$ _____

3. $4(5.6) + 5(6 - 3.5)$ _____

4. $4.2(10 - 6.5) + 18(4.2)$ _____

5. $5.2(4.5) + 3.5^2 - 2.2^2$ _____

6. $3.5^2 - 2.2^2 + 0.5^2 - 0.2^2$ _____

7. $1.5(5.3 - 2.3)^2$ _____

8. $3.6(12.7 - 7.7)^2$ _____

9. $0.5(7.4 - 3.4)^2 + 10(4.1)$ _____

10. $0.6(5.4 + 1.6)^2 - 10(1.2)$ _____

11. $10(7.6 - 1.7) + 100(7.1 - 0.1)$ _____

12. $100(0.5 - 0.3) + 10(9.2 + 0.8)$ _____

13. $(4.4 - 3.3)^2 + (2.5 + 2.5)^2 + (2.4 - 1.8)^2 + (1.7 + 3.3)^2$ _____

14. $2(4.5 - 3.3)^2 + 3(2.8 - 2.8)^2 + (2.1 - 1.8)^2 + 4.1(3.7 - 2.7)^2$ _____

Making Sense of Numbers   Unit 3 Decimals **107**

10-8 Changing to a Smaller Unit of Metric Measure

OBJECTIVE: Writing a measure given in one metric unit of measure as the same measure in a smaller metric unit

In the metric system, length and distance are measured in kilometers, meters, centimeters, and millimeters.

1 kilometer	= 1000 meters
1 meter	= 100 centimeters
1 centimeter	= 10 millimeters

In the metric system, capacity is measured in liters and milliliters.

1 liter = 1000 milliliters

In the metric system, mass is measured in kilograms and grams.

1 kilogram = 1000 grams

To change a measure in a larger unit to the same measure in a smaller unit, multiply by the appropriate power of 10. The three tables above list the powers of 10 that you will use.

EXAMPLE

Write each measure in the specified unit.
a. 2.5 meters = __?__ centimeters
b. 7.34 liters = __?__ milliliters
c. 14.26 kilograms = __?__ grams

Solution

a. 2.5 × 100 = 250   2.5 meters = 250 centimeters
b. 7.34 × 1000 = 7340   7.34 liters = 7340 milliliters
c. 14.26 × 1000 = 14,260   14.26 kilograms = 14,260 grams

Write each measure in the specified unit.

1. 3.7 meters = _____ centimeters
2. 2.5 centimeters = _____ millimeters
3. 14.1 liters = _____ milliliters
4. 4.11 kilograms = _____ grams
5. 1.27 kilometers = _____ meters
6. 24.2 meters = _____ centimeters
7. 1.106 liters = _____ milliliters
8. 2.125 liters = _____ milliliters
9. 0.3 kilograms = _____ grams
10. 0.34 kilometers = _____ meters
11. 0.625 liters = _____ milliliters
12. 0.884 kilometers = _____ meters
13. 0.4 kilometers = _____ centimeters
14. 0.25 kilometers = _____ centimeters

NAME _____ CLASS _____ DATE _____

10-9 Writing Numbers in Scientific Notation
UNIT 3

OBJECTIVE: Writing a number in scientific notation and writing a number given in scientific notation in standard form

The display below shows the same number in two forms, standard form and scientific notation.

$$\begin{array}{cc} \text{standard form} & \text{scientific notation} \\ 4320 & = \quad 4.32 \times 10^3 \end{array}$$

A number is written in **scientific notation** when it is written as a number between 1 and 10, excluding 10, multiplied by an integer power of 10. If the given number is greater than 10, such as 4320, the power of 10 is a counting number.

EXAMPLE 1 Write 12,560 in scientific notation.

Solution

Move the decimal point 4 places to the left so that there is just one digit to the left of the new location of the decimal point.
Use 4 as the needed power of 10.
In scientific notation, $12,560 = 1.256 \times 10^4$.   *4 places left*

EXAMPLE 2 Write 1.31×10^5 in standard form.

Solution

Move the decimal point 5 places to the right.
Add zeros as needed.
In standard form, $1.31 \times 10^5 = 131,000$.   *5 places right*

Write each number in scientific notation.

1. 20.2 _____
2. 312 _____
3. 1200 _____

4. 1345 _____
5. 12.68 _____
6. 182.4 _____

7. 100.4 _____
8. 12,500 _____
9. 120,500 _____

Write each number in standard form.

10. 1.24×10^2 _____
11. 7.42×10^1 _____
12. 9.5×10^4 _____

13. 7.05×10^3 _____
14. 1.08×10^4 _____
15. 2.2×10^5 _____

16. 7.25×10^3 _____
17. 5.56×10^4 _____
18. 9.84×10^1 _____

Making Sense of Numbers   Unit 3 Decimals

NAME _____ CLASS _____ DATE _____

11-1 Dividing a Decimal by a Power of 10
UNIT 3

OBJECTIVE: *Finding the quotient when a decimal is divided by a power of 10*

To divide a decimal by a power of 10, move the decimal point in the given decimal to the left as many places as there are zeros in the power of 10.

EXAMPLE 1 **Divide:** $34.5 \div 1000$

▶ **Solution**

There are three zeros in 1000. Locate the decimal point in 34.5, and then move the decimal point to the left three places. Add one 0.

Therefore, $34.5 \div 1000 = 0.0345$.

Add one 0.
↓
0 3 4.5
↶
3 places left

To divide a decimal by a power of 10, move the decimal point in the given decimal to the left as many places as indicated by the exponent in the power of 10.

EXAMPLE 2 **Divide:** $367.82 \div 10^2$

▶ **Solution**

The exponent in 10^2 is 2. Locate the decimal point in 367.82, and then move the decimal point to the left two places.

Therefore, $367.82 \div 10^2 = 3.6782$.

3 6 7.82
↶
2 places left

Divide.

1. $3234 \div 1000$ _____

2. $1854 \div 100$ _____

3. $2245 \div 100$ _____

4. $783.1 \div 100$ _____

5. $100.7 \div 1000$ _____

6. $3200.5 \div 10$ _____

7. $3.4 \div 1000$ _____

8. $7.5 \div 100$ _____

9. $888.8 \div 1000$ _____

10. $7.82 \div 100$ _____

11. $0.45 \div 10$ _____

12. $0.4 \div 1000$ _____

13. $567.1 \div 10^2$ _____

14. $3671.4 \div 10^3$ _____

15. $3000.1 \div 10^1$ _____

16. $125.18 \div 10^1$ _____

17. $450.4 \div 10^2$ _____

18. $1200.1 \div 10^3$ _____

19. $334.12 \div 10^1$ _____

20. $0.34 \div 10^1$ _____

21. $0.53 \div 10^2$ _____

22. $0.1 \div 10^3$ _____

23. $0.65 \div 10^1$ _____

24. $0.8 \div 10^2$ _____

NAME _____ CLASS _____ DATE _____

11-2 Dividing Decimals
UNIT 3

OBJECTIVE: *Dividing a decimal by another decimal*

To divide with decimals, transform the decimal division into a whole-number division.

When dividing by a whole number, place the decimal point in the quotient directly above the decimal point in the dividend.

When dividing by a decimal, move the decimal point in the divisor and the dividend enough places to make the divisor a whole number. Then divide as with a whole-number divisor.

EXAMPLE Divide.   a. 84.7 ÷ 7   b. 11.96 ÷ 2.3

Solution

a.
```
      12.1
   7)84.7
     7
     ―
     14
     14
     ――
      7
      7
      ―
      0
```

b. 2.3)11.96 →
```
       5.2
   23)119.6
      115
      ―――
       46
       46
       ――
        0
```

So, 84.7 ÷ 7 = 12.1.   So, 11.96 ÷ 2.3 = 5.2.

Divide.

1. 42.5 ÷ 5 _____

2. 72.18 ÷ 6 _____

3. 213.3 ÷ 9 _____

4. 530.4 ÷ 8 _____

5. 1266.9 ÷ 3 _____

6. 1863.5 ÷ 5 _____

7. 85.2 ÷ 12 _____

8. 55.5 ÷ 15 _____

9. 223.2 ÷ 18 _____

10. 124.8 ÷ 12 _____

11. 235.3 ÷ 13 _____

12. 355.3 ÷ 17 _____

13. 2.55 ÷ 1.5 _____

14. 32.66 ÷ 2.3 _____

15. 33.92 ÷ 6.4 _____

16. 35.88 ÷ 2.6 _____

17. 91.98 ÷ 7.3 _____

18. 129.05 ÷ 8.9 _____

19. 121.33 ÷ 1.1 _____

20. 204.96 ÷ 6.1 _____

21. 509.74 ÷ 7.7 _____

22. 240.45 ÷ 10.5 _____

23. 452.6 ÷ 12.4 _____

24. 1024.88 ÷ 18.4 _____

Making Sense of Numbers

NAME _____ CLASS _____ DATE _____

11-3 Decimals, Division, and Zeros
UNIT 3

OBJECTIVE: Dividing a decimal by another decimal when zero must be inserted in the quotient or dividend

Sometimes you must insert one or more zeros in the quotient when you divide with decimals.

EXAMPLE 1 Divide: 14.35 ÷ 7

Solution

3 is not divisible by 7. Insert 0.

$$7\overline{)14.35} \rightarrow \begin{array}{r}2.0\\7\overline{)14.35}\\\underline{14}\\3\end{array} \rightarrow \begin{array}{r}2.05\\7\overline{)14.35}\\\underline{14}\\35\\\underline{35}\\0\end{array}$$ So, 14.35 ÷ 7 = 2.05.

Sometimes you need to add one or more zeros to the dividend in order to continue and complete a division.

EXAMPLE 2 Divide: 2.5 ÷ 4

Solution

$$4\overline{)2.5} \rightarrow \begin{array}{r}.6\\4\overline{)2.5}\\\underline{24}\\1\end{array} \rightarrow \begin{array}{r}.62\\4\overline{)2.50}\\\underline{24}\\10\\\underline{8}\\2\end{array} \rightarrow \begin{array}{r}.625\\4\overline{)2.500}\\\underline{24}\\10\\\underline{8}\\20\\\underline{20}\\0\end{array}$$ So, 2.5 ÷ 4 = 0.625.

(Add 0. Add another 0.)

Divide.

1. 12.24 ÷ 4 _____
2. 30.54 ÷ 6 _____
3. 77.88 ÷ 11 _____

4. 66.18 ÷ 6 _____
5. 98.035 ÷ 7 _____
6. 66.012 ÷ 3 _____

7. 3.6 ÷ 8 _____
8. 48.2 ÷ 8 _____
9. 77.4 ÷ 12 _____

10. 57.6 ÷ 18 _____
11. 43.332 ÷ 2.4 _____
12. 12.334 ÷ 3.5 _____

13. 130 ÷ 24 _____
14. 607 ÷ 12 _____
15. 136 ÷ 11 _____

11-4 Estimating Decimal Quotients

UNIT 3

OBJECTIVE: Using whole numbers to estimate quotients of decimals

To estimate the quotient of two decimals, you can use numbers that are called *compatible*.
For example, you can estimate $13 \div 4$ as shown at right.

12 and 4 are compatible because $12 \div 4$ is a whole number.

$13 \div 4 \rightarrow 12 \div 4 \rightarrow 3$

EXAMPLE 1 Estimate $356.85 \div 16.85$ by using compatible numbers.

▸ **Solution**

If you round 356.85 to 360 and round 16.85 to 18, you get a pair of compatible numbers.
$$360 \div 18 = \frac{360}{18} = 20$$
An estimate of $356.85 \div 16.85$ is 20.

EXAMPLE 2 Estimate $133 \div 0.4$ by using compatible numbers.

▸ **Solution**

1. Write the quotient so that the divisor is a whole number.
$$133 \div 0.4 = 1330 \div 4$$
2. The numbers 1340 and 4 are compatible numbers.
$$1340 \div 4 = 335$$
An estimate of $133 \div 0.4$ is 335.

Estimate by using compatible numbers.

1. $122 \div 5.2$ _____
2. $161.2 \div 3.9$ _____
3. $142.3 \div 7.2$ _____

4. $172.1 \div 2.1$ _____
5. $542.4 \div 3.6$ _____
6. $354.8 \div 5.8$ _____

7. $49.1 \div 24.2$ _____
8. $54.8 \div 18.3$ _____
9. $1008.1 \div 10.8$ _____

10. $0.34 \div 0.7$ _____
11. $0.76 \div 0.3$ _____
12. $0.65 \div 0.4$ _____

13. $0.83 \div 0.12$ _____
14. $0.29 \div 0.14$ _____
15. $0.83 \div 0.9$ _____

16. $0.4 \div 0.16$ _____
17. $0.76 \div 0.15$ _____
18. $0.122 \div 0.11$ _____

19. $65.7 \div 0.23$ _____
20. $132.8 \div 0.4$ _____
21. $110.5 \div 0.55$ _____

22. $0.45 \div 0.6$ _____
23. $0.83 \div 0.7$ _____
24. $0.345 \div 0.11$ _____

NAME _____ CLASS _____ DATE _____

11-5 Solving Problems Involving Decimal Division

UNIT 3

OBJECTIVE: Using division with decimals to solve real-world problems

Division is often used to distribute a quantity.

EXAMPLE 1 Given that a school play costs $2587.50 to produce and the auditorium holds 450 people, what should each ticket holder pay so that production costs are paid for?

▶ **Solution**

Divide 2587.50 by 450. $450\overline{)2587.50}$ = 5.75

Each ticket should cost $5.75.

EXAMPLE 2 Find the length of a rectangle whose width is 5.6 feet and whose area is 115.92 square feet.

▶ **Solution**

Since the area of a rectangle is the product of length and width, divide the area by the width to find the length of the rectangle.

$$5.6\overline{)115.92} \rightarrow 56\overline{)1159.2} = 20.7$$

The length of the rectangle is 20.7 feet.

Solve.

1. Seven students contribute equally to a gift valued at $45.50. How much does each student contribute? _____

2. Find the width of a rectangle whose length is 7.3 feet and whose area is 111.69 square feet. _____

3. If a carton containing 24 boxes of candy costs $40.56, what is the cost of each box of candy? _____

4. If a worker earns a salary of $54,500 over a twelve month period, how much does the worker earn for one month? _____

5. A technician pours equal amounts of a 540.6 milliliter solution into 8 containers. How much solution will be in each container? _____

NAME _____ CLASS _____ DATE _____

11-6 Interpreting the Quotient
UNIT 3

OBJECTIVE: *Finding and then interpreting the quotient to solve real-world problems*

Division is often used to solve a real-world problem. However, the solution may be an interpretation of the quotient.

> **EXAMPLE**
>
> Give a reasonable answer to each question.
>
> a. If one bus can carry 35 people, how many buses are needed to carry 195 people?
>
> b. If 8 novels all the same price cost $79, what does one novel cost?
>
> c. A teacher has 340 counters to distribute among 23 students. How many counters does each student receive?
>
> ▶ **Solution**
>
> a. Divide 195 by 35. Then round up. $35\overline{)195}$ = 5 remainder 30
> Six buses are needed.
>
> b. Divide 79 by 8. Then round to the nearest cent. $8\overline{)79.000}$ = 9.875
> One novel costs $9.88.
>
> c. Divide 340 by 23. Then round down. $23\overline{)340.0}$ = 14.7 ...
> Each student will receive 14 counters.

Give a reasonable answer to each question.

1. How many boards each 3.5 feet long can be cut from a 16-foot long board?   _____

2. If 6 cartons of eggs costs $11.92, what is the cost of one carton of eggs?   _____

3. A student has $100 to spend on shirts. If each shirt costs $18, how many shirts can the student buy?   _____

4. A baker baked 150 donuts. If one box of donuts contains 12 donuts, how many boxes does the baker have to sell?   _____

5. How many teams of nine students each can be formed from a group of 130 students?   _____

6. How many tables are needed to seat 230 people for a dinner if each table can seat 8 people?   _____

Making Sense of Numbers

NAME _____ CLASS _____ DATE _____

11-7 Dividing Decimals and Fractions
UNIT 3

OBJECTIVE: *Finding a quotient involving a decimal and a fraction or mixed number*

Given a division involving a decimal and a fraction or mixed number, you may need to change a decimal to a fraction or a fraction to a decimal before beginning to divide.

EXAMPLE Divide. **a.** $15.6 \div \frac{2}{3}$ **b.** $4\frac{2}{5} \div 3.6$ **c.** $2.55 \div \frac{3}{4}$

Solution

a. Divide a decimal by the given fraction.
$$15.6 \div \frac{2}{3} = 15.6 \times \frac{3}{2} = 7.8 \times 3 = 23.4$$

b. Method 1: Use mixed numbers.
$$4\frac{2}{5} \div 3.6 = 4\frac{2}{5} \div 3\frac{3}{5} = \frac{22}{5} \times \frac{5}{18} = \frac{11}{9} = 1\frac{2}{9}$$

Method 2: Use decimals.
$$4\frac{2}{5} \div 3.6 = 4.4 \div 3.6 \quad \rightarrow \quad 3.6 \overline{)4.4}^{\,1.\overline{2}}$$

Note that the answer obtained by Method 1 is equivalent to the answer obtained by Method 2. That is, $1\frac{2}{9} = 1.\overline{2}$.

c. Write $\frac{3}{4}$ as a decimal.
$$2.55 \div \frac{3}{4} = 2.55 \div 0.75 \quad \rightarrow \quad 75\overline{)255.0}^{\,3.4}$$

Divide.

1. $9.4 \div \frac{2}{3}$ _____   2. $93.9 \div \frac{3}{5}$ _____   3. $14.7 \div \frac{7}{9}$ _____

4. $1\frac{2}{3} \div 1.4$ _____   5. $6\frac{1}{5} \div 0.4$ _____   6. $5\frac{3}{4} \div 0.25$ _____

7. $7.35 \div 1\frac{1}{2}$ _____   8. $8.44 \div 2\frac{4}{5}$ _____   9. $12.3 \div 2\frac{1}{4}$ _____

10. $0.6 \div \frac{1}{3}$ _____   11. $0.2 \div \frac{2}{3}$ _____   12. $0.9 \div \frac{2}{9}$ _____

13. $1\frac{2}{7} \div 1.1$ _____   14. $1\frac{1}{7} \div 0.4$ _____   15. $1\frac{3}{11} \div 0.2$ _____

16. $2\frac{1}{6} \div 2.6$ _____   17. $2\frac{5}{6} \div 2.4$ _____   18. $1\frac{5}{7} \div 14.4$ _____

11-8 Adding, Subtracting, Multiplying, and Dividing with Decimals

UNIT 3

OBJECTIVE: Finding the value of an expression involving addition, subtraction, multiplication, and division of decimals

To evaluate an expression involving addition, subtraction, multiplication, and division of decimals, follow the order of operations.

EXAMPLE Evaluate. a. $2.5(3.6 - 0.7) + 11.2$ b. $\dfrac{3.5(1 + 8.2) - 5}{0.4}$

Solution

a. $2.5(3.6 - 0.7) + 11.2 = 2.5(2.9) + 11.2$
$= 7.25 + 11.2$
$= 18.45$

b. $\dfrac{3.5(1 + 8.2) - 5}{0.4} = \dfrac{3.5(9.2) - 5}{0.4}$ *Work within parentheses.*

$= \dfrac{32.2 - 5}{0.4}$ *Multiply.*

$= \dfrac{27.2}{0.4}$ *Subtract.*

$= 68$ *Then divide.*

Evaluate.

1. $3(4.3) + 7(8.1)$ _____

2. $8(7.5) - 4(8.5)$ _____

3. $2(4.4) + 3(4.5) + 4(4.6)$ _____

4. $9(2.1) + 8(2.2) + 7(2.3)$ _____

5. $8(7.4) - 4(5.3) - 2(3.5)$ _____

6. $8.5(2.5) - 4(5) + 2(7.7)$ _____

7. $7(6.1)^2 - 3(5.6)^2$ _____

8. $3(4.1)^2 + 11(1.2)^2$ _____

9. $4(6.1 - 4.5)^2 - 3$ _____

10. $11 + 4(1.1 + 3.4)^2$ _____

11. $\dfrac{3.5(3.8 + 6.2) - 10}{0.5}$ _____

12. $\dfrac{2.4(13.7 - 3.7) - 10}{1.4}$ _____

13. $\dfrac{1.2(3.8 + 1.2)}{0.6} + 4.3$ _____

14. $\dfrac{11.5(3.8 - 0.2)}{1.2} - 7.1$ _____

15. $\dfrac{1.5(3.8 + 1.2)}{5(6.4 + 3.6)}$ _____

16. $\dfrac{4.5(3.8 - 1.2)}{0.9(6.4 + 3.6)}$ _____

17. $\left(\dfrac{11.8 + 3.2}{6.0 - 3.5}\right)^2$ _____

18. $\left(\dfrac{19.8 - 0.8}{6.0 + 3.5}\right)^2$ _____

Making Sense of Numbers

NAME _____ CLASS _____ DATE _____

11-9 Changing to a Larger Unit of Metric Measure
UNIT 3

OBJECTIVE: *Writing a measure given in one metric unit of measure as the same measure in a larger metric unit*

In the metric system, length and distance are measured in kilometers, meters, centimeters, and millimeters.

| 1 kilometer = 1000 meters |
| 1 meter = 100 centimeters |
| 1 centimeter = 10 millimeters |

In the metric system, capacity is measured in liters and milliliters.

1 liter = 1000 milliliters

In the metric system, mass is measured in kilograms and grams.

1 kilogram = 1000 grams

To change a measure in a smaller unit to the same measure in a larger unit, divide by a power of 10.

EXAMPLE Write each measure in the specified unit.
  a. 38 centimeters = __?__ meters
  b. 689 milliliters = __?__ liters
  c. 1750 grams = __?__ kilograms

Solution
  a. 38 ÷ 100 = 0.38   38 centimeters = 0.38 meter
  b. 689 ÷ 1000 = 0.689   689 milliliters = 0.689 liter
  c. 1750 ÷ 1000 = 1.75   1750 grams = 1.75 kilograms

Write each measure in the specified unit.

1. 95 centimeters = _____ meters

2. 32 millimeters = _____ centimeters

3. 155 milliliters = _____ liters

4. 5200 grams = _____ kilograms

5. 1300 meters = _____ kilometers

6. 143 centimeters = _____ meters

7. 1306 milliliters = _____ liters

8. 2120 milliliters = _____ liters

9. 30 grams = _____ kilograms

10. 980 meters = _____ kilometers

11. 625 milliliters = _____ liters

12. 8840 meters = _____ kilometers

13. 1400 centimeters = _____ meters

14. 25 centimeters = _____ meters

15. 2900 milliliters = _____ liters

16. 9850 grams = _____ kilograms

NAME _____ CLASS _____ DATE _____

11-10 Writing Numbers Between 0 and 1 in Scientific Notation
UNIT 3

OBJECTIVE: Writing a number between 0 and 1 in scientific notation and writing a number given in scientific notation in standard form

The display below shows the same number in two forms, standard form and scientific notation.

standard form   scientific notation
0.0043   = 4.3×10^{-3}

A number is written in **scientific notation** when it is written as a number between 1 and 10, excluding 10, multiplied by an integer power of 10. If the given number is between 0 and 1, such as 0.0043, the power of 10 is a negative integer.

EXAMPLE 1   Write 0.0078 in scientific notation.

▶ **Solution**

Move the decimal point 3 places to the right so that there is just one digit to the left of the new location of the decimal point.
Use -3 as the needed power of 10.
In scientific notation, $0.0078 = 7.8 \times 10^{-3}$.

0.0078
3 places right

EXAMPLE 2   Write 3.22×10^{-4} in standard form.

▶ **Solution**

Move the decimal point 4 places to the left.
Add zeros as needed.
In standard form, $3.22 \times 10^{-4} = 0.000322$.

0003.22
4 places left

Write each number in scientific notation.

1. 0.45 _____
2. 0.007 _____
3. 0.0345 _____

4. 0.0022 _____
5. 0.0035 _____
6. 0.0124 _____

7. 0.9999 _____
8. 0.2255 _____
9. 0.00034 _____

Write each number in standard form.

10. 5.1×10^{-2} _____
11. 7.29×10^{-3} _____
12. 9.95×10^{-3} _____

13. 1.55×10^{-1} _____
14. 3.5×10^{-1} _____
15. 1.1×10^{-4} _____

Making Sense of Numbers   Unit 3   Decimals   **119**

Unit 4 — Ratio, Proportion, and Percent

Chapter 12 Ratio and Proportion
- **12-1** Writing Ratios 123
- **12-2** Writing Rates 124
- **12-3** Solving Problems Involving Ratios and Rates 125
- **12-4** Solving Problems Involving Distance, Rate, and Time 126
- **12-5** Determining Whether Two Ratios are Equal 127
- **12-6** Solving Proportions 128
- **12-7** Solving Problems Involving Proportions 129
- **12-8** Solving Problems Involving Similar Geometric Figures 130

Chapter 13 Percent Fundamentals
- **13-1** Writing Percents Less Than 100% 131
- **13-2** Writing Percents Greater Than 100% 132
- **13-3** Writing Percents as Fractions 133
- **13-4** Writing Fractions as Percents 134
- **13-5** Writing Percents as Decimals 135
- **13-6** Writing Decimals as Percents 136
- **13-7** Recognizing Equivalent Fractions, Decimals, and Percents 137

Chapter 14 Operations Involving Percent
- **14-1** Finding a Percent of a Number 138
- **14-2** Estimating a Percentage of a Number 139
- **14-3** Solving Problems by Finding a Percentage of a Number 140
- **14-4** Finding the Percent Rate 141
- **14-5** Using Proportion to Find a Percent Rate 142
- **14-6** Solving Problems by Finding a Percent Rate 143
- **14-7** Finding a Base Number When its Percent Rate and Percentage are Known 144
- **14-8** Using Proportion to Find a Base Number 145
- **14-9** Solving Problems by Finding a Base Number 146

Chapter 15 Applications of Percent
- **15-1** Percent of Increase 147
- **15-2** Percent of Decrease 148
- **15-3** Calculating Tips and Total Cost 149
- **15-4** Calculating Sales Tax and Total Cost 150

15-5	Solving Discount Problems	151
15-6	Solving Successive Discount Problems	152
15-7	Solving Markup Problems	153
15-8	Solving Simple Interest Problems	154
15-9	Solving Compound Interest Problems	155
15-10	Solving Commission Problems	156
15-11	Finding Probabilities	157

NAME _____ CLASS _____ DATE _____

12-1 Writing Ratios
UNIT 4

OBJECTIVE: Writing a ratio to represent a comparison of two quantities

A **ratio** is the comparison of two quantities by division. For example, if there are 13 boys and 12 girls in one classroom, then the ratio of boys to girls is 13 to 12, also written 13 : 12, or $\frac{13}{12}$.

EXAMPLE 1 The length of a rectangle is 27 inches and its width is 1 foot 6 inches. Write the ratio of length to width.

▶ **Solution**

Convert 1 foot 6 inches into inches.

The width is 1 foot 6 inches, or 18 inches. $\quad \frac{\text{length}}{\text{width}} \rightarrow \frac{27}{18} = \frac{3}{2}$

The ratio of length to width is 3 to 2, 3 : 2, or $\frac{3}{2}$.

EXAMPLE 2 In a recent survey, 125 people expressed approval of a new civil project and 75 people expressed disapproval.
a. Find the ratio of those in favor to the total number in the survey.
b. Find the ratio of those opposed to the total number in the survey.

▶ **Solution**

a. $\dfrac{\text{number in favor}}{\text{total in survey}} \rightarrow \dfrac{125}{125 + 75} = \dfrac{125}{200} = \dfrac{5}{8}$

b. $\dfrac{\text{number opposed}}{\text{total in survey}} \rightarrow \dfrac{75}{125 + 75} = \dfrac{75}{200} = \dfrac{3}{8}$

Write each ratio as a fraction in lowest terms.

1. 9 students to 45 students _____   2. 1 foot 4 inches to 8 inches _____

3. 2 feet to 14 feet _____   4. 5 red chips to 25 blue chips _____

5. 8 vans to 56 cars _____   6. 240 votes to 360 votes _____

7. 18 gallons to 2.5 gallons _____   8. 18 books to 48 books _____

9. 98 grams to 14 grams _____   10. 90 birds to 10 birds _____

11. 21 bushes to 42 pots _____   12. 3 inches to 3 feet _____

13. 6 hours to 1 day _____   14. $24 to $18 _____

Making Sense of Numbers   Unit 4 Ratio, Proportion, and Percent   **123**

12-2 Writing Rates
UNIT 4

OBJECTIVE: *Writing a rate to represent a comparison of two different quantities*

A **rate** is a ratio that compares two unlike quantities. For example, a speed of 55 miles per hour is a rate because distance is compared to time. A **unit rate** is a ratio in which the denominator is one unit. For example, a price per pound is a unit rate.

EXAMPLE 1

Write the unit rate. Round as needed to the nearest cent.
$4.59 for 5 pounds

▶ **Solution**

$$\frac{\text{dollars}}{\text{pounds}} \rightarrow \frac{4.59}{5} \quad \text{Divide 4.59 by 5.} \quad 5\overline{)4.590}^{\,0.918}$$

The price per pound is about $0.92.

EXAMPLE 2

Write the unit rate. Round as needed to the nearest hundredth.
180 miles in 3.5 hours

▶ **Solution**

$$\frac{\text{miles}}{\text{hours}} \rightarrow \frac{180}{3.5} \quad \text{Divide 180 by 3.5.}$$

Since 180 ÷ 3.5 is about 51.43, the unit rate is about 51.43 miles per hour.

Write each unit rate. Round to the nearest hundredth as needed.

1. $220 for 40 hours

2. $12.45 for 12 pounds

3. $310.88 for 4 tires

4. 236 miles in 3.6 hours

5. $98 for 7 tickets

6. 72 boxes for $12

7. $630 for 8 days

8. 840 words in 20 minutes

9. $56 for 12 issues

10. 380 miles in 3.5 hours

11. 34 liters in 12 minutes

12. 18 tokens for 6 rides

NAME _____ CLASS _____ DATE _____

12-3 Solving Problems Involving Ratios and Rates
UNIT 4

OBJECTIVE: Using unit rates to solve real-world problems

Finding a unit rate can help answer questions about distance or cost.

EXAMPLE 1 A motorist drove 195 miles in 3.5 hours. Assuming a constant speed, find the motorist's speed in miles per hour.

▶ **Solution**

$\dfrac{\text{miles}}{\text{hours}} \to \dfrac{195}{3.5}$ Divide 195 by 3.5.

Since $195 \div 3.5 \approx 55.7$, the speed is about 55.7 miles per hour.

EXAMPLE 2 One brand (A) of detergent costs $4.99 for 50 fluid ounces. A second brand (B) of detergent costs $6.99 for 64 fluid ounces. Which brand has the lower unit price?

▶ **Solution**

Brand A: $\dfrac{\text{dollars}}{\text{fluid ounces}} \to \dfrac{4.99}{50}$ Brand B: $\dfrac{\text{dollars}}{\text{fluid ounces}} \to \dfrac{6.99}{64}$

The unit price for Brand A is $0.10 per fluid ounce and the unit price for Brand B is $0.11 per fluid ounce. Since $0.10 < 0.11$, Brand A has the lower unit price.

Solve each problem.

1. It took a technician 4.5 seconds to pour 270 milliliters of solution into a container. Find the flow rate per second. _____

2. In 2.4 minutes, a small plane descended 900 feet. If the rate of descent is constant, find the rate of descent per minute. _____

Which has the lower unit rate?

3. One brand (X) of fertilizer costs $12.99 for 10 pounds. A second brand (Y) of fertilizer costs $26.99 for 25 pounds. _____

4. One brand (K) of vegetable costs $1.89 for 16 ounces. A second brand (L) of vegetable costs $0.99 for 10 ounces. _____

5. Motorist R takes 3.2 hours to drive 200 miles. Motorist S takes 4.8 hours to drive 400 miles. _____

Making Sense of Numbers   Unit 4 Ratio, Proportion, and Percent

NAME _____ CLASS _____ DATE _____

12-4 Solving Problems Involving Distance, Rate, and Time

UNIT 4

OBJECTIVE: *Finding distance, rate, or time when two of the three quantities are known*

If a traveler drives at a constant speed, or rate, then distance, d, traveled, rate, r, and travel time, t, are related as shown below.

$$\text{distance} = \text{rate} \times \text{time} \qquad d = rt$$

EXAMPLE

a. How long will it take a motorist driving at 60 miles per hour to drive 330 miles?

b. At what speed should a motorist drive in order to drive 480 miles in 8 hours?

▶ **Solution**

Substitute known quantities into $d = rt$, and then solve for the unknown quantity by using division.

a. Distance and rate are known.
Time t is unknown.

$$330 = 60t$$

$$\frac{330}{60} = t \quad \text{Divide by 60.}$$

$$\frac{11}{2} = t$$

It will take 5.5 hours.

b. Distance and time are known.
Rate r is unknown.

$$480 = 8r$$

$$\frac{480}{8} = r \quad \text{Divide by 80.}$$

$$60 = r$$

Speed should be 60 miles per hour.

Use the formula $d = rt$ to find the unknown quantity. Round to the nearest hundredth as needed.

1. $d = 540$ miles and $t = 9$ hours $r = $ _____

2. $d = 620$ miles and $r = 54$ miles per hour $t = $ _____

3. $d = 291.5$ miles and $t = 7.5$ hours $r = $ _____

4. $d = 337.5$ miles and $r = 54$ miles per hour $t = $ _____

5. $d = 426.25$ miles and $t = 7\frac{3}{4}$ hours $r = $ _____

6. $d = 16\frac{1}{4}$ miles and $r = 6.5$ miles per hour $t = $ _____

7. $d = 17.36$ miles and $t = 1\frac{2}{5}$ hours $r = $ _____

NAME _____ CLASS _____ DATE _____

12-5 Determining Whether Two Ratios are Equal
UNIT 4

OBJECTIVE: Determining whether two given ratios are equal

Two ratios are equal if they have the same value.

EXAMPLE 1 Tell whether the ratios are equal.

a. $\frac{18}{27}$ and $\frac{2}{3}$ b. $\frac{4}{9}$ and $\frac{2}{3}$ c. $\frac{2}{3}$ and $\frac{3}{5}$

Solution

a. $\frac{18}{27} = \frac{18 \div 9}{27 \div 9} = \frac{2}{3}$. Therefore, $\frac{18}{27} = \frac{2}{3}$.

b. $\frac{2}{3} = \frac{2 \times 3}{3 \times 3} = \frac{6}{9}$. Since $\frac{4}{9} \neq \frac{6}{9}$, you may conclude that $\frac{4}{9} \neq \frac{2}{3}$.

c. $\frac{2}{3} = 0.\overline{6}$ and $\frac{3}{5} = 0.6$. Since $0.\overline{6} \neq 0.6$, $\frac{2}{3} \neq \frac{3}{5}$.

Another way to determine whether ratios $\frac{a}{b}$ and $\frac{c}{d}$ are equal is by comparing *cross products*, ad and bc.

If $ad = bc$, then you may conclude that $\frac{a}{b} = \frac{c}{d}$.

EXAMPLE 2 Tell whether the ratios are equal.   a. $\frac{18}{27}$ and $\frac{2}{3}$ b. $\frac{2}{3}$ and $\frac{3}{5}$

Solution

a. Since $18 \times 3 = 27 \times 2$, $\frac{18}{27} = \frac{2}{3}$.   b. Since $2 \times 5 \neq 3 \times 3$, $\frac{2}{3} \neq \frac{3}{5}$.

Tell whether the ratios are equal.

1. $\frac{1}{2}$ and $\frac{7}{14}$ _____

2. $\frac{1}{2}$ and $\frac{1}{3}$ _____

3. $\frac{3}{4}$ and $\frac{4}{3}$ _____

4. $\frac{15}{20}$ and $\frac{3}{4}$ _____

5. $\frac{3}{7}$ and $\frac{10}{21}$ _____

6. $\frac{18}{25}$ and $\frac{70}{100}$ _____

7. $\frac{49}{21}$ and $\frac{21}{9}$ _____

8. $\frac{10}{7}$ and $\frac{110}{77}$ _____

9. $\frac{48}{35}$ and $\frac{6}{7}$ _____

10. $\frac{1}{10}$ and $\frac{2}{11}$ _____

11. $\frac{18}{81}$ and $\frac{2}{9}$ _____

12. $\frac{13}{3}$ and $\frac{12}{2}$ _____

13. $\frac{17}{10}$ and $\frac{10}{17}$ _____

14. $\frac{121}{22}$ and $\frac{33}{6}$ _____

15. $\frac{15}{225}$ and $\frac{3}{45}$ _____

Making Sense of Numbers — Unit 4 Ratio, Proportion, and Percent

NAME _____ CLASS _____ DATE _____

12-6 Solving Proportions
UNIT 4

OBJECTIVE: *Solving a proportion for an unknown term*

A proportion is an equality of two ratios. The four quantities in the proportion are called *terms*. If the ratios are equal, then the proportion is true.

EXAMPLE 1 Tell whether the proportion $\frac{4}{9} = \frac{2}{3}$ is true or false.

▶ **Solution**
Since $4 \times 3 \neq 9 \times 2$, you may conclude that $\frac{4}{9} \neq \frac{2}{3}$.
Therefore, the ratios are not equal. The proportion is false.

If a proportion involves an unknown, represented by a variable, you can find the number that makes the proportion true. To solve a proportion, find the cross products and set them equal to each other. Solve the equation that results.

$$\text{If } \frac{a}{b} = \frac{c}{d}, \text{ then } ad = bc.$$

EXAMPLE 2 Solve $\frac{x}{8} = \frac{35}{40}$.

▶ **Solution**
To make the proportion true, the cross products must be equal.
$$\frac{x}{8} = \frac{35}{40}$$
$40x = 8 \times 35$ *Set cross products equal.*
$x = \frac{8 \cdot 35}{40} = 7$ *Divide each side by 40.*
Therefore, $x = 7$.

Tell whether the given proportion is true or false.

1. $\frac{15}{6} = \frac{45}{18}$ _____
2. $\frac{13}{7} = \frac{25}{14}$ _____
3. $\frac{35}{9} = \frac{15}{4}$ _____

Solve each proportion.

4. $\frac{x}{6} = \frac{30}{12}$ _____
5. $\frac{5}{6} = \frac{y}{30}$ _____
6. $\frac{a}{39} = \frac{18}{13}$ _____

7. $\frac{1}{21} = \frac{z}{3}$ _____
8. $\frac{3}{4} = \frac{t}{9}$ _____
9. $\frac{1}{13} = \frac{4}{a}$ _____

10. $\frac{4}{c} = \frac{8}{5}$ _____
11. $\frac{7}{n} = \frac{5}{9}$ _____
12. $\frac{9}{19} = \frac{18}{m}$ _____

128   Unit 4   Ratio, Proportion, and Percent

NAME _____ CLASS _____ DATE _____

12-7 Solving Problems Involving Proportions
UNIT 4

OBJECTIVE: Using proportions to solve real-world problems

When a constant rate is part of a real-world problem, you may be able to use a proportion to find the unknown quantity.

EXAMPLE If an inspector examines 20 light bulbs in 18 minutes, how many light bulbs will the inspector examine in 72 minutes?

▶ **Solution**

1. Write a proportion involving number of bulbs and time. Let x represent the number of bulbs examined in 72 minutes.

$$\frac{\text{number of bulbs}}{\text{time}} \rightarrow \frac{20}{18} = \frac{x}{72}$$

2. Solve the proportion for x. $\frac{20}{18} = \frac{x}{72}$

   $18x = 20 \cdot 72$ *Set cross products equal.*
   $x = 80$ *Divide each side by 18.*

The inspector will examine 80 bulbs in 72 minutes.

Solve each problem. Round answers as necessary.

1. If detergent costs $6.50 for 50 fluid ounces, what will be the cost of 120 fluid ounces?   _____

2. If a motorist drives 180 miles in 3.2 hours, how far will the motorist drive in 4.5 hours?   _____

3. If a student reads 18 pages of an assignment in 30 minutes, how many pages will the student read in 48 minutes?   _____

4. If 420 students enter a stadium in 25 minutes, how many students will enter the stadium in 35 minutes?   _____

5. How many students are in the reading club if the ratio of boys to girls is 5 to 4 and there are 35 boys in the club?   _____

6. If 3 CDs cost $39, how much will 7 CDs cost?   _____

7. If a motorist drives 220 miles in 3.8 hours, how long will it take the motorist to drive 550 miles?   _____

8. How many sandwiches can be bought with $21 if three sandwiches cost $9?   _____

Making Sense of Numbers   Unit 4   Ratio, Proportion, and Percent

NAME _____ CLASS _____ DATE _____

12-8
UNIT 4
Solving Problems Involving Similar Geometric Figures

OBJECTIVE: *Using proportions to find unknown lengths of sides in similar geometric figures*

Two geometric figures in the plane are *similar* if the ratios of the lengths of corresponding sides are equal.

EXAMPLE Triangles *ABC* and *XYZ* shown at right are similar triangles. Find *XY* and *YZ*.

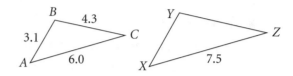

▶ **Solution**

$\dfrac{\text{Triangle } XYZ}{\text{Triangle } ABC} \rightarrow \dfrac{XY}{3.1} = \dfrac{7.5}{6.0}$

$6(XY) = 3.1 \times 7.56$
$XY = 3.875$
So, $XY = 3.875$.

$\dfrac{\text{Triangle } XYZ}{\text{Triangle } ABC} \rightarrow \dfrac{YZ}{4.3} = \dfrac{7.5}{6.0}$

$6(YZ) = 4.3 \times 7.5$
$YZ = 5.375$
So, $YZ = 5.375$.

Exercises 1–3: Figures *LKMN* and *PQRS* are similar.

1. Find *PQ*. _____

2. Find *QR*. _____

3. Find *RS*. _____

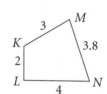
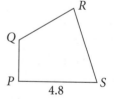

Exercises 4–6: Figures *CDEF* and *GHJK* are similar.

4. Find *DE*. _____

5. Find *EF*. _____

6. Find *FC*. _____

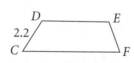
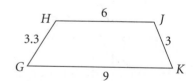

Exercises 7–9: Figures *UVWX* and *MATH* are similar.

7. Find *VW*. _____

8. Find *TH*. _____

9. Find *UX*. _____

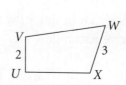
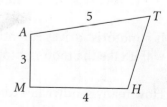

NAME _____ CLASS _____ DATE _____

13-3 Writing Percents as Fractions
UNIT 4

OBJECTIVE: *Representing a percent as a fraction in lowest terms*

You can write a percent less than 100% as a fraction in lowest terms.

EXAMPLE 1 | **Write each percent as a fraction in lowest terms.**
a. 42%   b. 0.5%

▶ **Solution**
Write each percent as a fraction with denominator 100.

a. 42% → $\dfrac{42}{100} = \dfrac{21}{50}$ b. 0.5% → $\dfrac{0.5}{100} = \dfrac{5}{1000} = \dfrac{1}{200}$

You can represent a percent greater than 100% as a mixed number with the fraction part in lowest terms.

EXAMPLE 2 | **Write 125% as a mixed number with the fraction in lowest terms.**

▶ **Solution**
Write 125% as a fraction with denominator 100.

125% → $\dfrac{125}{100} = \dfrac{5}{4} = 1\dfrac{1}{4}$

Write each percent as a fraction in lowest terms or as a mixed number with the fraction in lowest terms.

1. 1% _____   2. 5% _____   3. 20% _____   4. 25% _____

5. 60% _____   6. 75% _____   7. 80% _____   8. 100% _____

9. 150% _____   10. 140% _____   11. 160% _____   12. 350% _____

13. 1000% _____   14. 101% _____   15. 110% _____   16. 105% _____

17. 0.6% _____   18. 1.5% _____   19. 130.4% _____   20. 112.5% _____

21. $12\dfrac{1}{2}\%$ _____   22. $37\dfrac{1}{2}\%$ _____   23. $62\dfrac{3}{5}\%$ _____   24. $49\dfrac{2}{5}\%$ _____

25. $8\dfrac{1}{8}\%$ _____   26. $25\dfrac{3}{8}\%$ _____   27. $44\dfrac{1}{16}\%$ _____   28. $50\dfrac{7}{8}\%$ _____

29. $33\dfrac{1}{3}\%$ _____   30. $66\dfrac{2}{3}\%$ _____   31. $14\dfrac{2}{7}\%$ _____   32. $11\dfrac{1}{9}\%$ _____

Making Sense of Numbers   Unit 4   Ratio, Proportion, and Percent

NAME _____ CLASS _____ DATE _____

13-4 Writing Fractions as Percents
UNIT 4

OBJECTIVE: *Writing a fraction as a percent*

You can use equivalent fractions to write a given fraction as a percent.

EXAMPLE 1 Write each fraction or mixed number as a percent.

a. $\dfrac{3}{4}$ b. $1\dfrac{3}{5}$

Solution

a. $\dfrac{3}{4} = \dfrac{3 \times 25}{4 \times 25} = \dfrac{75}{100} = 75\%$ b. $1\dfrac{3}{5} = \dfrac{8}{5} = \dfrac{8 \times 20}{5 \times 20} = \dfrac{160}{100} = 160\%$

Sometimes you need to use division to write a fraction as a percent.

EXAMPLE 2 Write each fraction as a percent.

a. $\dfrac{5}{8}$ b. $\dfrac{1}{3}$

Solution

a. $\dfrac{5}{8} \rightarrow 8\overline{)5.00}^{\,0.625}$ b. $\dfrac{1}{3} \rightarrow 3\overline{)1.00}^{\,0.\overline{3}}$

$\dfrac{5}{8} = 0.625$, or 62.5% $\dfrac{1}{3} = 0.\overline{3}$, or $33\dfrac{1}{3}\%$

Write each fraction or mixed number as a percent.

1. $\dfrac{7}{10}$ _____   2. $\dfrac{13}{10}$ _____   3. $\dfrac{7}{20}$ _____   4. $\dfrac{3}{25}$ _____

5. $\dfrac{17}{25}$ _____   6. $\dfrac{12.5}{50}$ _____   7. $\dfrac{18.45}{50}$ _____   8. $\dfrac{16.25}{25}$ _____

9. $\dfrac{27}{20}$ _____   10. $\dfrac{32}{25}$ _____   11. $\dfrac{7}{4}$ _____   12. $\dfrac{9}{5}$ _____

13. $2\dfrac{1}{5}$ _____   14. $1\dfrac{3}{4}$ _____   15. $3\dfrac{4}{5}$ _____   16. $4\dfrac{3}{20}$ _____

17. $\dfrac{5}{12}$ _____   18. $\dfrac{7}{8}$ _____   19. $3\dfrac{5}{16}$ _____   20. $4\dfrac{11}{16}$ _____

21. $3\dfrac{1}{8}$ _____   22. $1\dfrac{7}{8}$ _____   23. $1\dfrac{2}{3}$ _____   24. $2\dfrac{5}{6}$ _____

25. $1\dfrac{5}{16}$ _____   26. $2\dfrac{7}{16}$ _____   27. $2\dfrac{1}{3}$ _____   28. $10\dfrac{1}{6}$ _____

NAME _____ CLASS _____ DATE _____

13-5 Writing Percents as Decimals
UNIT 4

OBJECTIVE: Writing a percent as a decimal

Recall that when you divide a number by 100, you move the decimal point two places to the left.

EXAMPLE 1 Write each percent as a decimal.
a. 6%   b. 7.3%   c. 136.4%

▶ **Solution**

a. $6\% = 6 \div 100 = 0.06$ b. $7.3\% = 7.3 \div 100 = 0.073$
c. $136.4\% = 136.4 \div 100 = 1.364$

Sometimes you need to change a fraction to a decimal before writing the given percent as a decimal.

EXAMPLE 2 Write each percent as a decimal.   a. $47\frac{3}{5}\%$ b. $33\frac{1}{3}\%$

▶ **Solution**

a. $47\frac{3}{5}\% = 47.6\% = 47.6 \div 100 = 0.476$

b. $33\frac{1}{3}\% = 33.\overline{3}\% = 0.33\overline{3} = 0.\overline{3}$ Recall that $\frac{1}{3} = 0.\overline{3}$.

Write each percent as a decimal.

1. 21% _____   2. 2.1% _____   3. 98.5% _____   4. 53.3% _____

5. 0.3% _____   6. 0.04% _____   7. 0.9% _____   8. 0.003% _____

9. 0.04% _____   10. 0.001% _____   11. 0.999% _____   12. 0.101% _____

13. 129% _____   14. 108% _____   15. 118.5% _____   16. 206.1% _____

17. $\frac{1}{2}\%$ _____   18. $\frac{1}{4}\%$ _____   19. $\frac{1}{40}\%$ _____   20. $\frac{3}{5}\%$ _____

21. $50\frac{1}{2}\%$ _____   22. $1\frac{1}{4}\%$ _____   23. $28\frac{3}{4}\%$ _____   24. $34\frac{4}{5}\%$ _____

25. $98\frac{5}{8}\%$ _____   26. $5\frac{3}{8}\%$ _____   27. $124\frac{1}{8}\%$ _____   28. $200\frac{7}{12}\%$ _____

29. $66\frac{2}{3}\%$ _____   30. $5\frac{2}{3}\%$ _____   31. $120\frac{1}{3}\%$ _____   32. $130\frac{5}{6}\%$ _____

Making Sense of Numbers   Unit 4   Ratio, Proportion, and Percent

13-6 Writing Decimals as Percents

UNIT 4

OBJECTIVE: Writing decimals as percents

To write a decimal as a percent, move the decimal point two places to the right, and then add the percent symbol (%).

EXAMPLE 1 Write each decimal as a percent.
 a. 0.48   b. 0.026   c. 0.625   d. 1.13

Solution

 a. 0.48 → 48%   b. 0.026 → 2.6%
 c. 0.625 → 62.5%   d. 1.13 → 113%

A number may be written as a combination of a decimal and a fraction. To change such a decimal to a percent, write the number as a decimal, and then proceed as in Example 1.

EXAMPLE 2 Write $0.14\frac{1}{8}$ as a percent.

Solution

$0.14\frac{1}{8}$ → 0.14125 → 14.125% → $14\frac{1}{8}\%$

Write each decimal or mixed decimal as a percent.

1. 0.5 _____
2. 0.05 _____
3. 0.005 _____
4. 0.56 _____

5. 0.982 _____
6. 0.1345 _____
7. 0.3395 _____
8. 0.9999 _____

9. 1.47 _____
10. 1.047 _____
11. 1.0047 _____
12. 2.5 _____

13. 1.999 _____
14. 1.001 _____
15. 1 _____
16. 2 _____

17. $0.50\frac{1}{2}$ _____
18. $0.40\frac{1}{2}$ _____
19. $0.99\frac{1}{4}$ _____

20. $0.37\frac{1}{8}$ _____
21. $0.25\frac{1}{8}$ _____
22. $1.25\frac{1}{8}$ _____

23. $1.04\frac{1}{5}$ _____
24. $0.02\frac{1}{3}$ _____
25. $1.09\frac{1}{4}$ _____

26. $1.333\frac{1}{10}$ _____
27. $1.025\frac{3}{10}$ _____
28. $1.184\frac{3}{4}$ _____

NAME _____ CLASS _____ DATE _____

13-7 Recognizing Equivalent Fractions, Decimals, and Percents
UNIT 4

OBJECTIVE: Writing equivalent fractions, decimals, and percents

The table below shows equivalence of frequently used fractions, decimals, and percents. Having worked with these, you should be able to change from any form given to an equivalent one.

Equivalence of Commonly Used Percents, Decimals, and Fractions

$20\% = 0.2 = \frac{1}{5}$	$15\% = 0.25 = \frac{1}{4}$	$12\frac{1}{2}\% = 0.125 = \frac{1}{8}$	$16\frac{2}{3}\% = 0.1\overline{6} = \frac{1}{6}$
$40\% = 0.4 = \frac{2}{5}$	$50\% = 0.5 = \frac{1}{2}$	$37\frac{1}{2}\% = 0.375 = \frac{3}{8}$	$33\frac{1}{3}\% = 0.\overline{3} = \frac{1}{3}$
$60\% = 0.6 = \frac{3}{5}$	$75\% = 0.75 = \frac{3}{4}$	$62\frac{1}{2}\% = 0.625 = \frac{5}{8}$	$66\frac{2}{3}\% = 0.\overline{6} = \frac{2}{3}$
$80\% = 0.8 = \frac{4}{5}$	$100\% = 1.00 = 1$	$87\frac{1}{2}\% = 0.875 = \frac{7}{8}$	$83\frac{1}{3}\% = 0.8\overline{3} = \frac{5}{6}$

EXAMPLE

a. Write the equivalent decimal and fraction for $62\frac{1}{2}\%$.

b. Write the equivalent percent and decimal for $\frac{7}{8}$.

Solution

a. From the table above, $62\frac{1}{2}\% = 0.625 = \frac{5}{8}$.

b. From the table above, $\frac{7}{8} = 87\frac{1}{2}\% = 0.875$.

Given each fraction, decimal, or percent, write the other two equivalent forms.

1. $\frac{2}{5}$ _____   2. $\frac{3}{8}$ _____   3. $\frac{1}{3}$ _____   4. $\frac{4}{5}$ _____

5. $\frac{1}{2}$ _____   6. $\frac{3}{4}$ _____   7. $\frac{5}{6}$ _____   8. $\frac{2}{3}$ _____

9. 0.8 _____   10. 0.125 _____   11. 0.4 _____   12. 0.375 _____

13. $0.8\overline{3}$ _____   14. $0.\overline{6}$ _____   15. $0.\overline{3}$ _____   16. $0.1\overline{6}$ _____

17. $62\frac{1}{2}\%$ _____   18. $33\frac{1}{3}\%$ _____   19. $37\frac{1}{2}\%$ _____   20. $83\frac{1}{3}\%$ _____

21. $162\frac{1}{2}\%$ _____   22. $133\frac{1}{3}\%$ _____   23. $137\frac{1}{2}\%$ _____   24. $183\frac{1}{3}\%$ _____

Making Sense of Numbers   Unit 4 Ratio, Proportion, and Percent

NAME _____ CLASS _____ DATE _____

14-1 Finding a Percent of a Number
UNIT 4

OBJECTIVE: Finding a percentage, given a percent rate and a base number

In a percent statement such as "50% of 60 is 30," 50 is the *percent rate*, 60 is the *base*, and 30 is the *percentage*. In this lesson, you will be given a percent rate and a base, and will be asked to find a percentage.

> **EXAMPLE** Find each percentage.
>
> a. What number is 40% of 75?   b. What number is 40% of 95?
>
> c. 4.5% of 1200 is what number?   d. $66\frac{2}{3}\%$ of 243 is what number?
>
> ▸ **Solution**
>
> a. Use a decimal.
>   What number is 40% of 75?
> $n = 0.4 \times 75$
> $n = 30$
>
> b. Use a fraction.
>   What number is 40% of 95?
> $n = \frac{2}{5} \times \frac{95}{1}$
> $n = 38$
>
> c. Use a decimal.
>   4.5% of 1200 is what number?
> $0.045 \times 1200 = n$
> $54 = n$
>
> d. Use an equivalent fraction.
> $66\frac{2}{3}\%$ of 243 is what number?
> $\frac{2}{3} \times 243 = n$
> $162 = n$

Find each percentage.

1. What number is 40% of 100? _____

2. What number is 3.5% of 100? _____

3. What number is 65% of 700? _____

4. What number is 11% of 600? _____

5. What number is 10% of 65? _____

6. What number is 10% of 12.2? _____

7. What number is 32.5% of 80? _____

8. What number is 67.5% of 120? _____

9. $33\frac{1}{3}\%$ of 360 is what number? _____

10. $16\frac{1}{6}\%$ of 258 is what number? _____

11. $12\frac{1}{2}\%$ of 160 is what number? _____

12. $62\frac{1}{2}\%$ of 720 is what number? _____

13. $37\frac{1}{2}\%$ of 100 is what number? _____

14. $87\frac{1}{2}\%$ of 888 is what number? _____

15. $16\frac{2}{3}\%$ of 315 is what number? _____

16. $11\frac{1}{9}\%$ of 81.09 is what number? _____

NAME _____ CLASS _____ DATE _____

14-2 Estimating a Percentage of a Number
UNIT 4

OBJECTIVE: Using fractions and whole numbers to estimate a percentage of a given number

To estimate a percentage of a number, use numbers that make multiplication easier. Sometimes it is easier to replace a percent rate or a base number with a fraction.

EXAMPLE 1 Estimate each percentage.
a. 24% of 120   b. 66% of 148

▶ **Solution**

a. 24% is about 25%. Use $\frac{1}{4}$ instead of 24%. $\frac{1}{4} \times 120 = 30$

b. 66% is about $66\frac{2}{3}$% and 148 is about 150.
Use $\frac{2}{3}$ for 66% and use 150 for 148. $\frac{2}{3} \times 150 = 100$

Sometimes it is easier to replace a percent rate or a base number with a decimal.

EXAMPLE 2 Estimate each percentage.
a. 9% of 87.5   b. 18.6% of 98.3

▶ **Solution**

a. 9% is about 10%. Use 0.1 instead of 9%. $0.1 \times 87.5 = 8.75$

b. 18.6% is about 20% and 98.3 is about 100.
Use 0.2 for 18.6% and use 100 for 98.3. $0.2 \times 100 = 20$

Estimate each percentage.

1. 24% of 80 _____
2. 33% of 33 _____
3. 76% of 12 _____

4. 19% of 80 _____
5. 73% of 70 _____
6. 16% of 66 _____

7. 2.1% of 66 _____
8. 1.2% of 93.2 _____
9. 0.8% of 17.4 _____

10. 9% of 18 _____
11. 17% of 75 _____
12. 79% of 1300 _____

13. 17.9% of 198 _____
14. 38.8% of 63 _____
15. 57.7% of 300 _____

16. $24\frac{1}{4}$% of 511 _____
17. $31\frac{3}{4}$% of 210 _____
18. $12\frac{3}{5}$% of 360 _____

19. $59\frac{5}{6}$% of 101 _____
20. $12\frac{2}{5}$% of 242 _____
21. $75\frac{1}{6}$% of 483 _____

Making Sense of Numbers   Unit 4 Ratio, Proportion and Percent   **139**

Solving Problems by Finding a Percentage of a Number

OBJECTIVE: *Finding a percentage of a number to solve real-world problems*

In many situations, you use percents to solve real-world problems.

EXAMPLE 1 If a stadium can seat 18,500 people and the stadium is 72% full, how many people are seated in the stadium?

▶ **Solution**

Find 72% of 18,500.
  72% × 18,500 = 0.72 × 18,500 = 13,320
There are 13,320 people seated in the stadium.

The total cost of a purchase including sales tax is found by multiplying cost by a percent greater than 100%.

EXAMPLE 2 With sales tax, an item costs 105% of the selling price. Find the total cost of a toaster that sells for $39.95.

▶ **Solution**

Find 105% of 39.95.
  105% × 39.95 = 1.05 × 39.95 = 41.9475
The total cost of the toaster is $41.95.

Find each percentage.

1. A student completed a project estimated to take 4.5 days in 120% of the estimated time. How long did the project take? _____

2. Shortly after a game ended, 75% of the 12,400 fans had left the stadium. How many fans left the stadium? _____

3. A car owner sold a $4000 car for 90% of what the owner had hoped to get for it. How much did the owner get for the car? _____

4. A student read 70% of a book that contained 564 pages. How many pages did the student read? _____

5. At the beginning of the year, an investor deposited $1250 in the bank. After one year, its value was 106.5% of the original amount. How much was in the account at year's end? _____

NAME _____ CLASS _____ DATE _____

14-4 Finding the Percent Rate
UNIT 4

OBJECTIVE: Finding the percent rate, given one base number and a given percentage of that number

To answer the question at right, translate words into symbols. Then use division to find the unknown.

> **What percent of 80 is 15?**

EXAMPLE

a. What percent of 80 is 15?   b. 36 is what percent of 24?

Solution

a. Rephrase the question. Let p represent the unknown percent.
15 is what percent of 80? → $15 = p \times 80$

$$\frac{15}{80} = \frac{80p}{80}$$

$$\frac{1}{6} = p$$

Therefore, 15 is $16\frac{2}{3}\%$ of 80.

b. 36 is what percent of 24?
Let p represent the percent. → $36 = p \times 24$

$$\frac{36}{24} = \frac{24p}{24}$$

$$1.5 = p$$

Therefore, 36 is 150% of 24.

Find each percent.

1. What percent of 70 is 35? _____

2. What percent of 48 is 12? _____

3. What percent of 200 is 5? _____

4. What percent of 360 is 72? _____

5. What percent of 140 is 4.2? _____

6. What percent of 450 is 76.5? _____

7. 30 is what percent of 90? _____

8. 160 is what percent of 20? _____

9. 180 is what percent of 45? _____

10. 3 is what percent of 0.75? _____

11. 1.8 is what percent of 1.2? _____

12. 35 is what percent of 25? _____

13. What percent of $8\frac{3}{4}$ is 5.25? _____

14. $1\frac{4}{5}$ is what percent of 5.4? _____

15. What percent of $8\frac{3}{4}$ is $3\frac{1}{2}$? _____

16. $2\frac{1}{2}$ is what percent of $7\frac{1}{2}$? _____

Making Sense of Numbers   Unit 4   Ratio, Proportion and Percent

NAME _____ CLASS _____ DATE _____

14-5 Using Proportion to Find a Percent Rate
UNIT 4

OBJECTIVE: Finding a percent rate, given a percentage and a base number

To answer the question at right, you can write and solve a proportion.

What percent of 80 is 20?

EXAMPLE   a. What percent of 80 is 20?   b. 39 is what percent of 26?

▶ **Solution**

a. Write a proportion. Let p represent the part of 100.

$$\frac{\text{part}}{\text{whole}} \rightarrow \frac{20}{80} = \frac{p}{100} \leftarrow \frac{\text{part}}{\text{whole}}$$

$$80p = 20 \times 100$$
$$p = 25$$

Therefore, 20 is 25% of 80.

b. 39 is what percent of 26? Let p represent the part of 100.

$$\frac{39}{26} = \frac{p}{100}$$

$$26p = 39 \times 100$$

$$p = 150$$

Therefore, 39 is 150% of 26.

Use a proportion to find each percent.

1. What percent of 8 is 6? _____
2. What percent of 125 is 24? _____
3. What percent of 20 is 16? _____
4. What percent of 160 is 140? _____
5. What percent of 56 is 7? _____
6. What percent of 108 is 9? _____
7. What percent of 35 is 42? _____
8. What percent of 333 is 55.5? _____
9. 80 is what percent of 100? _____
10. 40 is what percent of 100? _____
11. 10.2 is what percent of 12? _____
12. 12 is what percent of 10.2? _____
13. 10 is what percent of 120? _____
14. 8 is what percent of 56.6? _____
15. What percent of $6\frac{1}{2}$ is $2\frac{3}{5}$? _____
16. $6\frac{1}{2}$ is what percent of $2\frac{3}{5}$? _____
17. What percent of $5\frac{1}{3}$ is $7\frac{1}{9}$? _____
18. $2\frac{3}{4}$ is what percent of $4\frac{1}{8}$? _____

142   Unit 4   Ratio, Proportion, and Percent   *Making Sense of Numbers*

NAME _____ CLASS _____ DATE _____

14-6 Solving Problems by Finding a Percent Rate
UNIT 4

OBJECTIVE: Finding a percent rate to solve real-world problems

You can use division to find a percent when you are given two known quantities.

EXAMPLE 1 A motorist drove 540 miles as part of a 720-mile trip. What percent of the trip has been completed?

Solution

Let p represent the percent of the trip that has been completed.

$$\frac{540}{720} = \frac{p}{100}$$

$$720p = 540 \times 100$$

The motorist has completed 75% of the trip.

$$p = 75$$

EXAMPLE 2 An investor intended to invest $1000 but instead invested $1200. What percent of his intended deposit did he actually invest?

Solution

Let p represent the percent of $1000 actually invested.

$$\frac{1200}{1000} = \frac{p}{100}$$

$$1000p = 1200 \times 100$$

The depositor invested 120% of what he or she planned to invest.

$$p = 120$$

Solve each problem.

1. An investor withdrew $450 from an account containing $800. What percent of the amount in the account was withdrawn? _____

2. In a survey of 750 people, 400 people expressed favor for a city proposal. What percent of those surveyed favored the plan? _____

3. A jogger planned to jog 10 miles but jogged 13 miles instead. What percent of the planned jog did the jogger actually do? _____

4. A recipe calls for 18 ounces of flour to serve 12 people. What percent of this amount should the cook use to serve 8 people? _____

5. A modeler expects a model rocket to achieve a maximum altitude of 480 feet. If the rocket achieves a maximum altitude of 520 feet, what percent of the expectation is this? _____

Making Sense of Numbers

NAME _____ CLASS _____ DATE _____

14-7 Finding a Base Number When its Percent Rate and Percentage Are Known

OBJECTIVE: Finding a base number when a percent rate and a percentage are known

To answer the question at right, translate words into symbols. Then solve.

> If 20% of an unknown number is 7, what is the number?

EXAMPLE If 20% of an unknown number is 7, what is the number?

▶ **Solution**

Let n represent the unknown number.   20% of n is 7 → $0.2n = 7$

Method 1: Write a decimal as a fraction.

$$\frac{1}{5}n = 7$$

$$5 \times \frac{1}{5}n = 5 \times 7$$

$$n = 35$$

Method 2: Divide by a decimal.

$$\frac{0.2n}{0.2} = \frac{7}{0.2}$$

$$n = 7 \div 0.2 = 7 \div \frac{1}{5} = 7 \times 5 = 35$$

Find each base number, n.

1. 20% of n is 5. _____
2. 50% of n is 10.5. _____
3. 75% of n is 15. _____
4. 40% of n is 24. _____
5. 80% of n is 80. _____
6. 100% of n is 13.6. _____
7. 120% of n is 5. _____
8. 150% of n is 9. _____
9. 200% of n is 100. _____
10. 130% of n is 3.9. _____
11. 140% of n is 49. _____
12. 155% of n is 18.6. _____
13. 0.5% of n is 0.6. _____
14. 0.2% of n is 0.6. _____
15. $33\frac{1}{3}$% of n is 20. _____
16. $12\frac{1}{2}$% of n is 18. _____
17. $16\frac{2}{3}$% of n is 12.6. _____
18. $62\frac{1}{2}$% of n is 132.5. _____
19. $66\frac{2}{3}$% of n is 12,444. _____
20. $37\frac{1}{2}$% of n is 18,333. _____
21. $112\frac{1}{2}$% of n is 312. _____
22. $133\frac{1}{3}$% of n is 768. _____

14-8 Using Proportion to Find a Base Number

UNIT 4

OBJECTIVE: Using proportion to find a base number when a percent rate and a percentage are known

To find a base number when a percent rate and a percentage are known, you can use a proportion as explained below.

EXAMPLE 1   120 is 25% of what base number?

▶ **Solution**

Let n represent the unknown base number.

$$\frac{\text{part}}{\text{whole}} \rightarrow \frac{120}{n} = \frac{25}{100} \leftarrow \frac{\text{part}}{\text{whole}}$$

$$25n = 120 \times 100$$

$$\frac{25n}{25} = \frac{120 \times 100}{25}$$

$$n = 480$$

EXAMPLE 2   120 is 125% of what base number?

▶ **Solution**

Let n represent the unknown base number.

$$\frac{\text{part}}{\text{whole}} \rightarrow \frac{120}{n} = \frac{125}{100} \leftarrow \frac{\text{part}}{\text{whole}}$$

$$125n = 120 \times 100$$

$$\frac{125n}{125} = \frac{120 \times 100}{125}$$

$$n = 96$$

Use a proportion to find each base number.

1. 180 is 75% of what number? _____
2. 27 is 60% of what number? _____
3. 4.8 is 10% of what number? _____
4. 81 is 90% of what number? _____
5. 4.8 is 30% of what number? _____
6. 108 is 45% of what number? _____
7. 5 is 125% of what number? _____
8. 5.4 is 150% of what number? _____
9. 14 is 175% of what number? _____
10. 33 is 110% of what number? _____
11. 1 is 2.5% of what number? _____
12. 7.55 is 12.5% of what number? _____

NAME _____ CLASS _____ DATE _____

14-9 Solving Problems by Finding a Base Number
UNIT 4

OBJECTIVE: Finding a base number when a percent rate is known in order to solve real-world problems

Often, you write and solve an equation to find a base number after a percent of it is taken and the resulting percentage is known.

EXAMPLE A coat sold for $145, which was 80% of its original price. What was the original price?

▶ **Solution**

1. Rephrase the question. $145 is 80% of what price?
2. Let p represent the original price. $145 is 80% of p.
3. Solve an equation. $145 = 0.8p$

$$145 = 0.8p$$
$$145 = \frac{4}{5}p$$
$$\frac{5}{4} \cdot 145 = \frac{5}{4} \cdot \frac{4}{5}p \quad \text{Multiply both sides of the equation}$$
$$181.25 = p \quad \text{by } \frac{5}{4}, \text{ the reciprocal of } \frac{4}{5}.$$

The original price of the coat was $181.25.

Solve each problem.

1. After 60% of a liquid was removed from a container, 330 milliliters remained. How much did the container originally have? _____

2. A motorist drove 356 miles and this distance represents 25% of the total trip. How long is the total trip? _____

3. A coat was sold for $165.50, which was 70% of its original price. What was the original price? _____

4. After one year, $1750 was in a bank account. This represents 105% of the initial deposit. How much was the initial deposit? _____

5. How much does a worker need to earn so that $724, which is 20% of the monthly salary, can be used to pay the monthly rent? _____

6. A store manager sold 36 pairs of shoes, which is 120% of the original quantity in stock. How many pairs were originally in stock? _____

7. According to a survey, 360 people own homes. If this number is 45% of those surveyed, how many people were in the survey altogether? _____

NAME _____ CLASS _____ DATE _____

15-1 Percent of Increase
UNIT 4

OBJECTIVE: Finding a percent to represent the increase from one amount to a greater amount

There are two ways you can find the percent by which one quantity is greater than a second quantity.

EXAMPLE

Find the percent of increase.
original weekly pay: $240   new weekly pay: $280

▶ **Solution**

Method 1: Divide the amount of increase by the original weekly pay.
$$\frac{\text{pay increase}}{\text{original pay}} \rightarrow \frac{280 - 250}{250} = \frac{30}{250} = \frac{3}{25} = \frac{12}{100} = 12\%$$

Method 2: Subtract 100% from the ratio of the new pay to the original pay.
$$\frac{280}{250} - 100\% = 1.12 - 100\% = 112\% - 100\% = 12\%$$

By either method, the percent of increase is 12%.

Find each percent of increase.

1. original weekly pay: $300   new weekly pay: $350   _____

2. original height: 24 inches   new height: 30 inches   _____

3. original weight: 10 pounds   new weight: 11 pounds   _____

4. original distance: 16 miles   new distance: 26 miles   _____

5. original price: $17.50   new price: $35   _____

6. original length: 10 inches   new length: 13.4 inches   _____

7. original price: $12.95   new price: $31.08   _____

8. original weight: 500 grams   new price: 654 grams   _____

9. original pay: $96   new pay: $110.40   _____

10. original altitude: 1360 feet   new altitude: 1428 feet   _____

11. original volume: 4 cubic feet   new volume: 6 cubic feet   _____

Making Sense of Numbers   Unit 4   Ratio, Proportion, and Percent

NAME _____ CLASS _____ DATE _____

15-2 Percent of Decrease
UNIT 4

OBJECTIVE: Finding a percent to represent the decrease from one amount to a smaller amount

There are two ways you can find the percent by which one quantity is less than a second quantity.

EXAMPLE Find the percent of decrease.
original altitude: 2000 feet   new altitude: 1600 feet

▶ **Solution**

Method 1: Divide the amount of decrease in altitude by the original altitude.

$$\frac{\text{altitude decrease}}{\text{original altitude}} \rightarrow \frac{2000 - 1600}{2000} = \frac{400}{2000} = \frac{1}{5} = 20\%$$

Method 2: Subtract the ratio of the new altitude to the original altitude from 100%.

$$100\% - \frac{1600}{2000} = 100\% - \frac{4}{5} = 100\% - 80\% = 20\%$$

By either method, the percent of decrease is 20%.

Find each percent of decrease.

1. original altitude: 2400 feet   new altitude: 1600 feet   _____

2. original depth: 20 inches   new depth: 18 inches   _____

3. original weight: 18 pounds   new weight: 16 pounds   _____

4. original price: $75   new price: $70   _____

5. original price: $12.50   new price: $10   _____

6. original length: 48 inches   new length: 12 inches   _____

7. original depth: 12 feet   new depth: 2 feet   _____

8. original pay: $960   new pay: $800   _____

9. original altitude: 6000 feet   new altitude: 1000 feet   _____

10. original volume: 6 cubic feet   new volume: 4.5 cubic feet   _____

11. original length: 1 foot 2 inches   new length: 7 inches   _____

NAME _____ CLASS _____ DATE _____

15-3 Calculating Tips and Total Cost

OBJECTIVE: *Finding an amount to leave for a tip and the total cost of a meal*

For service rendered, a customer may leave a *tip* when paying for a meal. A rule of thumb is to leave a tip that is 15% of the cost of the meal when service is done well.

EXAMPLE 1 Find the amount of the tip for a meal that costs $34.22. Assume that the tip is 15% of the cost.

▶ **Solution**
Method 1: Calculate 15% of 34.22.
  15% of 34.22 = 0.15 × 34.22 = 5.133
Method 2: Use $\frac{1}{7}$ and 35 as estimates of 15% and 34.22.
  $\frac{1}{7}$ of 35 = $\frac{1}{7}$ × 35 = 5
The value of the tip is $5.13, or about $5.

The total cost of a meal is the sum of the tip and the meal cost.

EXAMPLE 2 Find the total cost of the meal in Example 1.

▶ **Solution**
Method 1: Add $5.13 and $34.22.   5.13 + 34.22 = 39.35
Method 2: Add $5 and $35.00.   5 + 35 = 40
The total cost is $39.35, or about $40.00.

Assume the tip is 15%. Use 0.15 to find the actual amount of tip and total cost. Then use $\frac{1}{7}$ to estimate the tip and total cost.

1. $21.95 _____

2. $98.75 _____

3. $50.30 _____

4. $110.46 _____

5. $13.80 _____

6. $235.68 _____

7. $7.05 _____

Making Sense of Numbers   Unit 4 Ratio, Proportion, and Percent   **149**

15-4 Calculating Sales Tax and Total Cost

UNIT 4

OBJECTIVE: Finding the amount of sales tax and total cost including the amount of tax

In many states, consumers pay a tax on certain purchases. The tax is a fixed percent of the purchase price. In one state, the sales tax may be 5% of the cost of an item.

EXAMPLE 1 If the sales tax is 5%, find the amount of tax on a table that costs $495.50.

▶ **Solution**

To find the amount of tax, calculate 5% of $495.50.
$$5\% \text{ of } \$495.50 \rightarrow 0.05 \times 495.5 = 24.775$$
The amount of tax is $24.78.

The total cost of an item is the sum of the purchase price and the amount of tax. There are two ways to find total cost.

EXAMPLE 2 Find the total cost of the table in Example 1.

▶ **Solution**

Method 1: To find the total cost, add the purchase price and the amount of tax.
$495.50 + $24.78 = $520.28
Method 2: Multiply the cost of the table by 105%.
$$105\% \text{ of } \$495.50 \rightarrow 1.05 \times 495.5 = 520.275$$
By either method, the total cost is $520.28.

Find the amount of tax and total cost.

1. sales tax 6%; purchase price: $102.45 _____

2. sales tax 4%; purchase price: $329.90 _____

3. sales tax 6.5%; purchase price: $39.95 _____

4. sales tax 5%; purchase price: $1200.66 _____

5. sales tax 6%; purchase price: $4356.99 _____

6. sales tax 4%; purchase price: $5488.75 _____

7. sales tax 5.5%; purchase price: $6885.44 _____

NAME _____ CLASS _____ DATE _____

15-5 Solving Discount Problems
UNIT 4

OBJECTIVE: Finding the amount of discount and reduced sale price

To encourage consumers to buy a product, sellers may offer a *discount*, a reduction of the original price to a lower sale price.

EXAMPLE 1 A coat ordinarily sells for $238.45. If the price is reduced by 20%, find the amount of the discount.

▶ **Solution**
    20% of 238.45 → 0.2 × 238.45 = 47.69
The amount of the discount is $47.69.

To find the new sale price after discount, apply either Method 1 or Method 2 below.

EXAMPLE 2 Find the reduced sale price of the coat in Example 1.

▶ **Solution**
Method 1: Subtract dollar amounts.
    $238.45 − $47.69 = 190.76
Method 2: Calculate 80% of the original price.
    80% of 238.45 → 0.8 × 238.45 = 190.76
By either method, the reduced sale price is $190.76.

Use any method to find discount and reduced sale price.

1. 20%; $120 _____
2. 25%; $250 _____
3. 40%; $480 _____
4. 50%; $12.50 _____
5. 10%; $380.30 _____
6. 10%; $18.42 _____
7. 30%; $111.10 _____
8. 50%; $1000.00 _____
9. $33\frac{1}{3}$%; $330 _____
10. $12\frac{1}{2}$%; $560 _____
11. $16\frac{2}{3}$%; $360 _____
12. $66\frac{2}{3}$%; $150 _____
13. $14\frac{3}{5}$%; $420.70 _____
14. $83\frac{1}{3}$%; $720 _____
15. 20.5%; $268.50 _____
16. 18.5%; $337.80 _____

Making Sense of Numbers   Unit 4   Ratio, Proportion, and Percent   **151**

NAME _____ CLASS _____ DATE _____

15-6 Solving Successive Discount Problems
UNIT 4

OBJECTIVE: *Finding the result of applying one discount after another*

Often a seller may discount an item and then apply a second discount to the reduced sale price. This results in what is called *successive discounts*.

EXAMPLE A stereo system ordinarily sells for $485.49. A discount of 20% is applied and is followed by a 25% discount on the reduced price. Find the final selling price.

▶ **Solution**

First find the reduced sale price after applying the 20% discount.
$$485.49 - 0.2 \times 485.49 = 388.392$$
Then find the reduced sale price after applying the 25% discount to $388.39.
$$388.39 - 0.25 \times 388.39 = 291.2925$$
The final sale price is $291.29.

You can also solve the problem in the example by calculating the product below.
$$(100\% - 20\%)(100\% - 25\%) \times 485.49 = 0.8 \times 0.75 \times 485.49 = 291.29$$

Find the final selling price after the given successive discounts.

1. ordinary price: $312.50; 20% then 25%   _____

2. ordinary price: $420.50; 20% then 20%   _____

3. ordinary price: $685.40; 40% then 10%   _____

4. ordinary price: $788.70; 50% then 50%   _____

5. ordinary price: $248.10; 10% then 90%   _____

6. ordinary price: $56.10; $33\frac{1}{3}$% then 20%   _____

7. ordinary price: $66.50; $16\frac{2}{3}$% then 25%   _____

8. ordinary price: $186.40; $12\frac{1}{2}$% then $12\frac{1}{2}$%   _____

9. ordinary price: $1478.95; $14\frac{2}{7}$% then 40%   _____

NAME _____ CLASS _____ DATE _____

15-7 Solving Markup Problems
UNIT 4

OBJECTIVE: Finding the amount of markup and the new selling price

To pay expenses and make a profit, a seller will buy a product for one price, mark the price up, and sell the product for a higher price.

EXAMPLE 1 A store owner buys a product for $12.50 and marks the price up 60%. Find the amount of markup.

▶ **Solution**
Calculate 60% of 12.50. $0.6 \times 12.5 = 7.5$ or $\frac{3}{5} \times 12.5 = 7.5$
By either method, the amount of markup is $7.50.

To find the selling price after markup, add the amount of markup to the original price or multiply the original price by 100% plus the percent of markup.

EXAMPLE 2 Find the final selling price of the product in Example 1.

▶ **Solution**
Method 1: Add markup and original price.
    $7.50 + $12.50 = $20.00
Method 2: Multiply original price by 160%.
    160% of $12.50 = $1.6 \times 12.5 = 20$
By either method, the final selling price is $20.00.

Find the amount of markup and final selling price.

1. original price: $35.60; markup: 80%   _____

2. original price: $64.20; markup: 100%   _____

3. original price: $99.00; markup: 95%   _____

4. original price: $591.22; markup: 84%   _____

5. original price: $78.95; markup: 120%   _____

6. original price: $33.10; markup: 150%   _____

7. original price: $278.66; markup: $133\frac{1}{3}$%   _____

Making Sense of Numbers   Unit 4   Ratio, Proportion, and Percent

NAME _____ CLASS _____ DATE _____

15-8 Solving Simple Interest Problems
UNIT 4

OBJECTIVE: Finding the amount of simple interest earned and total deposit accumulation

A bank pays a depositor a certain percent for the use of the depositor's money. The amount paid the depositor is called *interest*. If the percent is applied only to the amount of deposit, the interest is called *simple interest*.

> **Simple Interest Formulas**
>
> Let P represent the initial deposit, r represent the interest rate as a decimal, t represent the number of years the money is on deposit, and A represent the sum of the deposit and interest earned.
>
> $$I = Prt \qquad A = P(1 + rt)$$

EXAMPLE

An investor deposits $1200 into an account that pays 5% simple interest. Find the amount of interest earned over 1.5 years and the final amount in the account.

▶ **Solution**

interest: $I = Prt = 1200 \times 0.05 \times 1.5 = 90$
amount: $A = P(1 + rt) = 1200(1 + 0.05 \times 1.5) = 1290$
The deposit earns $90 and the final amount will be $1290.

Find the amount of interest earned and the final amount.

1. $P = \$1180$, $r = 6\%$, and $t = 2$ years $I = $ _____ $A = $ _____

2. $P = \$1350$, $r = 6\%$, and $t = 2.4$ years $I = $ _____ $A = $ _____

3. $P = \$5000$, $r = 6.5\%$, and $t = 1.75$ years $I = $ _____ $A = $ _____

4. $P = \$10{,}000$, $r = 6.2\%$, and $t = 1.8$ years $I = $ _____ $A = $ _____

5. $P = \$7500$, $r = 5.25\%$, and $t = 1.3$ years $I = $ _____ $A = $ _____

6. $P = \$11{,}580$, $r = 6.8\%$, and $t = 10.5$ years $I = $ _____ $A = $ _____

7. $P = \$1180$, $r = 6\%$, and $t = 2.5$ years $I = $ _____ $A = $ _____

8. $P = \$3360$, $r = 6.3\%$, and $t = 3\frac{1}{4}$ years $I = $ _____ $A = $ _____

9. $P = \$2450$, $r = 5\frac{1}{4}\%$, and $t = 1\frac{3}{4}$ years $I = $ _____ $A = $ _____

NAME _____ CLASS _____ DATE _____

Solving Compound Interest Problems

UNIT 4

OBJECTIVE: Finding the amount in an account after compound interest is applied

A bank pays a depositor a certain percent for the use of the depositor's money. The amount paid to the depositor is called *interest*. If the interest rate is applied to the amount of deposit and current interest earned, the interest is called *compound interest*.

> **Compound-Interest Formula**
>
> Let P represent initial deposit, r represent the interest rate as a decimal, t represent the number of years money is on deposit, and A represent the sum of the deposit and interest earned.
>
> $$A = P(1 + r)^t$$

EXAMPLE   An investor deposits $1600 into an account that pays 5% compound interest. Find the amount in the account after 2 years.

▶ **Solution**

Apply the compound-interest formula.
$A = P(1 + r)^t = 1600(1 + 0.05)^2 = 1600(1.05)^2 = 1764$
After 2 years, the account will contain $1764.

Find the amount, A, in the account that earns compound interest.

1. $P = \$1000$, $r = 5\%$, and $t = 1$ year   _____

2. $P = \$1200$, $r = 6\%$, and $t = 2$ years   _____

3. $P = \$5000$, $r = 6\%$, and $t = 3$ years   _____

4. $P = \$10{,}000$, $r = 4\%$, and $t = 4$ years   _____

5. $P = \$7500$, $r = 4.25\%$, and $t = 2$ years   _____

6. $P = \$12{,}000$, $r = 6.8\%$, and $t = 1$ year   _____

7. $P = \$5400$, $r = 6\%$, and $t = 4$ years   _____

8. $P = \$2260$, $r = 6.6\%$, and $t = 1$ year   _____

9. $P = \$4000$, $r = 5\frac{1}{2}\%$, and $t = 2$ years   _____

10. $P = \$3550$, $r = 4\frac{1}{4}\%$, and $t = 2$ years   _____

Making Sense of Numbers   Unit 4 Ratio, Proportion, and Percent   **155**

NAME _____ CLASS _____ DATE _____

15-10 Solving Commission Problems
UNIT 4

OBJECTIVE: *Finding commission and total pay*

Many people sell goods and receive a percent of the amount sold as income. This percent of amount sold is called *commission*. Some people earn a combination of salary and commission.

> **EXAMPLE**
>
> Find the total pay for each salesperson.
> a. commission of 5.5% on $108,500 sold
> b. $600 per month plus 3.5% on $108,500 sold that month
>
> ▶ **Solution**
>
> a. Calculate 5.5% of 108,500. $0.055 \times 108,500 = 5967.50$
>   Total pay is $5967.50.
> b. Add 600 to 3.5% of 108,500. $600 + 0.035 \times 108,500 = 4397.50$
>   Total pay is $4397.50.

Find the total pay.

1. commission of 4.5% on $222,500 sold   _____

2. commission of 1.5% on $456,500 sold   _____

3. commission of 2.5% on $133,600 sold   _____

4. commission of 3.55% on $1,450,600 sold   _____

5. commission of 5.5% on $108,500 sold   _____

6. commission of $3\frac{1}{4}$% on $448,100 sold   _____

7. $700 per month plus 1.25% on $96,400 sold that month   _____

8. $450 per month plus 1.4% on $85,000 sold that month   _____

9. $360 per month plus 2.45% on $92,050 sold that month   _____

10. $510 per month plus $1\frac{3}{5}$% on $81,020 sold that month   _____

11. $360 per month plus $2\frac{5}{8}$% on $73,520 sold that month   _____

12. $245.50 per month plus $1\frac{7}{8}$% on $64,880 sold that month   _____

13. $198.75 per month plus $2\frac{1}{5}$% on $45,550 sold that month   _____

156   Unit 4   Ratio, Proportion, and Percent   *Making Sense of Numbers*

NAME _____ CLASS _____ DATE _____

15-11 Finding Probabilities
UNIT 4

OBJECTIVE: Finding the probability of an event and how many occurrences of an event can be expected

Probability is a measure of the likelihood that some *event* will happen.

EXAMPLE 1

A bag contains 5 black marbles, 12 blue marbles, 17 red marbles, and 2 white marbles. If one marble is chosen at random, find the probability that the marble is blue.

▶ **Solution**

In all, there are 5 + 12 + 17 + 2, or 36 marbles. There are 12 blue marbles in the bag of 36 marbles.

$$\text{probability of choosing blue} \rightarrow \frac{12}{36} = \frac{1}{3}$$

The probability of choosing blue is 1 out of 3, or $33\frac{1}{3}\%$.

Using multiplication, you can predict the number of times a blue marble might be selected.

EXAMPLE 2

Refer to Example 1. In this experiment, one trial consists of choosing a marble and then replacing it. If a marble is chosen and then replaced, how many times might blue be chosen in 150 trials?

▶ **Solution**

If the probability of choosing blue is 1 out of 3, then you can expect to choose blue one-third of 150 times, or 50 times.

$$\frac{1}{3} \times 150$$

Find the probability of choosing the specified marble from a bag. Write each probability as a fraction in lowest terms.

1. 13 black, 11 blue, 6 red, and 10 white marbles; red _____

2. 42 black, 18 blue, 7 red, and 13 white marbles; black _____

3. 17 black, 18 blue, 15 red, and 30 white marbles; blue _____

4. 24 black, 18 blue, 18 red, and 18 white marbles; white _____

Predict the number of occurrences for each number of trials.

5. 100 trials, Exercise 1 _____   6. 160 trials, Exercise 2 _____

7. 320 trials, Exercise 3 _____   8. 403 trials, Exercise 4 _____

Making Sense of Numbers

Unit 5 Integers

Chapter 16 Integer Fundamentals
- **16-1** Positive and Negative Numbers 161
- **16-2** Comparing and Ordering Integers 162
- **16-3** Finding Opposites and Absolute Values 163

Chapter 17 Addition of Integers
- **17-1** Adding Two Integers With Like Signs 164
- **17-2** Adding Two Integers With Unlike Signs 165
- **17-3** Adding Three or More Integers 166
- **17-4** Solving Problems Involving Integer Addition 167

Chapter 18 Subtraction of Integers
- **18-1** Subtracting Integers 168
- **18-2** Solving Problems Involving Integer Subtraction 169
- **18-3** Adding and Subtracting With Integers 170

Chapter 19 Multiplication of Integers
- **19-1** Multiplying Integers 171
- **19-2** Adding, Subtracting, and Multiplying With Integers 172
- **19-3** Solving Problems Involving Integer Multiplication 173

Chapter 20 Division of Integers
- **20-1** Dividing Integers 174
- **20-2** Solving Problems Involving Integer Division 175
- **20-3** Adding, Subtracting, Multiplying, and Dividing With Integers 176

Making Sense of Numbers

Unit Five

16-1 Positive and Negative Numbers

UNIT 5

OBJECTIVE: Writing positive and negative numbers in various situations

In many situations, a quantity is represented by a positive number or a negative number. The symbols (+) and (−) are used to designate positive and negative numbers, respectively.

EXAMPLE 1 Represent each situation by a positive or negative number.
a. a decrease of 5 degrees   b. a gift of $7   c. a debt of $11

▶ **Solution**

a. The decrease is represented by −5.
b. The gift of $7 is represented by +7, or simply 7.
c. The debt is represented by −11.

Positive numbers and negative numbers can be represented on a number line. Positive numbers are represented as points to the right of 0 and negative numbers are represented as points to the left of 0.

EXAMPLE 2 Represent each number on a number line.   a. −4   b. −2   c. 0   d. 4

▶ **Solution**

Sketch a diagram like the following. This is a number line.

To place 4 on the number line, put a dot at the tick that is 4 units to the right of 0. The number line below shows −4, −2, 0, and 4.

Represent each situation by a positive or negative number.

1. forward 7 steps _____   2. backward 7 steps _____

3. up 11 feet _____   4. down 18 miles _____

5. a loss of $112 _____   6. a gain of 196 points _____

Represent each number on the given number line below.

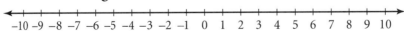

7. −7   8. −3   9. 7   10. −1   11. 2   12. −8

13. −2   14. 10   15. −9   16. −6   17. 1   18. 9

Making Sense of Numbers   Unit 5 Integers   **161**

NAME _____ CLASS _____ DATE _____

16-2 Comparing and Ordering Integers
UNIT 5

OBJECTIVE: *Comparing two integers and writing a list of integers in order from least to greatest*

An *integer* is any number in the list . . . . , −3, −2, −1, 0, 1, 2, 3, 4, ... All counting numbers and 0 are integers.

Recall that when you compare two numbers, you decide which number is greater than (>) the other and which number is less than (<) the other. Just as you can compare two counting numbers, you can compare two integers.

EXAMPLE 1 Write < or > to complete each comparison.
a. −5 __?__ 2   b. −1 __?__ −4

▶ **Solution**
Use a number line.

a.

−5 −4 −3 −2 −1 0 1 2 3 4

−5 is to the left of 2.   −5 < 2

b.

−5 −4 −3 −2 −1 0 1 2 3 4

−1 is to the right of −4.   −1 > −4

Recall that when you order a list of numbers, you often write a new list with the numbers written from least to greatest.

EXAMPLE 2 Write −4, 3, 4, 0, −2, and 5 in order from least to greatest.

▶ **Solution**
Use a number line.

−5 −4 −3 −2 −1 0 1 2 3 4 5

Use sorting.

negative   0   positive
−4 −2   0   3 4 5

In order from least to greatest, the list is −4, −2, 0, 3, 4, and 5.

Write < or > to complete each comparison.

1. −7 ____ 0   2. −113 ____ −73   3. −11 ____ −17   4. 23 ____ 0

Write each list of integers in order from least to greatest.

5. −5, 6, 7, −4, 0, −6 _____   6. 18, −18, 7, 0, −4, −5 _____

7. 11, 5, 4, −4, −5, −11 _____   8. 7, −3, −4, −2, 0, 3, 6 _____

9. −6, 3, 0, 2, −7, 8, −10 _____   10. 3, 100, −200, 6, −543 _____

162   Unit 5   Integers   *Making Sense of Numbers*

NAME _____ CLASS _____ DATE _____

16-3 Finding Opposites and Absolute Values
UNIT 5

OBJECTIVE: *Finding the opposite and absolute value of an integer*

Every integer has an *opposite*, or additive inverse.

-3 is the opposite of 3.   3 is the opposite of -3.

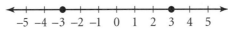

EXAMPLE 1 Find the opposite of each integer.   a. 4   b. -7 c. 0

> **Solution**
> a. opposite of 4: -4 b. opposite of -7: 7   c. opposite of 0: 0

The *absolute value* of a number x, denoted $|x|$, is the distance between x and 0 on the number line.

The absolute value of -4 is 4.   The absolute value of 4 is 4.

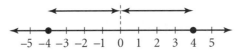

EXAMPLE 2 Find the absolute value of each integer.   a. 5   b. -6

> **Solution**
> a. The graph of 5 on the number line is 5 units to the right of 0. Therefore, the absolute value of 5 is 5. $|5| = 5$
>
> b. The graph of -6 on the number line is 6 units to the left of 0. Therefore, the absolute value of -6 is 6. $|-6| = 6$

Find the opposite and the absolute value of each integer.

1. 7 _____   2. -7 _____   3. -4 _____

4. -100 _____   5. 24 _____   6. 10 _____

7. 45 _____   8. 54 _____   9. 33 _____

10. 5 _____   11. 19 _____   12. -35 _____

13. -99 _____   14. -20 _____   15. 44 _____

16. -71 _____   17. 133 _____   18. 89 _____

19. 1237 _____   20. -1800 _____   21. -39 _____

22. 26 _____   23. 15,333 _____   24. 51 _____

Making Sense of Numbers

NAME _____ CLASS _____ DATE _____

17-1 Adding Two Integers With Like Signs

UNIT 5

OBJECTIVE: *Finding the sum of two integers that have like signs*

You can use a number line to add two integers.

EXAMPLE 1 Use a number line to find the sum $-3 + (-4)$.

▶ **Solution**

Draw an arrow from 0 to -3 on the number line. Starting at -3, draw an arrow pointing left and 4 units long. The sum is -7.

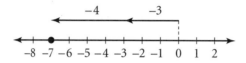

You can use the following rule to add two integers with like signs.

To add two integers with like signs:
1. Find the absolute value of each integer.
2. Add absolute values.
3. Attach the sign of both integers.

EXAMPLE 2 Find each sum.   a. $-11 + (-12)$ b. $8 + 13$

▶ **Solution**

a. Add 11 and 12 to get 23. Since both numbers are negative, the sum is negative. Therefore, $-11 + (-12) = -23$.
b. Add 8 and 13 to get 21. Since both numbers are positive, $8 + 13 = 21$.

Add by using the number line method from Example 1 or the rule from Example 2.

1. $-5 + (-6)$ _____
2. $7 + 11$ _____
3. $17 + 0$ _____
4. $0 + 21$ _____

5. $100 + 1$ _____
6. $-8 + (-8)$ _____
7. $7 + 35$ _____
8. $-7 + (-7)$ _____

9. $-45 + (-8)$ _____
10. $-2 + (-11)$ _____
11. $-9 + (-9)$ _____

12. $-6 + (-14)$ _____
13. $-5 + (-5)$ _____
14. $-1 + (-11)$ _____

15. $-8 + (-15)$ _____
16. $-76 + (-184)$ _____
17. $-102 + (-67)$ _____

164   Unit 5   Integers   *Making Sense of Numbers*

NAME _____ CLASS _____ DATE _____

17-2 Adding Two Integers With Unlike Signs
UNIT 5

OBJECTIVE: *Finding the sum of two integers when they have unlike signs*

You can use a number line to add two integers with unlike signs.

EXAMPLE 1   Use a number line to find the sum $-4 + 9$.

▶ **Solution**

Draw an arrow from 0 to -4 on the number line. Starting at -4, draw an arrow pointing right and 9 units long. The sum is 5.

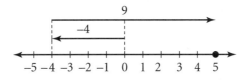

You can use the following rule to add two integers with unlike signs.

To add two integers with unlike signs:

1. Find the absolute value of each integer.
2. Subtract the smaller absolute value from the larger one.
3. Attach the sign of the number with greater absolute value.

EXAMPLE 2   Find each sum.   a. $11 + (-19)$ b. $-18 + 23$

▶ **Solution**

a. Subtract the absolute value of 11 from
the absolute value of -19. $19 - 11 = 8$
Since -19 has the greater absolute value,
the sum will be negative. $11 + (-19) = -8$

b. Subtract the absolute value of 18 from
the absolute value of -23. $23 - 18 = 5$
Since 23 has the greater absolute value,
the sum will be positive. $-18 + 23 = 5$

Add.

1. $-18 + 98$ _____
2. $17 + (-75)$ _____
3. $-125 + 125$ _____

4. $17 + (-18)$ _____
5. $18 + (-88)$ _____
6. $111 + (-111)$ _____

7. $20 + (-200)$ _____
8. $13 + (-17)$ _____
9. $-65 + 66$ _____

Making Sense of Numbers   Unit 5   Integers   **165**

17-3 Adding Three or More Integers

UNIT 5

OBJECTIVE: Finding the sum of three or more integers

To find the sum of three or more integers, follow the order of operations.

EXAMPLE 1 Add $-12 + 15 + (-7)$.

Solution

$-12 + 15 + (-7) = 3 + (-7)$ Add: $-12 + 15$
$ = -4$ Add: $3 + (-7)$

To find the sum of three or more integers, you can rearrange the numbers in the sum. Group the positive numbers and the negative numbers as illustrated in Example 2.

EXAMPLE 2 Add $-11 + 5 + (-1) + 3$.

Solution

$-11 + 5 + (-1) + 3 = -11 + (-1) + 5 + 3$ Group negative numbers. Group positive numbers.
$ = -12 + 8$ Add numbers in each group.
$ = -4$

Add.

1. $-2 + 3 + (-4)$ _____
2. $-15 + 15 + (-7)$ _____
3. $42 + 30 + (-100)$ _____
4. $-12 + 13 + (-12)$ _____
5. $-15 + (-15) + (-7)$ _____
6. $32 + 30 + (-100)$ _____
7. $12 + (-13) + (-1)$ _____
8. $-37 + 0 + (-37)$ _____
9. $2 + 0 + (-2)$ _____
10. $-8 + 18 + (-10)$ _____
11. $35 + 35 + (-57)$ _____
12. $-2 + (-20) + (-83)$ _____
13. $-7 + 8 + (-5)$ _____
14. $-13 + 19 + 47$ _____
15. $-89 + (-7) + (-13)$ _____
16. $7 + (-8) + 11 + 10 + (-3)$ _____
17. $-6 + (-18) + (-1) + 13$ _____
18. $-7 + (-7) + 7 + 7 + (-11)$ _____

NAME _____ CLASS _____ DATE _____

17-4 Solving Problems Involving Integer Addition
UNIT 5

OBJECTIVE: Using addition of integers to solve real-world problems

Addition of integers often plays a role in solving problems involving net increase or decrease in some quantity.

EXAMPLE 1 At regular intervals between 9:00 A.M. and 2:00 P.M., the following temperature changes in degrees Fahrenheit were recorded.

$$2°F, -3°F, 1°F, 3°F, -1°F, -1°F$$

What was the net change in temperature from 9:00 A.M. to 2:00 P.M.?

▶ **Solution**

Find the sum: $2 + (-3) + 1 + 3 + (-1) + (-1) = 1$
The temperature at 2:00 P.M. was 1°F warmer than at 9:00 A.M.

EXAMPLE 2 The table below shows deposits and withdrawals from a checking account. Find the net change in the account's balance.

deposits	$350	$229	$367
withdrawals	$135	$980	$136

▶ **Solution**

Add deposits, add withdrawals, and then subtract withdrawals from deposits.

$(350 + 229 + 367) - (135 + 980 + 136) = 946 - 1251 = -305$

There was a net decrease of $305.

Find each net change.

1. changes in temperature (°F): 2, −3, 1, 3, −1   _____

2. deposits: $235, $398; withdrawals: $220, $144, $18, $180   _____

3. changes in depth (inches): 3, −3, −4, 5, 4, 6, −11   _____

4. changes in volume (cubic inches): 11, −10, −20, −31 −45, −56   _____

5. changes in area (square feet): 131, −100, −100, −128, 450   _____

6. changes in population (millions): 11, −10, −1, 8, 10, 12   _____

7. changes in inventory (dozens): 17, −16, 18, −20, 22, 23   _____

Making Sense of Numbers

NAME _____ CLASS _____ DATE _____

18-1 Subtracting Integers
UNIT 5

OBJECTIVE: *Finding the difference when one integer is subtracted from another*

The subtraction of one number, b, from another number, a, is defined in terms of addition. To subtract b from a, add the opposite of b to a.

$$\underset{\text{subtraction}}{a - b} = \underset{\text{addition}}{a \;+} \;\underset{\text{opposite of }b}{(-b)}$$

To subtract one integer from another integer, rewrite the subtraction expression as an addition expression, and then add.

EXAMPLE Find each difference. a. $7 - 12$ b. $18 - (-17)$ c. $-14 - (-15)$

Solution

a. $7 - 12 = 7 + (-12)$ Rewrite subtraction as addition.
            $= -5$ The opposite of 12 is -12.
                              Add -12 to 7.

b. $18 - (-17) = 18 + 17$ Rewrite subtraction as addition.
              $= 35$ The opposite of -17 is 17.
                              Add 17 to 18.

c. $-14 - (-15) = -14 + 15$ Rewrite subtraction as addition.
               $= 1$ The opposite of -15 is 15.
                              Add 15 to -14.

Find each difference.

1. $1 - 3$ _____
2. $7 - 18$ _____
3. $-10 - 22$ _____

4. $-15 - 15$ _____
5. $3 - (-4)$ _____
6. $-8 - (-12)$ _____

7. $-9 - (-3)$ _____
8. $-19 - (-5)$ _____
9. $100 - 101$ _____

10. $230 - 424$ _____
11. $154 - 245$ _____
12. $777 - 888$ _____

13. $108 - (-81)$ _____
14. $303 - (-303)$ _____
15. $-111 - (-608)$ _____

16. $100 - 200$ _____
17. $-171 - 281$ _____
18. $-245 - (-245)$ _____

19. $389 - 389$ _____
20. $1459 - 1459$ _____
21. $134 - (-134)$ _____

NAME _____ CLASS _____ DATE _____

18-2 Solving Problems Involving Integer Subtraction
UNIT 5

OBJECTIVE: Finding the difference when one integer is taken from another to solve real-world problems

Subtraction of integers plays a role in solving many real-world problems. You may need to interpret the answer.

EXAMPLE 1 A customer orders 18 computer games from a store that has 12 games on hand. How many games must the store order to meet the demand?

▶ **Solution**

Take 18 games from 12 games on hand.
  Subtract. $12 - 18 = -6$
The store manager must order 6 games to meet the demand.

EXAMPLE 2 On a cold day, the temperature at 3:00 A.M. was 34°F. By 4:00 A.M., the temperature had dropped 4°F. How much below freezing (32°F) was the temperature at 4:00 A.M.?

▶ **Solution**

temperature at 4:00 A.M.: $34°F - 4°F = 30°F$

Subtract 32°F from 30°F. $30°F - 32°F = -2°F$
At 4:00 A.M. the temperature was 2°F below freezing.

Solve each problem.

1. How many refrigerators must a manager order if the store has 13 refrigerators on hand and a customer wants 20 refrigerators? _____

2. A diving bird on a cliff 400 feet above sea level dives 415 feet to catch a fish. How far below the surface of the water is the fish? _____

3. A rocket fired upward from a cliff ascended 320 feet, descended 412 feet, and then hit the ground. How tall is the cliff? _____

4. A bank customer tried to withdraw $368 from an account containing $250. Use subtraction to show that the withdrawal cannot be made. _____

Making Sense of Numbers

NAME _____ CLASS _____ DATE _____

18-3 Adding and Subtracting With Integers
UNIT 5

OBJECTIVE: Simplifying an expression involving both addition and subtraction of integers

To find the value of an expression involving both addition and subtraction of integers, follow the order of operations.

EXAMPLE 1 Simplify $-17 + 6 + (-7) + 13$.

Solution

Method 1: Use the order of operations.
$$-17 + 6 + (-7) + 13 = -11 + (-7) + 13 \quad \text{Add: } -17 + 6 = -11$$
$$= -18 + 13 \quad \text{Add: } -11 + (-7) = -18$$
$$= -5$$

Method 2: Group -17 and -7. Group 6 and 13.
$$-17 + 6 + (-7) + 13 = -17 + (-7) + 6 + 13$$
$$= -24 + 19$$
$$= -5$$

Remember to simplify any expressions within parentheses first.

EXAMPLE 2 Simplify $-[12 + (-15)] - [7 - (12)]$.

Solution

$$-[12 + (-15)] - (7 - 12) = -(-3) - (7 - 12) \quad 12 + (-15) = -3$$
$$= -(-3) - (-5) \quad 7 - 12 = -5$$
$$= 3 + 5 \quad -(-3) = 3$$
$$= 8$$

Simplify.

1. $-5 + 6 - (-7)$ _____

2. $10 - 13 - [2 + (-4)]$ _____

3. $-[-3 + (-24) - 30]$ _____

4. $-5 + 6 - (2 - 7)$ _____

5. $-9 - (-9) - (-3 + 7)$ _____

6. $10 - (-10) - 18 + 1$ _____

7. $-5 + 9 + 5 - 9$ _____

8. $-(4 - 7) - (-2 + 3)$ _____

9. $7 + (-8) - (-5 - 1)$ _____

10. $12 - [-2 - (-3)]$ _____

11. $-[-7 - (-7)]$ _____

12. $3 + (-11) + 11$ _____

13. $10 - [2 + (-5)]$ _____

14. $-[3 - (-5)] - (-3)$ _____

170 Unit 5 Integers

Making Sense of Numbers

NAME _____ CLASS _____ DATE _____

19-1 Multiplying Integers
UNIT 5

OBJECTIVE: *Finding the product of two integers*

When finding the product of two integers, there are three possibilities.

- The factors have like signs. The product will be positive.
- The factors have unlike signs. The product will be negative.
- The product of 0 and any integer is 0.

To multiply, find the product as if both factors were positive. Then decide whether the product is positive, negative, or zero.

EXAMPLE 1 Multiply: **a.** -7×4 **b.** $(-7)(-9)$ **c.** 0×24

Solution

a. $7 \times 4 = 28$ unlike signs   Therefore, $-7 \times 4 = -28$.
b. $7 \times 9 = 63$ like signs   Therefore, $(-7)(-9) = 63$.
c. $0 \times 24 = 0$ the product of zero and any integer is zero

You can multiply three or more integers using the rules above.

EXAMPLE 2 Multiply: $5(-2)(-3)$

Solution

$5(-2)(-3) = (-10)(-3)$ $5(-2) = -10$
$ = 30$ $(-10)(-3) = 30$

Multiply.

1. 7×8 _____
2. 1×8 _____
3. 11×0 _____

4. $0 \times (-20)$ _____
5. $-7 \times (-7)$ _____
6. $-6 \times (-12)$ _____

7. -10×20 _____
8. -6×13 _____
9. $9 \times (-9)$ _____

10. $2 \times (-46)$ _____
11. $(-11)^2$ _____
12. $(-12)^2$ _____

13. -4×4 _____
14. $4 \times (-4)$ _____
15. $-(-5)^2$ _____

16. $(-2) \times 5 \times (-3)$ _____
17. $(-4) \times (-4) \times (-5)$ _____

18. $6 \times (-2) \times (-3)$ _____
19. $(-6) \times 1 \times (-7)$ _____

20. $(-3) \times (-2) \times 11$ _____
21. $(-3)^2(-2)^2$ _____

Making Sense of Numbers

NAME _____ CLASS _____ DATE _____

19-2 Adding, Subtracting, and Multiplying With Integers
UNIT 5

OBJECTIVE: Simplifying an expression involving addition, subtraction, and multiplication with integers

To simplify an expression involving multiple operations with integers, follow the order of operations.

EXAMPLE 1 Simplify $-3[4-(-5)]$.

Solution

$$
\begin{aligned}
-3[4-(-5)] &= -3(4+5) \quad &\text{Work within parentheses first.} \\
&= -3(9) \quad &\text{Add.} \\
&= -27 \quad &\text{Multiply.}
\end{aligned}
$$

EXAMPLE 2 Simplify $2[4+(-7)] - 5(-3-1)^2$.

Solution

$$
\begin{aligned}
2[4+(-7)]-5(-3-1) &= 2(-3)-5(-4)^2 \quad &\text{Work within parentheses.} \\
&= -6-80 \quad &\text{Multiply.} \\
&= -86 \quad &\text{Subtract.}
\end{aligned}
$$

Simplify.

1. $3(-4+5)$ _____
2. $-4(1-7)$ _____
3. $6(-3+7)$ _____

4. $5(-6-6)$ _____
5. $7(-8+5)$ _____
6. $-10(-10+10)$ _____

7. $3-2(7-11)$ _____
8. $-10-4(-4+4)$ _____
9. $17+2(-7-7)$ _____

10. $-6[-3+(-3)]+7[-3+(-4)]$ _____
11. $-2(5-7)-2(7-5)+2(-5+7)$ _____

12. $3(-5+4)^2+(-5-1)^2+3(7-8)^2$ _____
13. $3(1+4)^2-(-1-1)^2-3(3-3)^2$ _____

14. $[4+(-5)-7+5]^2$ _____
15. $(-3-5-1-1)^2$ _____

16. $[1+(-1)-1+4]^2-(5-5)^2$ _____
17. $[8+(-8)-1+1]^2+(-2-5)^2$ _____

18. $(-4)^2+(-2)^3+(-1)^3+(-2)^3$ _____
19. $(-5)^2-(-5)^3+(-1)^3-(-1)^3$ _____

20. $[-6+(-8)]^2[-4-(-6)]^2$ _____
21. $[4-(-1)]^2[-7+(-2)]^2$ _____

22. $[-2+(-7)]^2[-3-(-5)]^2+(-1)$ _____
23. $[-1-(-1)]^3[-1-(-1)]^2-(-1)$ _____

19-3 Solving Problems Involving Integer Multiplication

UNIT 5

OBJECTIVE: Using multiplication of integers to solve real-world problems

You can use multiplication of integers to solve problems involving gains and losses.

EXAMPLE 1 On six separate occasions, a bank customer withdrew $50 and made no deposits. What was the net change in the customer's balance?

▶ **Solution**

Represent the withdrawal as -50. To find the net change, multiply.
$$6(-50) = -300$$
The net change is a decrease of $300 in the customer's balance.

EXAMPLE 2 Five customers each ordered 4 boxes of light bulbs from a supplier that had 18 boxes on hand. How many boxes must the supplier order to meet demand?

▶ **Solution**

boxes needed for customers: $5 \times 4 = 20$
supplier shortage: $20 - 18 = -2$
The supplier needs to order 2 boxes of light bulbs.

Solve each problem.

1. A technician decreased the temperature in a storage room by 25°F each hour for 3 hours. If the temperature initially was 64°F, what was the temperature 3 hours after the decrease was started? _____

2. Six customers each ordered 16 boxes of light bulbs from a supplier that had 90 boxes on hand. How many boxes must the supplier order to meet demand? _____

3. A technician decreased the temperature of a reaction as below.

after hour:	1	2	3	4	5	6
change:	−3°F	−3°F	−3°F	−4°F	−4°F	−4°F

Initial temperature was 33°F. Find the final temperature. _____

4. Rework Exercise 3 using the temperatures below.
   −3°F, −4°F, −3°F, −4°F, −3°F, −3°F, −5°F, −5°F, −5°F _____

Making Sense of Numbers

20-1 Dividing Integers

UNIT 5

OBJECTIVE: Finding the quotient when one integer is divided by another

Recall that division can appear in the two forms shown below.

$$\text{dividend} \div \text{divisor} \qquad \frac{\text{dividend}}{\text{divisor}}$$

When finding the quotient of two integers, there are three possibilities.

- The dividend and divisor have like signs. The quotient will be positive.
- The dividend and divisor have unlike signs. The quotient will be negative.
- The number 0 divided by any nonzero number is 0.

To divide, find the quotient as if both dividend and divisor were positive. Then decide whether the quotient is positive, negative, or zero.

EXAMPLE Divide: a. $-42 \div 7$ b. $42 \div 7$ c. $\frac{-84}{-4}$ d. $\frac{0}{12}$

Solution

a. $42 \div 7 = 6$ unlike signs   Therefore, $-42 \div 7 = -6$.
b. $42 \div 7$ like signs   Therefore, $42 \div 7 = 6$.
c. $\frac{84}{4} = 21$ like signs   Therefore, $\frac{-84}{-4} = 21$.
d. $\frac{0}{12} = 0$ zero divided by any nonzero number is zero

Divide.

1. $-60 \div 10$ _____
2. $-72 \div (-36)$ _____
3. $-35 \div 5$ _____

4. $144 \div 12$ _____
5. $\frac{-34}{17}$ _____
6. $\frac{-45}{-5}$ _____

7. $\frac{48}{-6}$ _____
8. $\frac{-39}{13}$ _____
9. $\frac{600}{60}$ _____

10. $\frac{625}{-25}$ _____
11. $\frac{-169}{-13}$ _____
12. $\frac{98}{-49}$ _____

13. $-120 \div (-12)$ _____
14. $-12 \div (-12)$ _____
15. $0 \div (-11)$ _____

16. $0 \div 1000$ _____
17. $\frac{0}{-3}$ _____
18. $\frac{0}{143}$ _____

19. $\frac{-1024}{64}$ _____
20. $\frac{-49}{-49}$ _____
21. $98 \div 14$ _____

NAME _____ CLASS _____ DATE _____

20-2 Solving Problems Involving Integer Division
UNIT 5

OBJECTIVE: *Finding the quotient of two integers to help solve real-world problems*

Division of integers occurs in problems involving distribution of some quantity.

EXAMPLE 1 A pilot wants to descend 1200 feet in 3 minutes. If descent is constant, how far will the pilot descend in 1 minute?

▶ **Solution**

Represent the descent as -1200 feet. Divide by time, 3 minutes.

$$\frac{\text{descent}}{\text{time}} \rightarrow \frac{-1200}{3} = -400$$

The pilot will descend 400 feet per minute.

EXAMPLE 2 A technician wants to remove 640 milliliters of solution from a container and put four equal amounts of it into four smaller containers. How much should be put into each small container?

▶ **Solution**

Represent the amount to be removed as -640. Divide into 4 equal parts.

$$\frac{\text{removal}}{\text{number of containers}} \rightarrow \frac{-640}{4} = -160$$

The technician should remove 160 milliliters for each container.

Solve each problem by using integer division.

1. Rework Example 1 given a descent of 2500 feet in 5 minutes. _____

2. Rework Example 2 given 343 milliliters and 7 containers. _____

3. A bank customer expects to withdraw $6600 in 11 equal amounts. How much will each withdrawal be? _____

4. If the temperature fell 18°F in 9 hours and fell the same amount each hour, what was the temperature drop each hour? _____

5. A store manager needs to take 24 cartons from inventory for 8 customers each asking for the same amount. How many cartons should each customer receive? _____

6. Workers removed 120 cubic yards of dirt from a construction site. How many trucks were filled if each truck holds 8 cubic yards? _____

Making Sense of Numbers

NAME _____ CLASS _____ DATE _____

20-3 Adding, Subtracting, Multiplying, and Dividing With Integers

UNIT 5

OBJECTIVE: *Simplifying an expression involving multiple operations with integers*

Recall that when you simplify a numerical expression, you follow the order of operations.

EXAMPLE 1 Simplify. a. $\dfrac{-5+17}{-3}$ b. $\dfrac{6-24}{-6}$

▶ **Solution**

a. $\dfrac{-5+17}{-3} = \dfrac{12}{-3} = -4$ Add, then divide.

b. $\dfrac{6-24}{-6} = \dfrac{-18}{-6} = 3$ Subtract, then divide.

EXAMPLE 2 Simplify $\dfrac{-5(-1-5)}{-2}$.

▶ **Solution**

$\dfrac{-5(-1-5)}{-2} = \dfrac{-5(-6)}{-2}$ Subtract.

$= \dfrac{30}{-2}$ Multiply.

$= -15$ Divide.

Simplify.

1. $\dfrac{-1+3}{-2}$ _____

2. $\dfrac{4-20}{-4}$ _____

3. $\dfrac{-16+16}{11}$ _____

4. $\dfrac{-1+13}{4-8}$ _____

5. $\dfrac{-1-25}{-4-9}$ _____

6. $\dfrac{-15+15}{-10-10}$ _____

7. $\dfrac{6[11-(-7)]}{3(5-1)}$ _____

8. $\dfrac{-5[10-(-3)]}{3(-4)-1}$ _____

9. $\dfrac{-15(-5-7)}{-3(-7+1)} + 1$ _____

10. $\dfrac{[3-(-1)]^2}{2[5-(-3)]} + \dfrac{(4-3)^2}{(-3+4)^2}$ _____

11. $\dfrac{25[4-(-1)]^2}{-5(8-3)} + \dfrac{(7-6)^2}{(-6+7)^2}$ _____

12. $\dfrac{50[3-(-5)]^2}{25(5+3)} - \dfrac{(7-3)^2}{(-3+5)^2}$ _____

13. $\dfrac{-75[5-(-7)]}{3(6-4)^2} - \dfrac{(10-5)^2}{(-3+8)^2}$ _____

14. $\dfrac{(-2)^2+(-2)^3+(-2)^4}{3(-4)}$ _____

15. $\dfrac{(-3)^2-(-3)^3+(-3)^4}{117} + (-3)^3 + (-3)^4$ _____

176 Unit 5 Integers   *Making Sense of Numbers*

Unit 6 — Rational and Irrational Numbers

Chapter 21 Rational Number Fundamentals

- **21-1** Recognizing and Writing Rational Numbers 179
- **21-2** Comparing and Ordering Rational Numbers 180
- **21-3** Finding Opposites and Absolute Values of Rational Numbers 181

Chapter 22 Addition and Subtraction of Rational Numbers

- **22-1** Adding Rational Numbers 182
- **22-2** Problems Involving Rational Number Addition 183
- **22-3** Subtracting Rational Numbers 184
- **22-4** Problems Involving Rational Number Subtraction 185

Chapter 23 Multiplication and Division of Rational Numbers

- **23-1** Multiplying Rational Numbers 186
- **23-2** Problems Involving Rational Number Multiplication 187
- **23-3** Using Integer Exponents to Multiply Rational Numbers 188
- **23-4** Dividing Rational Numbers 189
- **23-5** Problems Involving Rational Number Division 190
- **23-6** Using Integer Exponents to Divide Rational Numbers 191

Chapter 24 Square Roots

- **24-1** Finding Squares and Rational Square Roots 192
- **24-2** Approximating Irrational Square Roots 193

Making Sense of Numbers

Unit Six

21-1 Recognizing and Writing Rational Numbers

OBJECTIVE: Classifying numbers and writing numbers as rational numbers

Integers are numbers in the list ..., −3, −2, −1, 0, 1, 2, 3, ...
A rational number is any quotient of two integers with nonzero denominator, $\frac{p}{q}$, where $q \neq 0$.

Counting numbers are numbers in the list 1, 2, 3, 4, ...
Whole numbers are numbers in the list 0, 1, 2, 3, ...

Counting numbers, whole numbers, integers, and rational numbers are related as shown at right.

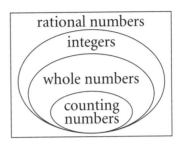

EXAMPLE

Classify each number in as many ways as possible.

a. −4   b. 0.45   c. $-2\frac{1}{3}$

Solution

a. Since −4 is in the list ..., −3, −2, −1, 0, 1, 2, 3, ..., it is an integer.
Since $-4 = \frac{-4}{1}$, it is also a rational number.

b. Since $0.45 = \frac{45}{100} = \frac{9}{20}$, it is a rational number, but not an integer.

c. The number $-2\frac{1}{3}$ can be written as $-\left(2+\frac{1}{3}\right)$, or $-\frac{7}{3}$.
This number is a rational number, $\frac{-7}{3}$, or $\frac{7}{-3}$, but not an integer.

Classify each number in as many ways as possible.

1. 3 _____

2. 0 _____

3. −5 _____

4. 0.1 _____

5. $-4\frac{2}{5}$ _____

6. −4.1 _____

7. $8\frac{2}{3}$ _____

Making Sense of Numbers   Unit 6 Rational and Irrational Numbers   **179**

NAME _____ CLASS _____ DATE _____

21-2 Comparing and Ordering Rational Numbers
UNIT 6

OBJECTIVE: *Comparing two rational numbers and writing a list of rational numbers in order from least to greatest*

Recall that when you compare two numbers, you decide which number is greater than (>) the other and which number is less than (<) the other. Just as you can compare two counting numbers or integers, you can compare two rational numbers.

EXAMPLE 1 Compare by writing < or >. a. $\frac{2}{3}$ ___?___ $-\frac{7}{12}$ b. $-\frac{3}{4}$ ___?___ -0.7

▶ Solution

a. $\frac{2}{3} > -\frac{7}{12}$ *A positive number is always greater than a negative number.*

b. $-\frac{3}{4} < -0.7$ $-\frac{3}{4} = -0.75$ and $-0.75 < -0.7$

Recall that when you order the numbers in a list, you often write a new list with the numbers from least to greatest.

EXAMPLE 2 Write $-2\frac{1}{2}, \frac{1}{4}, -3.75,$ and 2 in order from least to greatest.

▶ Solution

Use a number line. In order from least to greatest, the list is $-3.75, -2\frac{1}{2}, \frac{1}{4},$ and 2.

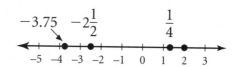

Compare by writing < or >.

1. $-\frac{4}{5}$ ___ $-\frac{3}{5}$ 2. $-1\frac{2}{3}$ ___ $-1\frac{2}{7}$ 3. 0.3 ___ -0.65 4. $3\frac{2}{5}$ ___ -0.6

Write each list of rational numbers in order from least to greatest.

5. $-2\frac{1}{5}, \frac{1}{3}, -3.5, 0, 2.25,$ and -2 _____

6. $-3\frac{1}{4}, -3.2, -1, -2\frac{1}{2},$ and $-3\frac{1}{10}$ _____

7. $-1\frac{1}{2}, -2\frac{1}{2}, -4\frac{1}{4}, 2.7,$ and -2 _____

180   Unit 6 Rational and Irrational Numbers   Making Sense of Numbers

NAME _____ CLASS _____ DATE _____

21-3 Finding Opposites and Absolute Values of Rational Numbers
UNIT 6

OBJECTIVE: Finding the opposite and absolute value of a rational number

Every rational number has an *opposite*, or additive inverse.

$-2\frac{1}{4}$ is the opposite of $2\frac{1}{4}$. $2\frac{1}{4}$ is the opposite of $-2\frac{1}{4}$.

The *absolute value* of a number x, denoted $|x|$, is the distance between x and 0 on the number line. Both $-2\frac{1}{4}$ and $2\frac{1}{4}$ have absolute value $2\frac{1}{4}$ since both numbers are the same distance from 0.

EXAMPLE Find the opposite and absolute value of each rational number.

a. -4.13 b. 0.457 c. $\frac{3}{11}$ d. $-4\frac{2}{3}$

Solution

Opposites:
a. opposite of -4.13 is 4.13
b. opposite of 0.457 is -0.457
c. opposite of $\frac{3}{11}$ is $-\frac{3}{11}$
d. opposite of $-4\frac{2}{3}$ is $4\frac{2}{3}$

Absolute Values:
$|-4.13| = 4.13$
$|0.457| = 0.457$
$\left|\frac{3}{11}\right| = \frac{3}{11}$
$\left|-4\frac{2}{3}\right| = 4\frac{2}{3}$

Find the opposite and the absolute value of each rational number.

1. -5 _____
2. 39 _____
3. -18 _____
4. -1 _____
5. 200 _____
6. -44 _____
7. 9.1 _____
8. -1.7 _____
9. -0.2 _____
10. $-4\frac{3}{5}$ _____
11. $-\frac{7}{10}$ _____
12. $10\frac{1}{2}$ _____
13. 2.56 _____
14. -2.04 _____
15. 0.1 _____
16. $1\frac{1}{3}$ _____
17. $-\frac{4}{7}$ _____
18. $6\frac{4}{5}$ _____

Making Sense of Numbers   Unit 6   Rational and Irrational Numbers   **181**

NAME _____ CLASS _____ DATE _____

22-1 Adding Rational Numbers
UNIT 6

OBJECTIVE: Finding the sum of two or more rational numbers

To find the sum of two rational numbers, follow the rules for adding two integers. You will also need to recall how to add fractions and mixed numbers.

EXAMPLE 1 Add: $\frac{3}{4} + \left(-\frac{4}{5}\right)$

Solution

$\frac{3}{4} + \left(-\frac{4}{5}\right) = \frac{3 \times 5}{4 \times 5} + \left(-\frac{4 \times 4}{5 \times 4}\right) = \frac{15}{20} + \left(-\frac{16}{20}\right)$ The LCM of 4 and 5 is 20.

$= \frac{15 + (-16)}{20}$ Add as with fractions.

$= \frac{-1}{20}$, or $-\frac{1}{20}$ Add integer numerators.

The number $-2\frac{1}{2}$ can be written as $-\left(2\frac{1}{2}\right)$. Therefore, $-2\frac{1}{2} = -\frac{5}{2}$.

EXAMPLE 2 Add: $-2\frac{1}{2} + \left(-1\frac{2}{3}\right)$

Solution

$-2\frac{1}{2} + \left(-1\frac{2}{3}\right) = -\frac{5}{2} + \left(-\frac{5}{3}\right)$

$= -\frac{5 \times 3}{2 \times 3} + \left(-\frac{5 \times 2}{3 \times 2}\right) = \frac{-15}{6} + \left(\frac{-10}{6}\right)$ The LCM of 2 and 3 is 6.

$= \frac{-15 + (-10)}{6}$ Add as with fractions.

$= \frac{-25}{6}$, or $-6\frac{1}{4}$ Add integer numerators.

Add.

1. $\frac{1}{2} + \left(-\frac{3}{4}\right)$ _____

2. $-\frac{1}{5} + \left(-\frac{5}{6}\right)$ _____

3. $-\frac{3}{7} + \frac{1}{5}$ _____

4. $-4.6 + (-4.9)$ _____

5. $6.8 + (-12.7)$ _____

6. $-3.8 + (-12.4)$ _____

7. $3\frac{1}{2} + \left(-4\frac{1}{4}\right)$ _____

8. $-2\frac{3}{5} + \left(-2\frac{1}{4}\right)$ _____

9. $3\frac{5}{6} + \left(-3\frac{3}{4}\right)$ _____

182 Unit 6 Rational and Irrational Numbers

Making Sense of Numbers

NAME _____ CLASS _____ DATE _____

22-2 Problems Involving Rational Number Addition
UNIT 6

OBJECTIVE: Finding the sum of two rational numbers to solve real-world problems

You can use addition of rational numbers to solve problems.

EXAMPLE If 2.5 pounds of sand are removed from a container and then 4.7 more pounds are removed, find the net change in the amount of sand in the container.

▶ **Solution**
Represent weight of sand removed as a negative number. Then add.
$$-2.5 + (-4.7) = -7.2$$
Altogether 7.2 pounds of sand were removed.

Solve each problem.

1. Rework the Example above, with 10.5 pounds of sand removed and 13.8 pounds added to the container.

2. Rework the Example above, with 29.5 pounds of sand removed and 23.1 pounds added to the container.

3. An airplane descends 1200 feet and then ascends 490 feet. Find the net change in altitude.

4. An airplane descends 1840 feet, descends another 640 feet, and then ascends 490 feet. Find the net change in altitude.

5. A bank customer withdraws $120.79, $238.22, and $110.15 from an account. Find the net change in the account's balance.

6. The water level in a creek rose $2\frac{1}{4}$ feet, and then fell $2\frac{3}{4}$ feet. Find the net change in water level.

7. If a number is decreased by 46.7 and then increased by 17.1, by how much did the original number increase or decrease?

8. If a number is decreased by $13\frac{1}{3}$ and then increased by $17\frac{1}{5}$, by how much did the original number increase or decrease?

9. A bank customer withdraws $20.54, $138.43, and deposits $39.10. Find the net change in the account's balance.

Making Sense of Numbers   Unit 6 Rational and Irrational Numbers

NAME _____ CLASS _____ DATE _____

22-3 Subtracting Rational Numbers
UNIT 6

OBJECTIVE: *Finding the difference when one rational number is subtracted from another*

To find the difference of two rational numbers, follow the rules for subtracting integers. You will also need to recall how to subtract fractions and mixed numbers.

EXAMPLE 1 Subtract: $\dfrac{3}{5} - \left(-\dfrac{2}{3}\right)$

▶ **Solution**

$\dfrac{3}{5} - \left(-\dfrac{2}{3}\right) = \dfrac{3 \times 3}{5 \times 3} - \left(-\dfrac{2 \times 5}{3 \times 5}\right) = \dfrac{9}{15} - \left(-\dfrac{10}{15}\right)$ *The LCM of 5 and 3 is 15.*

$= \dfrac{9 - (-10)}{15}$ *Subtract as with fractions.*

$= \dfrac{19}{15}, \text{ or } 1\dfrac{4}{15}$ *Subtract integer numerators.*

The number $-2\dfrac{1}{2}$ can be written as $-\left(2\dfrac{1}{2}\right)$. Therefore, $-2\dfrac{1}{2} = -\dfrac{5}{2}$.

EXAMPLE 2 Subtract: $-2\dfrac{1}{2} - \left(3\dfrac{3}{5}\right)$

▶ **Solution**

$-2\dfrac{1}{2} - \left(3\dfrac{3}{5}\right) = -\dfrac{5 \times 5}{2 \times 5} - \left(\dfrac{18 \times 2}{5 \times 2}\right) = -\dfrac{25}{10} - \left(\dfrac{36}{10}\right)$ *The LCM of 2 and 5 is 10.*

$= \dfrac{-25 - 36}{10}$ *Subtract as with fractions.*

$= \dfrac{-61}{10}, \text{ or } -6\dfrac{1}{10}$ *Subtract integer numerators.*

Subtract.

1. $2 - 5\dfrac{3}{4}$ _____

2. $3 - 6\dfrac{2}{3}$ _____

3. $\dfrac{2}{5} - 1\dfrac{3}{5}$ _____

4. $1\dfrac{1}{3} - 3\dfrac{2}{3}$ _____

5. $4\dfrac{2}{3} - 5\dfrac{4}{5}$ _____

6. $3\dfrac{1}{3} - 1\dfrac{2}{3}$ _____

7. $2\dfrac{2}{3} - 3\dfrac{1}{4}$ _____

8. $-2\dfrac{4}{5} - 1\dfrac{1}{3}$ _____

9. $-3\dfrac{1}{5} - 5\dfrac{4}{5}$ _____

NAME _____ CLASS _____ DATE _____

22-4 Problems Involving Rational Number Subtraction

OBJECTIVE: Subtracting one rational number from another to solve real-world problems

Subtraction of rational numbers can help solve real-world problems.

EXAMPLE Find the net change in a bank account's balance if $425.35 is deposited and a check for $745.66 is written.

▶ **Solution**

Subtract as shown at right. Since the amount of the check is greater than the amount of the deposit, the answer will be negative.

$425.35 - 745.66 = -320.31$

The net change is a decrease of $320.31.

```
  745.66
− 425.35
  ──────
  320.31
```

Solve each problem.

1. Find the net change in a bank account's balance if $230.75 is deposited and a check for $700.22 is written. _____

2. A share of stock changed in value from $42\frac{3}{8}$ points to $39\frac{1}{8}$ points. Find its net change in value. _____

3. The temperature of a chemical reaction dropped 12.3°F from an initial temperature of 7°F. Find the final temperature. _____

4. A dieter weighing 212 pounds lost $24\frac{3}{10}$ pounds. Find the dieter's weight after the weight loss. _____

5. A submarine initially 365.5 feet below sea level rises 130.8 feet. Find the submarine's final depth. _____

6. What number results from taking $18\frac{3}{5}$ from $12\frac{1}{3}$? _____

7. What is the total before sales tax for two purchases of $10.50 and $8.00, given that the customer has a $2.25 coupon? _____

8. What number results from taking 39.9 from 10 and then taking 47.1 from the difference? _____

Making Sense of Numbers   Unit 6   Rational and Irrational Numbers   **185**

NAME _____ CLASS _____ DATE _____

23-1 Multiplying Rational Numbers
UNIT 6

OBJECTIVE: *Finding the product of two or more rational numbers*

To find the product of two rational numbers, use what you know about multiplication of integers together with what you know about multiplying fractions and mixed numbers.

EXAMPLE 1 Multiply: $\frac{2}{5} \times \left(-2\frac{1}{4}\right)$

Solution

$$\frac{2}{5} \times \left(-2\frac{1}{4}\right) = \frac{2}{5} \times \left(-\frac{9}{4}\right)$$

$$= \frac{2 \times (-9)}{5 \times 4} = \frac{\overset{1}{\cancel{2}} \times (-9)}{5 \times \underset{2}{\cancel{4}}} \quad \text{Divide by 2.}$$

$$= \frac{1 \times (-9)}{5 \times 2} = \frac{-9}{10}, \text{ or } -\frac{9}{10} \quad \text{Multiply integers.}$$

You can multiply three rational numbers as easily as two rational numbers.

EXAMPLE 2 Multiply: $\frac{3}{10} \times \left(-1\frac{2}{5}\right) \times \frac{-5}{14}$

Solution

$$\frac{3}{10} \times \left(-1\frac{2}{5}\right) \times \frac{-5}{14} = \frac{3}{10} \times \left(\frac{-7}{5}\right) \times \frac{-5}{14}$$

$$= \frac{3}{10} \times \frac{\overset{-1}{\cancel{-7}}}{\underset{1}{\cancel{5}}} \times \frac{\overset{-1}{\cancel{-5}}}{\underset{2}{\cancel{14}}} \quad \begin{array}{l}\text{Divide 5 and } -5 \text{ by 5.}\\ \text{Divide } -7 \text{ and 14 by 7.}\end{array}$$

$$= \frac{3}{10} \times \frac{-1}{1} \times \frac{-1}{2}$$

$$= \frac{3(-1)(-1)}{(10)(1)(2)} = \frac{3}{20}$$

Multiply.

1. $\frac{3}{5} \times \left(-1\frac{1}{3}\right)$ _____

2. $-1\frac{3}{4} \times \left(-2\frac{2}{3}\right)$ _____

3. $-2\frac{3}{5} \times \frac{2}{7}$ _____

4. $-11\frac{3}{5} \times 0$ _____

5. $-2\frac{4}{5} \times \left(4\frac{1}{7}\right)$ _____

6. $-2\frac{1}{9} \times \left(-1\frac{2}{7}\right)$ _____

7. $2\frac{7}{10} \times \left(-1\frac{2}{9}\right) \times \left(\frac{1}{-2}\right)$ _____

8. $-2\frac{1}{7} \times \left(-1\frac{3}{10}\right) \times \left(\frac{1}{-3}\right)$ _____

NAME _____ CLASS _____ DATE _____

23-2 Problems Involving Rational Number Multiplication

UNIT 6

OBJECTIVE: Finding the product of two rational numbers to solve real-world problems

Multiplication of rational numbers can help solve problems involving quantities represented by positive and negative rational numbers.

> **EXAMPLE** A submarine captain plans to descend 300 feet per minute from an initial depth of 222.5 feet below the water surface. Find the submarine's depth after 2.5 minutes of descent.
>
> **Solution**
> Represent initial depth as -222.5 and descent per minute as -300.
> Calculate $-222.5 + 2.5(-300)$.
> $\quad -222.5 + 2.5(-300) = -222.5 - 750 \quad$ Multiply.
> $\quad \quad \quad \quad \quad \quad \quad \quad \quad = -972.5 \quad$ Subtract.
> The submarine's depth will be 972.5 feet below the surface.

Solve each problem.

1. Solve the Example above with an initial depth of 180.4 feet and a descent for 2.6 minutes. _____

2. A bank customer made 4 equal withdrawals of $182.50 each. How much was withdrawn in all? _____

3. A technician has a 500-milliliter salt solution. She needs to remove 5 equal amounts to put into small containers. If each small container is to receive 75.5 milliliters, how much is left in the large container? _____

4. A diving bird 195 feet above the water surface dives at the rate of 68.4 feet per second. How far below the water surface is the bird after 3 seconds? _____

5. An engineer opens a pipe that drains a tank at 40 gallons per minute. If the tank contains 633.75 gallons when the pipe is opened, how much is in the tank after 4.5 minutes? _____

6. An airplane descends at 420 feet per minute from an altitude of 1200 feet above a cliff that is 345 feet tall. How far below the top of the cliff is the plane after 3 minutes? _____

Making Sense of Numbers

NAME _____ CLASS _____ DATE _____

23-3
Unit 6

Using Integer Exponents to Multiply Rational Numbers

OBJECTIVE: Using rules of exponents to simplify products involving rational numbers

Two rules of exponents can help you simplify products involving rational numbers.

Two Rules of Exponents

Suppose that a and b are nonzero rational numbers and that m and n are integers.

Product rule: $a^m \cdot a^n = a^{m+n}$ Power of a quotient rule: $\left(\dfrac{a}{b}\right)^n = \dfrac{a^n}{b^n}$

EXAMPLE   Simplify $\left(-\dfrac{1}{2}\right)^2 \left(-\dfrac{1}{2}\right)^3$.

Solution

$\left(-\dfrac{1}{2}\right)^2 \left(-\dfrac{1}{2}\right)^3 = \left(-\dfrac{1}{2}\right)^{2+3} = \left(-\dfrac{1}{2}\right)^5$ Use $-\dfrac{1}{2}$ as the base and $2 + 3$, or 5, as the exponent.

$= \left(\dfrac{-1}{2}\right)^5$

$= \dfrac{(-1)^5}{2^5}$ Use $\left(\dfrac{a}{b}\right)^n = \dfrac{a^n}{b^n}$.

$= \dfrac{-1}{32}$, or $-\dfrac{1}{32}$ $(-1)^5 = -1$ and $2^5 = 32$

Simplify.

1. $\left(\dfrac{1}{2}\right)^2 \left(\dfrac{1}{2}\right)^2$ _____

2. $\left(\dfrac{2}{3}\right)^1 \left(\dfrac{2}{3}\right)^2$ _____

3. $\left(-\dfrac{2}{3}\right)^2 \left(-\dfrac{2}{3}\right)^2$ _____

4. $\left(-\dfrac{4}{5}\right)^2 \left(-\dfrac{4}{5}\right)^1$ _____

5. $\left(\dfrac{6}{5}\right)^1 \left(\dfrac{6}{5}\right)^1$ _____

6. $\left(-\dfrac{4}{3}\right)^1 \left(-\dfrac{4}{3}\right)^2$ _____

7. $\left(\dfrac{5}{3}\right)^1 \left(\dfrac{5}{3}\right)^3$ _____

8. $\left(-\dfrac{7}{2}\right)^1 \left(-\dfrac{7}{2}\right)^2$ _____

9. $\left(\dfrac{1}{2}\right)^4 \left(\dfrac{1}{2}\right)^6$ _____

10. $\left(\dfrac{2}{5}\right)^1 \left(\dfrac{2}{5}\right)^3$ _____

11. $\left(-\dfrac{5}{2}\right)^2 \left(-\dfrac{5}{2}\right)^2$ _____

12. $\left(1\dfrac{1}{2}\right)^2 \left(1\dfrac{1}{2}\right)^3$ _____

NAME _____ CLASS _____ DATE _____

23-4 Dividing Rational Numbers
UNIT 6

OBJECTIVE: Finding the quotient when one rational number is divided by another

To find the quotient of two rational numbers, use what you know about division of integers together with what you know about dividing fractions and mixed numbers.

EXAMPLE 1 Simplify: $\frac{4}{5} \div \left(-\frac{28}{15}\right)$

Solution

$$\frac{4}{5} \div \left(-\frac{28}{15}\right) = \frac{4}{5} \times \left(-\frac{15}{28}\right) \qquad \text{Multiply by the reciprocal, } -\frac{15}{28}.$$

$$= \frac{\cancel{4}^1}{\cancel{5}_1} \times \frac{-\cancel{15}^3}{\cancel{28}_7} = -\frac{3}{7} \qquad \begin{array}{l}\text{Divide 4 and 28 by 4.}\\ \text{Divide 5 and } -15 \text{ by 5.}\end{array}$$

To simplify an expression involving both multiplication and division, follow the order of operations.

EXAMPLE 2 Simplify: $\frac{4}{7} \div \left(-\frac{7}{10}\right) \times \left(-\frac{21}{8}\right)$

Solution

$$\frac{4}{7} \div \left(-\frac{7}{10}\right) \times \left(-\frac{21}{8}\right) = \frac{4}{7} \times \left(-\frac{10}{7}\right) \times \left(-\frac{21}{8}\right) \qquad \text{Multiply by the reciprocal, } \frac{-10}{7}.$$

$$= \frac{\cancel{4}^1}{7} \times \left(-\frac{10}{7}\right) \times \left(\frac{-\cancel{21}^3}{\cancel{8}_2}\right) \qquad \begin{array}{l}\text{Divide 4 and 8 by 4.}\\ \text{Divide 7 and } -21 \text{ by 7.}\end{array}$$

$$= \frac{1}{7} \times \left(\frac{-\cancel{10}^5}{1}\right) \times \left(-\frac{3}{\cancel{2}_1}\right) = \frac{15}{7} = 2\frac{1}{7} \qquad \begin{array}{l}\text{Divide 2 and } -10\\ \text{by 2.}\end{array}$$

Simplify.

1. $-\frac{4}{5} \div \left(-\frac{21}{25}\right)$ _____

2. $-2\frac{4}{5} \div \left(-3\frac{1}{7}\right)$ _____

3. $-\frac{3}{5} \div 1\frac{1}{5}$ _____

4. $-3\frac{1}{5} \div \left(-2\frac{2}{15}\right)$ _____

5. $2\frac{1}{3} \div \left(-1\frac{6}{15}\right)$ _____

6. $1\frac{1}{10} \div \left(1\frac{1}{2}\right)$ _____

7. $-2\frac{1}{3} \div 1\frac{2}{15}$ _____

8. $-2\frac{1}{7} \div \left(-2\frac{1}{7}\right)$ _____

9. $0 \div \left(-7\frac{1}{7}\right)$ _____

10. $-\frac{4}{7} \div \left(-\frac{1}{3}\right) \div \left(-\frac{16}{49}\right)$ _____

11. $\frac{2}{3} \times \left(-1\frac{4}{7}\right) \div \left(-\frac{2}{3}\right)$ _____

Making Sense of Numbers

NAME _____ CLASS _____ DATE _____

23-5 Problems Involving Rational Number Division
UNIT 6

OBJECTIVE: Using division of rational numbers to solve real-world problems

You can use division of rational numbers to solve real-world problems.

EXAMPLE A technician noticed temperature differences as shown in the table below. Find the average temperature change per hour.

time	4:00 A.M.	5:00 A.M.	6:00 A.M.	7:00 A.M.	8:00 A.M.	9:00 A.M.
temperature	−2.5°F	−1.5°F	−2.2°F	−2.9°F	2.1°F	2.2°F

▶ **Solution**

To find the average, add temperature differences, and then divide by 6.

$$\frac{-2.5 + (-1.5) + (-2.2) + (-2.9) + 2.1 + 2.2}{6} = \frac{-4.8}{6} = -0.8$$

The average temperature difference was −0.8°F.

Solve each problem.

1. Solve the Example above using the following table.   average temperature: _____

time	1:00 A.M.	2:00 A.M.	3:00 A.M.	4:00 A.M.	5:00 A.M.	6:00 A.M.
temperature	−2.1°F	−1.1°F	−2.1°F	2.1°F	2.1°F	2.9°F

2. Solve the Example above using the following table.   average temperature: _____

time	2:00 P.M.	3:00 P.M.	4:00 P.M.	5:00 P.M.	6:00 P.M.	7:00 P.M.
temperature	−2.8°F	−3.5°F	−2.2°F	−0.8°F	0.6°F	0.9°F

3. The table below shows variation in water depth in inches. Find the average variation in depth.   average variation: _____

time	2:00 P.M.	3:00 P.M.	4:00 P.M.	5:00 P.M.	6:00 P.M.	7:00 P.M.
variation	−3.4 in.	−3.4 in.	−4.5 in.	−5.0 in.	−6.0 in.	−7.5 in.

4. Find the average of $-2\frac{3}{4}$, $-3\frac{3}{4}$, $2\frac{1}{2}$, and $5\frac{1}{2}$.   _____

5. A bank customer made the withdrawals shown in the list below. Find the average amount of withdrawal.   _____
$132.50, $220.45, $324.45, $112.78, $188.96

NAME _____ CLASS _____ DATE _____

23-6 Using Integer Exponents to Divide Rational Numbers

UNIT 6

OBJECTIVE: Using rules of exponents to simplify quotients involving rational numbers

Two rules of exponents can help you simplify quotients involving rational numbers.

Two Rules of Exponents

Suppose that a and b are nonzero rational numbers and that m and n are integers.

Quotient rule: $\dfrac{a^m}{a^n} = a^{m-n}$ Power of a quotient rule: $\left(\dfrac{a}{b}\right)^n = \dfrac{a^n}{b^n}$

EXAMPLE Simplify $\left(-\dfrac{3}{2}\right)^4 \div \left(-\dfrac{3}{2}\right)^2$.

Solution

$\left(-\dfrac{3}{2}\right)^4 \div \left(-\dfrac{3}{2}\right)^2 = \left(-\dfrac{3}{2}\right)^{4-2} = \left(-\dfrac{3}{2}\right)^2$ Use $-\dfrac{3}{2}$ as the base and $4 - 2$, or 2, as the exponent.

$\qquad = \dfrac{(-3)^2}{2^2}$ Use $\left(\dfrac{a}{b}\right)^n = \dfrac{a^n}{b^n}$.

$\qquad = \dfrac{9}{4}$, or $2\dfrac{1}{4}$ $(-3)^2 = 9$ and $2^2 = 4$

Simplify.

1. $\left(\dfrac{1}{3}\right)^4 \div \left(\dfrac{1}{3}\right)^3$ _____

2. $\left(-\dfrac{2}{3}\right)^5 \div \left(-\dfrac{2}{3}\right)^2$ _____

3. $\left(-\dfrac{2}{7}\right)^3 \div \left(-\dfrac{2}{7}\right)^2$ _____

4. $\left(\dfrac{4}{7}\right)^5 \div \left(\dfrac{4}{7}\right)^3$ _____

5. $\left(\dfrac{6}{5}\right)^{11} \div \left(\dfrac{6}{5}\right)^{11}$ _____

6. $\left(-\dfrac{4}{5}\right)^6 \div \left(-\dfrac{4}{5}\right)^3$ _____

7. $\left(\dfrac{5}{11}\right)^3 \div \left(\dfrac{5}{11}\right)^1$ _____

8. $\left(-\dfrac{9}{2}\right)^4 \div \left(-\dfrac{9}{2}\right)^2$ _____

9. $\left(\dfrac{7}{13}\right)^7 \div \left(\dfrac{7}{13}\right)^6$ _____

10. $\left(-\dfrac{11}{3}\right)^4 \div \left(-\dfrac{11}{3}\right)^3$ _____

11. $\left(\dfrac{1}{3}\right)^{15} \div \left(\dfrac{1}{3}\right)^{12}$ _____

12. $\left(-\dfrac{1}{15}\right)^8 \div \left(-\dfrac{1}{15}\right)^6$ _____

Making Sense of Numbers   Unit 6 Rational and Irrational Numbers

24-1 Finding Squares and Rational Square Roots

UNIT 6

OBJECTIVE: Finding the square of a rational number and the square root of a perfect square

Recall that the expression a^2 represents the product of a with itself, or $a \cdot a$.

EXAMPLE 1 Simplify. a. $\left(-\frac{5}{7}\right)^2$ b. $\left(-2\frac{1}{3}\right)^2$

▶ **Solution**

a. $\left(-\frac{5}{7}\right)^2 = \left(-\frac{5}{7}\right)\left(-\frac{5}{7}\right) = \frac{25}{49}$ b. $\left(-2\frac{1}{3}\right)^2 = \left(-\frac{7}{3}\right)\left(-\frac{7}{3}\right) = \frac{49}{9} = 5\frac{4}{9}$

If there is a number, x, such that $x^2 = a$, then x is called a *square root* of a. A rational number is a *perfect square* if its square roots are rational numbers.

EXAMPLE 2 Find all the square roots of each number. a. 144   b. $\frac{49}{64}$

▶ **Solution**

a. Since $12 \times 12 = 144$ and $(-12) \times (-12) = 144$, the square roots of 144 are 12 and -12, denoted ± 12.

b. Since $7 \times 7 = 49$ and $8 \times 8 = 64$, one square root of $\frac{49}{64}$ is $\frac{7}{8}$. The other square root is $-\frac{7}{8}$.

Simplify.

1. $\left(-\frac{1}{2}\right)^2$ _____   2. $\left(1\frac{1}{2}\right)^2$ _____   3. $(-0.3)^2$ _____

4. $\left(3\frac{1}{3}\right)^2$ _____   5. $\left(-5\frac{1}{2}\right)^2$ _____   6. $(-1.3)^2$ _____

Find all the square roots of each number.

7. 25 _____   8. 1 _____   9. 100 _____

10. $\frac{49}{64}$ _____   11. $\frac{81}{100}$ _____   12. $\frac{144}{25}$ _____

13. $\frac{400}{9}$ _____   14. $\frac{9}{16}$ _____   15. $\frac{225}{100}$ _____

192 Unit 6 Rational and Irrational Numbers   Making Sense of Numbers

NAME _____ CLASS _____ DATE _____

24-2 Approximating Irrational Square Roots
UNIT 6

OBJECTIVE: *Finding a decimal approximation to a square root that is not rational*

If a rational number is not a perfect square, then its square roots are irrational numbers. You can approximate the roots by finding rational number approximations.

Two integers are consecutive if they differ by 1. The integers 7 and 8 are consecutive. The integers 7 and 9 are not.

EXAMPLE 1 Find two consecutive integers between which $\sqrt{52}$ lies.

▶ **Solution**
Note that $7^2 = 49$ and $8^2 = 64$. Since $49 < 52 < 64$, $\sqrt{52}$ is between 7 and 8.

Using trial and error, you can find a decimal approximation to a square root.

EXAMPLE 2 Approximate $\sqrt{52}$ to the nearest tenth.

▶ **Solution**
Since $\sqrt{52}$ is closer to 7 than it is to 8, test 7.2 and 7.3.
$$7.2^2 = 51.84 \qquad 7.3^2 = 53.29$$
So, $\sqrt{52}$ is between 7.2 and 7.3.

Since $\sqrt{52}$ is closer to 7.2 than it is to 7.3, test 7.21 and 7.22.
$$7.21^2 = 51.9841 \qquad 7.22^2 = 52.1284$$

Since 7.21^2 is closer to 52 than 7.22^2 is, $\sqrt{52}$ is closer to 7.21 than it is to 7.22.

To the nearest tenth, $\sqrt{52}$ is about 7.2.

Approximate each square root to the nearest tenth. First find two consecutive integers between which the square root lies, as in Example 1, and then calculate an approximation, as in Example 2.

1. $\sqrt{2}$ _____   2. $\sqrt{3}$ _____   3. $\sqrt{7}$ _____   4. $\sqrt{11}$ _____

5. $\sqrt{10}$ _____   6. $\sqrt{15}$ _____   7. $\sqrt{30}$ _____   8. $\sqrt{83}$ _____

9. $\sqrt{120}$ _____   10. $\sqrt{163}$ _____   11. $\sqrt{269}$ _____   12. $\sqrt{399}$ _____

Making Sense of Numbers   Unit 6   Rational and Irrational Numbers